APPROACHES TO

CLINICAL SUPERVISION:

ALTERNATIVES FOR

IMPROVING INSTRUCTION

APPROACHES TO

CLINICAL SUPERVISION:

ALTERNATIVES FOR

IMPROVING INSTRUCTION

Edward Pajak

Christopher-Gordon Publishers, Inc.
Norwood, MA

Chapter 5: Material from *The Educational Imagination: On the Design and Evaluation of Educational Programs, 2nd Edition*, New York, Macmillan Publishers Inc., reprinted by permission of Elliot W. Eisner.

Christopher-Gordon Publishers, Inc.
450 Washington Street
Norwood, MA 02062

Printed in the United States of America

10 9 8 7 6 5 4 3 2 1   98 97 96 95 94 93

ISBN 0-926842-27-7

To Zachary

Contents

Preface

Teachers today are visited in their classrooms by supervisors, administrators, and other teachers more often than ever before. In a growing number of schools and districts, the image of an isolated and professionally lonely teacher is fading from memory. In schools where people are dedicated to improving instruction for students, what goes on behind classroom doors is increasingly considered a legitimate subject for professional discussion and critical analysis.

Consensus is growing that classroom observation can be invigorating and valuable for both teachers and schools. But those who have responsibility for observing classrooms and providing feedback to teachers (i.e., supervisors, principals, and teachers) may be unclear about how best to accomplish these tasks and about the advice that various experts in the field have to offer. Furthermore, a number of circumstances make it difficult for practitioners and students of supervision to gain access to information that they need to make professionally sound judgments. These circumstances are:

- Many texts on clinical supervision, including the original works of Goldhammer, Mosher and Purpel, and Cogan are no longer in print.
- The term "clinical supervision" appears to have different meanings for different authors.
- New terms, like "coaching," have entered the literature and are also used in a variety of ways by different authors.
- Several contemporary versions of clinical supervision are not available in a single source.
- The number of clinical supervision models has mushroomed to the point that a small library of journals and books would be necessary to gain familiarity with them all.

What appears to be happening is that the notion of clinical supervision is "deconstructing," to borrow a term from modern philosophy. While this process no doubt began immediately after the publication of Goldhammer's 1969 edition of *Clinical Supervision*, the deconstruction of the concept has gained momentum in recent years. The meanings originally expressed by Goldhammer and Cogan are increasingly remote from our thinking. Contributions of other pioneers like Mosher and Purpel now are all but forgotten. During the last decade, new interventions, terms, practices, interpretations, and emphases have led to the invention and dispersal of new meanings of clinical supervision.

This book assumes a positive legitimacy of classroom observation and conferencing with teachers. It makes available in one volume the most enduring, influential, popular, and respected models of clinical supervision. Readers are strongly urged to seek out the original sources for those approaches that are of particular interest to them, however, in order to experience the full richness of these models and to consider them in light of their own personal meanings and professional practice. References are included at the end of each chapter.

A number of people have contributed to this book in a variety of ways. Hiram Howard, president of Christopher-Gordon Publishers, and I first envisioned a book that would describe a diversity of approaches to clinical supervision several years ago over coffee at a meeting of the American Educational Research Association. Hiram and Susanne Canavan, also with Christopher-Gordon, have been very supportive during the time it has taken to complete this project. I thank them for their patience and expert counsel.

My colleagues in the Department of Educational Leadership at the University of Georgia have also been supportive and encouraging of my efforts. I especially want to thank Carl Glickman, Jo Roberts, and Duncan Waite, who were kind enough to use a preliminary draft of this book as a text in their supervision classes and share their students' responses with me. They, along with my colleague, Ray Bruce, offered helpful suggestions that were incorporated into the final document.

I am grateful as well to the members of the supervision community outside of Georgia who reacted to one or more chapters. Noreen Garman and Helen Hazi provided excellent critiques of very rough drafts of Chapters 2 and 4. Dave Champagne, who taught with both Goldhammer and Cogan at Harvard and the University of Pittsburgh, was the first and most enthusiastic reviewer of the earliest version of the entire manuscript. Art Blumberg, Art Costa, Robert Garmston, and Carl Glickman helped me clarify the ideas described in the chapters addressing their respective work. Several anonymous reviewers also contributed useful insights and recommendations which I appreciate.

This book has benefitted from the suggestions of graduate assistants and students in several of my classes. My thanks go out to all of you collectively. I especially value the thoughtful criticism of Phillip Payne, whose straightforward questions and comments have improved the book considerably. I am also grateful to Mrs. Donna Bell, who prepared the figures, organized the final manuscript draft, and kept me on schedule.

Finally, I thank my family, Diane, Alexandra, and Zachary, for their encouragement and patient understanding.

E.P.
December 1992

Introduction

The Evolution of Clinical Supervision

Introduction - The Evolution of Clinical Supervision

"Effective teaching" and "reflective teaching," "peer coaching" and "cognitive coaching," "developmental supervision" and "differentiated supervision," are a few of the terms and concepts that have emerged in the education literature in just the last decade. Teachers, supervisors, and administrators may at times feel overwhelmed and even confused by the wide variety of models that now exists for improving classroom instruction through observation and conferencing. Finding the time to study and compare these different versions of clinical supervision can be a problem for practitioners, no matter how dedicated they may be. Busy educators may hurriedly select one approach to classroom observation and feedback under the mistaken belief that they are all basically the same, while overlooking other possibilities that better suit their particular philosophical beliefs and school setting.

This book is intended to clarify what each of the most popular approaches to clinical supervision has to offer and to help educators make informed choices among the options that are available to them. Informed choices will enable educators to successfully meet the pressing instructional challenges posed by today's changing organizational and social contexts of schooling while preserving and even enhancing the dignity of the teaching profession.

A Brief History of Supervision in Education

The seminal source for both supervision and administration as areas of study and practice in education appears to be a book entitled *Chapters on School Supervision* (1895), by William Payne, a Michigan school superintendent. Authors of most texts in the late 19th and early 20th centuries concentrated on the inspection function of supervision. They mainly described methods for improving the efficiency and objectivity of tasks that supervisors were expected to perform. This included monitoring and overseeing the curriculum and instruction, and evaluating teacher performance and student achievement (Bolin, 1987).

The influence of Frederick Taylor's industrial logic on educational administration in the early 20th century is well known (Callahan, 1962; Tyack, 1974). Taylor's principles of scientific management included (1) the identification and enforcement of one best way of accomplishing a task, (2) the separation of the planning of work from its execution, and (3) the direct linkage of pay to performance. While it would be incorrect to suggest that Taylor's work had no influence on educational supervision, its effect in the early years is often greatly overestimated by modern authors. Indeed, industrial logic appears to have been only one competing theme in the literature of educational supervision.

Early in the 20th century, supervision in the United States began to develop an identity separate from administration. As early as 1914, Edward C. Elliott described supervision as closely related to "the democratic motive of American education" (1914, p. 2). He distinguished "administrative efficiency" which demanded "centralization of administrative power," from "supervisory efficiency," which required *"decentralized, cooperative, expert,* supervision" (p. 78). Individuality and creativity were stifled in schools, Elliott argued, when administrative control was misapplied to the work of teachers and the accomplishments of students. During the 1920s, other authors in supervision testified to the importance of democracy as a guiding principle in education (e.g., Hosic, 1920; Barr & Burton, 1926; Burton, 1927; Ayer & Barr, 1928; Stone, 1929). Significantly, Barr and Burton noted in their 1926 text, *The Supervision of Instruction*, that Taylor's principles of scientific management have "never been especially popular" in education and seem "to have had little influence" (1926, p. 75).

According to Callahan and Button (1964) scientific management had comparatively less influence on supervision than it had on administration because "the problems of supervision and teaching method were not readily amenable to investigation in the management frame of reference nor with the techniques available." The field of supervision distinguished itself from administration during the 1930s, they suggest, by aligning itself instead with the process of curriculum development and "a new organization, the Association for Supervision and Curriculum Development" (Callahan & Button, 1964, p. 90).

John Dewey's combination of democracy and scientific thinking had a much greater influence on the evolution of supervision in education than is generally acknowledged (Glanz, 1992). Dewey's definition of scientific problem solving differed greatly from that of Taylor, however, and should not be confused with scientific management (McNeil, 1982; McKernan, 1987). When Dewey called for the application of the scientific method to educational problems, he was referring to reflective inquiry as a guide to practice (1910; 1929). Consciously reasoned, cooperative problem-solving, rather than rules generated by science, was a major early guiding principle of supervision in education. Drawing directly on Dewey's work, for example, Barr and Burton devoted an entire chapter to encouraging "reflective thought" among teachers and administrators through experimentation in classrooms and schools (1926, p. 351).

During the 1930s, publications of the National Education Association's Department of Supervisors and Directors of Instruction, a predecessor of the Association for Supervision and Curriculum Development, emphasized involvement of teachers in decisions related to instruction, as well as group deliberation and experimentation for solving problems. Drawing heavily on this literature, Barr, Burton, and Brueckner announced in their 1938 text, *Supervision*, that they were deliberately setting out to replace the old concept of the supervisor as an inspector with responsible leadership that would rely on scientific reason and experimentation for enlightenment and direction. Democratic supervision, according to this view, recognized the worth of individuals and emphasized flexibility in organization, free participation by all, and pursuit of the common good.

From the 1940s to the early 1960s, the literature of supervision continued to promote cooperative problem solving and urged educational leaders to be concerned about the personal development of those they led (Pajak, 1993). "Leadership from an educational viewpoint" was considered "synonymous with stimulating people to participate in planning, executing, and evaluating the experiences" through which they learned and worked together (DSDI, 1943). Promoting democracy among students and faculty was considered central to the purposes of supervision in education. It was argued that democracy should not only guide the governance of schools, it should provide direction to curriculum and instruction as well. True to the thinking of Dewey, democracy was portrayed as action oriented, with individuals joining their energies in pursuit of intelligent solutions through problem-centered groups.

At the mid-point of the 20th century the literature of supervision proclaimed that all individuals and groups in the school and community have leadership potential that should be exercised in accomplishing the common goal of making schools, homes, and communities better places in which to live. Leadership was something that emerged from within the group to meet the challenges of the situation at hand. Supervision was the process that facilitated the emergence of leadership in others (ASCD, 1951; 1960).

A drastic redefinition of supervision occurred during the 1960s, however, due to a greater federal role in education, an increase in the size and complexity of schools and school districts, and the institution of collective bargaining in many states (Pajak, 1993). The 1957 orbiting of the Soviet satellite Sputnik led to unprecedented national interest in education in the United States, first as a means of regaining technological superiority and second as an instrument of social policy. The appropriation of billions of dollars to fund federal programs like Operation Head Start, the Vocational Education Act, the Elementary and Secondary Education Act, and federal policies like the war on poverty and racial integration of schools significantly impacted public education in the mid-1960s. Innovations like the new math, team teaching, audiovisual equipment, bilingual education, and open classrooms were also introduced at this time.

The increasing size and complexity of schools and school districts in the United States during the 1960s and 1970s required district office supervisors to devote more time and attention to organizational goals, long-range planning, and change strategies (Ogletree, 1972; Alfonso, Firth, and Neville, 1975). At the same time, collective bargaining effectively usurped the supervisor's traditional tools of group planning and problem solving. Decisions affecting curriculum and the instructional program were reinterpreted as conditions of employment and supervisors were caught in a no-man's land between management and labor (Kinsella, Klopf, Shafer, & Young, 1969).

By the early 1960s, supervisors were being urged by some authors to think of themselves as "change agents." This meant being more concerned with whether their behavior was effective in convincing others "that a new course of action is a better one" than with whether their behavior was democratic (McCoy, 1961). Supervisors-as-change-agents were to clarify their positions and share their objectives with teachers only *after* identifying problems, establishing priorities, discerning importance, and deciding who, where, and how interventions would be introduced (Cunningham, 1963). Teachers were no longer considered a source of creative ideas and solutions, but a problem of resistance that had to be overcome. Supervisors were to keep teachers informed so that they understood the rationale for the innovation and how its implementation should occur (Toepfer, 1973).

The emergence of clinical supervision may be viewed as an evolutionary adaptation that helped preserve the traditional values of supervision – e.g., decentralized, rational, cooperative problem solving – within the environment of sweeping educational change that prevailed during the 1960s. Clinical supervision de-emphasized issues of large-scale curriculum implementation and school-wide change, and it refocused supervision's legacy of democracy, cooperative planning, problem solving, and action research on *classroom* events and processes.

The Origin of Clinical Supervision

Clinical supervision was invented by Morris Cogan at Harvard University in the mid-1950s. At that time, Cogan and others were coordinating Harvard's Master of Arts in Teaching program which prepared liberal arts graduates for careers as teachers. A central feature of this program was a closely supervised student teaching experience. Both the students who enrolled in the Master of Arts program and their university supervisors, however, recognized that the internship was not providing a satisfactory induction into the role of teacher. In response to this need for a more meaningful and productive student teaching experience, Cogan developed the concept and techniques that comprised clinical supervision.

The practice of planning, observing a lesson, and then meeting with the teacher afterward in a conference to discuss strengths and weaknesses was certainly not new in the 1950s. In fact, the sequence of a "preteaching conference," a "classroom visit," and a "follow-up conference" was suggested as a means of encouraging self-analysis by teachers as early as 1925 (Anderson, Barr, & Bush, 1925). Cogan, however, elaborated extensively on this three-step procedure. He viewed clinical supervision as a vehicle for developing professionally responsible teachers who were capable of analyzing their own performance, who were open to change and assistance from others, and who were, above all, self-directing.

As already noted, the emergence of clinical supervision in the 1960s represented a break from the problem-focused, group strategies that had dominated supervisory practice and theory during the 1950s and earlier. Clinical supervision retained an emphasis on reflective problem-solving, but it focused efforts directly on individual classrooms as the targets and teachers as the agents of change.

Robert Goldhammer studied as a graduate student with Cogan at Harvard in the early 1960s and became actively involved in the practice and further refinement of clinical supervision. In 1964, Cogan accepted a faculty position at the University of Pittsburgh, taking Goldhammer and several other talented doctoral students along with him. Their intention was to recreate the Harvard Master of Arts in Teaching program in this new setting. Both Pittsburgh and Harvard remained centers for the continued development and study of clinical supervision for many years.

After arriving in Pittsburgh, Goldhammer completed his doctoral dissertation. He analyzed data that he had collected while working as a supervisor in the Harvard program. Due to Goldhammer's untimely death in 1968, the final editing of his book, *Clinical Supervision: Special Methods for the Supervision of Teachers* (1969), was completed by Robert H. Anderson, who was then on the faculty at Harvard. Anderson subsequently published two later editions of Goldhammer's book with Robert Krajewski (1980; in press).

Ralph Mosher and David Purpel, meanwhile, had continued working in the Harvard Master of Arts program after Cogan's departure for Pittsburgh. In 1972, they coauthored a book entitled, *Supervision: The*

Reluctant Profession, which combined clinical supervision with ego counseling and emphasized advantages of working with teachers in groups. Thus, a second book about clinical supervision appeared in press before Cogan's fully developed rationale made its debut.

Although Cogan spoke and wrote extensively about clinical supervision for fifteen years prior to the publication of his book in 1973, much of this work is not readily accessible. According to people who knew him well, Cogan was unwilling to publish his ideas until he felt they were perfected. It is said that Cogan wrote four drafts of the manuscript for his 1973 publication, *Clinical Supervision*, before he was satisfied that it was ready for public scrutiny. Even then, he referred to his work rather tentatively as a "rationale," as opposed to a finished "model" of clinical supervision, apparently anticipating further refinement.

More Recent Developments in Supervision

In the foreword to the first edition of Robert Goldhammer's book, which introduced many people to clinical supervision in 1969, Robert H. Anderson optimistically declared that clinical supervision could potentially transform instructional supervisory practice. Although it has never entirely dominated supervision in education, clinical supervision certainly has been a major force in shaping it. Anderson lamented the absence of significant literature at that time upon which classroom supervision might be based. Today, more than twenty years after the publication of Goldhammer's book, a wide range of approaches to classroom observation and conferencing exists from which practitioners may choose.

Unlike many innovations in education clinical supervision has exhibited an almost unparalleled staying power and resiliency. Though its guise may have changed over the years as various authors have reinterpreted and elaborated on the basic framework, clinical supervision has remained vital for more than two decades. Such survival is no mean feat in the volatile and competitive marketplace of ideas in education.

To help the reader understand the development and the diversity of approaches to classroom supervision available today, four categories or families of models are presented in *Figure I-1*.

Essentially, the four categories of classroom supervision described in *Figure I-1* – original clinical, humanistic/artistic, technical/didactic, and developmental/reflective – represent different perspectives on the processes of classroom observation and feedback, and the nature of the relationship between teachers and those who observe them. Each of the four families and the approaches associated with them are introduced in this chapter and discussed more extensively throughout this book. Beginning with the original models of clinical supervision that appeared in the late 1960s and early 1970s, the evolution of clinical supervision is traced through the 1980s and early 1990s.

Families and Associated Authors	Approximate Years of Emergence	Major Principles
Original Clinical Models Goldhammer Mosher & Purpel Cogan	1960s to early 1970s	Collegiality and mutual discovery of meaning
Humanistic/Artistic Models Blumberg Eisner	mid 1970s to early 1980s	Positive and productive interpersonal relations with holistic understanding of classroom events
Technical/Didactic Models Acheson & Gall Hunter Joyce & Showers	early to mid 1980s	Effective teaching strategies, technique, and organizational expectations
Developmental/Reflective Models Glickman Costa & Garmston Schon Zeichner & Liston Garman Smyth Retallick Bowers & Flinders	mid 1980s to early 1990s	Teacher cognitive development, introspection, and discovery of context - specific principles of practice

Figure I-1
FAMILIES OF CLINICAL SUPERVISION

The Original Clinical Models

The writings of Robert Goldhammer, Ralph Mosher and David Purpel, and Morris Cogan, when considered independently or collectively, reflect what seems today to be a curious blending of empiricism, phenomenology, behavioralism, developmentalism, and technique. The eclectic nature of their work is probably due, at least in part, to the fact that these scholars were charting new territory and breaking new ground at a time when the entire field of education was heady with theoretical perspectives. The conceptual view inherent in these original models, which was built on contemporary psychological theory, is an important source of their strength and vigor. The diversity of philosophical viewpoints represented in them provided the seeds for many subsequent variations on the clinical supervision theme in later years. These original models of clinical supervision and the humanistic/artistic approaches that followed in the mid 1970s and early 1980s generally emphasized the importance of positive collegial relationships between supervisors and teachers in promoting teacher growth and in facilitating the collaborative discovery of meaning in classroom events.

Artistic/Humanistic Models

The writings of Arthur Blumberg and Elliott Eisner in the mid 1970s and early 1980s contrast somewhat with the empirical orientation and emphasis on procedure that are evident in the original models of clinical supervision. Blumberg speaks directly to this point, with a view that comes close to existentialism. He claims that the interpersonal relationship between teachers and supervisors is of primary essence in supervision, not the fidelity with which supervisors follow a series of predetermined phases or stages. Eisner argues that the application of empirical procedures in supervision threatens to displace the vital elements of intuition, artistry, and idiosyncracy from both teaching and supervision. Supervisors, according to Eisner, should function as connoisseurs and critics who help teachers understand the artistry of their teaching through rich descriptions and intuitive, aesthetic interpretations of classroom reality.

Technical/Didactic Models

The technical/didactic models of supervision that appeared during the early-to-mid 1980s emphasize the mastery of discrete techniques and the achievement of organizational goals. Philosophically, they stand in opposition to the humanistic/artistic approaches that preceded them. They accentuate the step-by-step procedures introduced in the original clinical models. Keith Acheson and Meredith Gall's three stage clinical sequence – planning, observation, and conferencing – for example, is subdivided into thirty-two distinct supervisory techniques. The models of Madeline Hunter and of Bruce Joyce and Beverly Showers also emphasize technique and employ classroom observation as a source of feedback to reinforce one or more predetermined models of teaching to which teachers are encouraged to conform. Classroom observation and conferencing are primarily used, in other words, as means of instructing or coaching teachers on the proper enactment of certain behaviors comprising preselected teaching strategies that have been documented as "effective" by researchers in education.

Developmental/Reflective Models

Advocates of the developmental/reflective approaches to supervision that appeared in the mid-to-late 1980s and early 1990s seek to go beyond changing teachers' behaviors. They call instead for supervisors to influence the thinking processes and sensitivities of teachers in order to help them improve. Some of these models draw on cognitive and developmental psychology for inspiration, others on the philosophy of John Dewey, and on modern social, political, economic, and moral criticism of society. All proponents of developmental/reflective models, however, call on the supervisor to encourage teacher introspection in order to discover context-specific principles of practice. Like Goldhammer, Mosher and Purpel, and Cogan, these authors tend to be advocates of phenomenology who want to help teachers understand their own practice and motivations within the contexts of their classrooms. But the modern authors go beyond the original models by urging consideration of the organizational, social, political, cultural, and ethical contexts of teaching and learning as well.

Supervision Models Omitted

Several perspectives on classroom supervision are not addressed extensively in this book and a brief explanation is in order. The most notable omission, for example, may be the revised Goldhammer, Anderson, and Krajewski (1980, in press) version of clinical supervision. The reason for its absence is that the second and third editions of Goldhammer's book primarily clarify and streamline processes described in the first edition. To their credit, Anderson and Krajewski refrain from altering the basic framework that Goldhammer developed, though they do give it a more technical orientation. At any rate, the difference between Goldhammer's first edition and more recent editions by Robert H. Anderson and Robert J. Krajewski were not deemed so great as to warrant separate treatment. Readers are encouraged to seek out both the earliest and more recent editions.

Glatthorn's (1984; 1990) "differentiated" approach is also omitted because it represents an eclectic synopsis of several versions of clinical supervision rather than an original interpretation. His views appear to be related to the developmental/reflective perspective, but Glatthorn endorses clinical supervision as one possibility among several alternatives that he considers appropriate for teachers at different stages in their professional careers.

General supervision textbooks, such as those of Alfonso, Firth, and Neville, Harris, Oliva, Lovell and Wiles, Lucio and McNeil, Sergiovanni and Starratt, and others are also noticeably absent. While some of these authors address the topic of clinical supervision in their books, it is not the central focus of their work.

Current Trends and Future Directions

Information and telecommunication technologies are drastically reshaping economic, political, and social realities around the world. Some suggest that the very nature of knowledge itself may be changing, along with its production, control, and dissemination. Educators are being asked to rethink and restructure how schools operate, how teachers relate to students, to one another, to parents and families, to communities, to business, and to government. New ways of thinking about classroom supervision are sorely needed to confront these contemporary issues.

Two very different rallying points for education reform are now prominent. Both stem, however, from advances in information processing and telecommunications. The first rallying point is the challenge posed by a technologically sophisticated global economy. According to the business management theorist, Peter Drucker (1989), each nation's economic competitiveness in today's knowledge-based world depends primarily on its schools' capacity to prepare knowledgeable, self-disciplined individuals who accept responsibility for life-long learning, and who possess strong analytical, interpersonal, and communication skills.

The second rallying point stems from concerns about social justice, public responsibility, multicultural and gender-related issues, and the environment. The new technologies are not only redefining curriculum and instruction, they are changing the social, economic, and political context of schooling throughout the world. At the moment, some of these changes seem to be for the worse.

As unpleasant as it is to admit, large numbers of students come to school today who are alienated, chemically dependent, physically, emotionally, and sexually abused, pregnant, hungry, malnourished, diseased, poor, homeless, and often violent. Educators must somehow address the fact that many families and communities no longer provide the conditions that students need for personal and academic growth. Curriculum theorist Henry Giroux points out that many citizens in traditional western democracies, especially the United States, are resolutely apathetic about social, political, and ethical issues. Above all, Giroux fears, "American youth are both unconcerned and largely ill-prepared to struggle for and keep democracy alive in the twenty-first century" (1991, p. 46).

Major differences exist between the positions expressed by Drucker (1989) and Giroux (1989) that should not be dismissed. These authors do agree, however, on several crucial points concerning education:

- Both believe that schools are increasingly important to the future of individuals as well as society because knowledge and the capacity to use it represent power. For Drucker the power of knowledge is economic, while for Giroux, knowledge represents political power.

- Drucker and Giroux also agree that schools should prepare students to accept responsibility for their own lives, to acquire information and produce knowledge independently, to think critically and creatively, and to be able to solve important problems.

- Finally, both warn that our democratic society cannot well tolerate the growing disparity between the advantaged who acquire, possess, and control knowledge, and the disadvantaged who do not.

Educators and policymakers are currently struggling with the problem of how best to restructure schools to meet these new demands. Beginning in the late 1950s and continuing through the 1980s, public education in the United States became increasingly bureaucratized, with decisions shifting away from schools and district offices to federal agencies, state legislatures, and state departments of education. This centralized bureaucratic organization was intended to achieve increased efficiency and more equal educational opportunity for students.

By the mid-1980s educators and policy makers became aware, however, that bureaucratic organization was creating obstacles to school success. These obstacles included poor communication and minimal cooperation between teachers and administrators, lack of teacher participation in decision making, little autonomy for teachers and administrators, isolation of teachers from their professional colleagues, organizational rigidity, poor morale, and elaborate evaluation systems that were unrelated to events in classrooms and schools (Pajak, 1992).

Beginning in the late 1980s and continuing into the 1990s, an alternative to the "bureaucratic paradigm" emerged. This emerging form of organization is characterized by decentralized structures, participative decision making, school-based management, collegiality, and teacher empowerment. Principals exercise greater autonomy in many districts, while leadership teams comprised of teachers, administrators, and often community members collectively make decisions about school governance. A key element of this emerging form of school organization is that mentor teachers and peer coaches induct new colleagues into the teaching profession, and improve instruction and implement innovations through frequent observation in one another's classrooms. In this emerging form of supervision, data collected during observations provides a basis for ongoing professional dialogue among the members of a learning community.

According to the business magazine, *Fortune*, the most successful corporations of the 1990s will be "learning organizations" that are capable of adapting quickly in a diverse and rapidly changing environment (Dumaine, 1989; 1991). Most educators agree that learning involves more than simply absorbing information. Learning is an organic process of thinking and creative expression. Indeed, modern businesses and schools are beginning to resemble organic systems more than mechanical ones. Although the maximally adaptive learning organization is still an ideal, many businesses and schools are already moving toward less bureaucratic, decentralized structures and are using problem-focused teams to improve their performance (Senge, 1990a, 1990b). Such practices are very similar to Dewey's notion of cooperative, democratic action as a shared, educative force.

Some educators may respond that most schools already emphasize learning all the time. Actually, schools are intended to be *teaching* organizations, and are not necessarily *learning* organizations. Most schools are designed mainly to transmit information, but they are not currently prepared to generate or invent it. Even schools that teach well may learn poorly. In schools that have the capacity for organizational learning, good practice is constantly reinforced, improved, and internalized through ongoing experimentation and feedback. The 1980s focused on getting schools to *teach* better. Schools today and in the future will have to *learn* better as well.

The world recently crossed the threshold of an era that is both disruptive and full of promise. Schools, as information-based organizations will remain at the forefront of change for the forseeable future. The challenge facing educators in the 1990s and beyond is how to facilitate collective learning in classrooms and schools so that new knowledge and creative innovations are generated and internalized (Cohen, Lotan, & Leechor, 1989; Schlecty, 1990; Fullan, 1991; Garmston, 1991), thus enabling schools to better meet the needs of students and adapt to the demands of a diverse and rapidly changing environment.

Clinical supervision can generate much useful information and knowledge about instruction and the classroom context, especially when feedback is provided by a teacher's colleagues. This process not only supports instructional improvement and professional growth of individuals, it can contribute to the learning capability of groups of teachers *and* the entire school community. Classroom observation and feedback can be implemented, however, in a manner that is consistent with *either* the bureaucratic or the learning form of organization. The framework and questions presented below (Pajak, 1992) may be useful to groups of educators in thinking about changes that may be needed or desirable in the way that classroom observation and feedback is practiced in their schools or districts.

Bureaucratic Organization

Classrooms are visited most often by principals under a bureaucratic organization, primarily to evaluate teacher performance. Such classroom visits are infrequent, except for beginning teachers who are having difficulty. Central office staff visit occasionally to "show the flag" or may be called on to observe teachers who are having chronic difficulty in order to secure further documentation for their dismissal. Teachers are expected to exhibit a set of predetermined behaviors that are supposed to indicate effective teaching. Most teachers view their classrooms as "sacred ground" and resent intrusions from outsiders.

Learning Community

In a school that operates as a learning community, teachers engage in peer coaching and visit each other's classrooms often in order to help improve instruction. Beginning teachers are paired with master teachers who serve as mentors. Less competent teachers are able to learn from observing others and may feel subtle pressure from their peers to improve their classroom performance. The emphasis, however, is on generating data and engaging in conversations about teaching with colleagues to develop a store of professional knowledge through instructionally-focused action research.

Some Questions to Consider When Moving Toward a Learning Community

- Where are we now and where do we want to be in terms of how classroom observation and conferencing are practiced in our school or district? In terms of how educators relate to one another? How data collected during observations is used?
- What forces are likely to help and hinder our progress?
- What series of steps is necessary for us to get to where we want to be?
- Who needs to be involved in these efforts?
- What resources are currently available?

- How will we know when and how well we have achieved our goal?

The following set of questions may be useful to individuals in selecting a model of supervision that "fits best" for them and for their schools:

Some Questions to Consider When Selecting a Model of Clinical Supervision

- How might this model of supervision contribute to the learning of students in my classroom or school?
- What does this model of supervision imply about teachers and the way they should be treated?
- Do I feel comfortable with this model of supervision as a teacher? Would I want to be supervised in this way? Why or why not?
- Would I feel comfortable using this model of supervision as a mentor or peer coach? Why or why not?
- Would I feel comfortable using this model of supervision as a supervisor or principal? Why or why not?
- What might I learn about myself as a teacher from this model?
- What might I learn about myself as a supervisor of teachers from this model?
- Would this model of supervision work in my school? Why or why not?

You, the reader, may want to consider these and other questions as you read and think about the various approaches to clinical supervision described in the chapters that follow. In the final chapter, more will be said about choosing or constructing a model and how classroom observation and feedback can contribute to schools becoming learning communities.

References

Alfonso, R.J., Firth, G.R., & Neville, R.F. (1975). *Instructional supervision: A behavior system*. Boston: Allyn and Bacon.

Anderson, C.J., Barr, A.S., & Bush, M.G. (1925). *Visiting the teacher at work*. New York: D. Appleton-Century.

Association for Supervision and Curriculum Development (1951). *Instructional supervision in small schools*. Washington, D.C.: Association for Supervision and Curriculum Development, National Education Association.

Association for Supervision and Curriculum Development (1960). *Leadership for improving instruction*, 1960 Yearbook. Washington, D.C.: Association for Supervision and Curriculum Development.

Ayer, F.C. & Barr, A.S. (1928). *The organization of supervision: An analysis of the organization and administration of supervision in city school systems*. New York: Appleton.

Barr, A. S. & Burton, W. H. (1926). *The supervision of instruction*. New York: D. Appleton-Century.

Barr, A. S., Burton, W. H., & Brueckner, L. J. (1938). *Supervision: Principles and practices in the improvement of instruction*. New York: D. Appleton-Century.

Bolin, F. (1987). On defining supervision. *The Journal of Curriculum and Supervision*, 2 (4), 368-380.

Burton, W.H. (1927). *Supervision and the improvement of teaching*. New York: D. Appleton-Century.

Callahan, R. (1962). *Education and the cult of efficiency*. Chicago: University of Chicago Press.

Callahan, R. E. & Button, H. W. (1964). Historical change of the role of the man in the organization: 1865-1950. In, Daniel E. Griffiths, (Ed.). *Behavioral Science and Educational Administration*, The Sixty-third Yearbook of the National Society for the Study of Education, Part II. Chicago: University of Chicago Press.

Cogan, M.L. (1973). *Clinical supervision*. Boston: Houghton Mifflin.

Cohen, E.G., Lotan, R.A., & Leechor, C. (1989). Can classrooms learn? *Sociology of Education*, 62 (April), 75-94.

Cunningham, L.L. (1963). Effecting change through leadership, *Educational Leadership*, 21 (2): 75-79.

Department of Supervisors and Directors of Instruction (1943). *Leadership at work*. Washington, D.C.: Department of Supervisors and Directors of Instruction, NEA.

Dewey, J. (1910). *How we think*. Boston: D.C. Heath.

Dewey, J. (1929). *The sources of a science of education*. New York: Horace Liveright.

Drucker, P.F. (1989). *The new realities*. New York: Perennial Library.

Dumaine, B. (1989). What leaders of tomorrow see. *Fortune, 120* (1), 48-62.

Dumaine, B. (1990). The bureacracy busters. *Fortune, 123* (13), 36-38.

Elliott, E. C. (1914). *City school supervision.* New York: World Book.

Fullan, M.G. with Steigelbauer, S. (1991). *The new meaning of educational change.* New York: Teachers College Press.

Garmston, R. (1991). Staff developers as social architects, *Educational Leadership, 49* (3), 64-65.

Giroux, H.A. (1989). Rethinking education reform in the age of George Bush, *Phi Delta Kappan, 70* (9), 728-730.

Giroux, H.A. (1991). *Postmodernism, feminism, and cultural politics: Redefining educational boundaries.* Albany: State University of New York Press.

Glanz, J. (1992). Curriculum development and supervision: Antecedents for collaboration and future possibilities. *Journal of Curriculum and Supervision, 7* (3), 226-244.

Glatthorn, A. (1984). *Differentiated supervision.* Alexandria, VA: Association for Supervision and Curriculum Development.

Glatthorn, A. (1990). *Supervisory leadership: Introduction to instructional supervision.* Glenview, IL: Scott, Foresman/Little, Brown.

Goldhammer, R. (1969). *Clinical supervision: Special methods for the supervision of teachers.* New York: Holt, Rinehart, & Winston.

Goldhammer, R., Anderson, R.H., & Krajewski, R.J. (1980). *Clinical supervision: Special methods for the supervision of teachers,* 2nd edition. New York: Holt, Rinehart, & Winston.

Goldhammer, R., Anderson, R.H., & Krajewski, R.J. (in press). *Clinical supervision: Special methods for the supervision of teachers,* 3rd edition. New York: Holt, Rinehart, & Winston.

Hosic, J.F. (1920). The democratization of supervision. *School and Society, 11,* 331-336.

Kinsella, B. W., Klopf, G. J., Shafer, H. T., & Young, W. T. (1969). *The supervisor's role in negotiation.* Washington, D. C.: Association for Supervision and Curriculum Development.

McCoy, R.F. (1961). *American school administration.* New York: McGraw-Hill.

McKernan, J. (1987). Action research and curriculum development. *Peabody Journal of Education, 64* (2), 6-19.

McNeil, J.D. (1982). A scientific approach to supervision. In T. J. Sergiovanni (Ed.), *Supervision of teaching,* 1982 Yearbook. Washington, D.C.: Association for Supervision and Curriculum Development.

Mitchell, B. (1990). Children, youth, and restructured schools: views from the field. In, B. Mitchell and L.L. Cunningham (Eds.) *Educational leadership and changing contexts of families, communities, and schools,* Eighty-ninth Yearbook of the National Society for the Study of Education, Part II. Chicago: University of Chicago Press.

Mosher, R.L. & Purpel, D.E. (1972). *Supervision: The reluctant profession.* Boston: Houghton Mifflin.

Ogletree, J.R. (1972). Changing supervision in a changing era. *Educational Leadership, 29* (6), 507-510.

Pajak, E. (1992). A view from the central office. In, C.D. Glickman, (Ed.), *Supervision in transition.* The 1992 ASCD Yearbook. Alexandria, VA: Association for Supervision and Curriculum Development.

Pajak, E. (1993). Conceptions of supervision and leadership: Change and continuity. In, Gordon Cawelti (Ed.). *Challenges and Achievements of American Education,* 1993 ASCD Yearbook. Alexandria, VA: Association for Supervision and Curriculum Development.

Payne, W. H. (1875). *Chapters on school supervision.* New York: Wilson, Hinkle.

Schlechty, P.C. (1990). *Schools for the 21st century.* San Francisco, CA: Jossey Bass.

Senge, P.M. (1990a). The leader's new work: Building learning organizations. *Sloan Management Review,* Fall 1990, pp. 7-23.

Senge, P.M. (1990b). *The fifth discipline: The art and practice of the learning organization.* New York: Doubleday/Currency.

Stone, C.R. (1929). *Supervision of the elementary school.* Boston: Houghton-Mifflin.

Toepfer, C.F. (1973). The supervisor's responsibility for innovation. *Educational Leadership, 30* (8), 740-743.

Tyack, D. (1974). *The one best system: A history of American urban education.* Cambridge, MA: Harvard University Press.

Section One

The Original Clinical Supervision Models

The three approaches to clinical supervision described in Section One shared common roots during the 1950s and 1960s in Harvard's Master of Arts in Teaching program, which was designed specifically to induct new teachers into the teaching profession. Techniques for conducting classroom observations, collecting data, and holding conferences appeared decades earlier in the education literature. But the books by Goldhammer, Mosher and Purpel, and Cogan represent the earliest comprehensive descriptions of theoretically based, field-tested approaches to working with teachers on improving instruction in classrooms.

Goldhammer, Mosher and Purpel, and Cogan offered perspectives that are congruent in many respects. For example, they all are greatly concerned with the quality of the interaction between the teacher and supervisor. The bases of a collegial relationship, which they favor, include trust and a willingness to share and to understand personal meanings, understandings, and frames of reference. All three versions portray clinical supervision as providing support for teachers with an aim toward increasing professional responsibility and openness, and the capacity for self-analysis and self-direction. Clinical supervision is intended, furthermore, to help teachers perfect their personal styles by recognizing and building on existing strengths instead of calling attention to deficits and shortcomings. This requires an acceptance by the supervisor of each teacher's unique style of teaching and a willingness to enter into dialogue with the assumption that the teacher is professionally competent.

Contributions of clinical supervision to teacher development are described by Goldhammer, Mosher and Purpel, and Cogan in considerable detail. Goldhammer describes a sequence of skill acquisition as the professional identity emerges, proceeding from technical primacy to compassion and naturalness. He cautions that judgments and even friendly advice from a supervisor should be avoided when working with novices until they acquire self-confidence. Mosher and Purpel are very much concerned with the stress that beginning teachers experience as they establish professional identities. They recommend ego counseling as a way of helping new teachers confront the strain created by the discrepancies they experience among personal intentions, job expectations, and actual performance in the classroom. Cogan observes that many veteran teachers display little progress after having acquired early in their careers a few survival strategies that simply let them get by from day to day. Clinical supervision is depicted by all of these authors as a democratic, dialogic enterprise that encourages teachers to consider alternatives and select their behaviors rationally on the basis of probable impact on students.

According to Goldhammer and Cogan, feedback provided to teachers relative to their performance should be strictly for the improvement of teaching and not for evaluation. This practical inquiry is supported by various tools. The verbatim transcript is the preferred method of data collection for both authors, although Cogan discusses the use of a number of observation instruments and electronic recording devices. Mosher and Purpel strongly favor video and audio recordings because of their "stop action" and "instant replay" capabilities. Analysis of data, according to all three approaches involves the identification of classroom patterns and critical incidents which suggest hypotheses regarding the relationship between teacher behavior and student outcomes.

A central concern of Goldhammer, Mosher and Purpel, and Cogan was overcoming meaningless, ritualistic behavior between teachers and students, and between supervisors and teachers. The strategies they proposed sought to replace ritualism with conscious, rational thinking. Deliberative reasoning and collaborative planning, however, necessitate attention to feelings as well as facts. Behavioral objectives are balanced in these approaches to clinical supervision, therefore, with a strong emphasis on interpersonal process outcomes. While human relationships are subjected to analysis and conscious choice, these authors all recognize that human beings also invent social reality and create meanings.

The models of clinical supervision proposed by Goldhammer and Cogan include a strong dose of humility for the supervisor. The inevitability of uncertainty and unpredictability in the classroom is heavily emphasized, implying that absolutes simply do not exist. The supervisor is expected by both authors to engage regularly in an examination of his or her personal motives and biases in order to contribute to his or her own professional improvement. Telling a teacher what is right or wrong, or good and bad, about his teaching is a temptation to be avoided, Goldhammer and Cogan warn, though it may save time by eliminating thoughtful analysis and even provide a passing moment of exhilaration for the supervisor.

Despite many similarities, the perspectives of Goldhammer, Mosher and Purpel, and Cogan are clearly distinctive. The rationales provided for clinical supervision, for example, differ in their initial foci. Goldhammer begins his rationale by expressing concern for students and the irrelevant experiences they often encounter in school. He follows with a scathing indictment of the meaninglessness of much of what occurs in classrooms and offers clinical supervision as a way of making instruction more consciously purposeful and responsive to students' needs.

Mosher and Purpel view clinical supervision as inextricably bound up with the content of teaching. They argue that clinical supervisors must be curriculum specialists, first and foremost, who help teachers improve *what* as well as *how* they teach. Cogan, in contrast, distances clinical supervision from curriculum and focuses his rationale primarily on organizational and professional issues. He offers clinical supervision as a means of disseminating and institutionalizing innovations more effectively, and professionalizing the teaching corps.

Another difference among the three models is the degree of emphasis each places on the relative importance of external versus subjective realities. All are concerned with observable behaviors and meanings, and the relationship between them, as expressed in each teacher's unique style. Cogan urges the supervisor to focus attention primarily on teacher behaviors, however, arguing that a change in style will naturally follow. Goldhammer sees a need to go beyond what he called "superficial behavior" and, along with Mosher and Purpel, favors a more intense self examination by the teacher. Goldhammer's and Mosher and Purpel's models therefore incorporate counseling, while Cogan argues against probing too deeply into the teacher's professional identity.

The models also differ in the emphasis they give to supervision of groups of teachers. Both Goldhammer and Cogan allude only to possible benefits of supervising teachers in groups. Mosher and Purpel expand the idea tremendously with detailed suggestions on how the clinical model can be adapted to this purpose. Along with the emphasis on curricular content and the use of videotaping, the application of clinical supervision to groups of teachers who analyze one another's lessons gives Mosher and Purpel's model of clinical supervision a contemporary feel and relevance. It also places them most clearly in the supervision tradition of cooperative group problem solving and understanding.

As the reader will discover in later chapters, the three models of clinical supervision presented in Section One are truly seminal. Many contemporary themes are foreshadowed in the work of Goldhammer, Mosher and Purpel, and Cogan. Seeking out the original editions of these works and studying them closely will be well worth the reader's time and effort.

Chapter 1

Robert Goldhammer's Clinical Model

The Model at Work

Mrs. Smith is on her on her way to observe Mr. Miller, a first year teacher who has been experiencing some difficulty in getting his class to run smoothly. As she walks down the hallway toward his classroom, Mrs. Smith recalls the preobservation conference they had several days earlier.

During the preobservation conference Mrs. Smith noticed that Mr. Miller was nervous and seemed uncertain as he described the lesson she was to observe. Mrs. Smith was primarily interested in understanding his overall frame of reference concerning teaching, but she quickly realized that this teacher needed some help. She therefore asked Mr. Miller to describe the sequence of tasks that he had planned for the students. He responded that he would like some suggestions from her. When Mrs. Smith offered some ideas, however, Mr. Miller objected that they "would never work" with the students in his class.

At that point Mrs. Smith immediately changed her strategy and avoided giving Mr. Miller any further direct advice. His behavior, both passive and defensive, alerted her that it was more important to respond to his emotional state. She tried to communicate support and general acceptance to Mr. Miller so that he would calm down enough to begin thinking about his teaching in a rational way.

Mrs. Smith suggested that they role play the lesson informally, with her playing the part of the students. Gaining control of the situation seemed to put Mr. Miller at ease. The two of them then acted out the sequence of events he had in mind for the class. When they were finished, Mr. Miller had a clearer idea of what he was going to do.

Before the preconference ended, Mrs. Smith and Mr. Miller agreed on when the classroom observation would take place. She explained that she would make as complete a record as possible of everything that he and his students said, as well as an objective account of their nonverbal behavior. Mr. Miller promised that he would further refine the lesson plan they had sketched out.

Mrs. Smith thought a moment about Miss Jones, who taught across the hall from Mr. Miller. Miss Jones was also a first year teacher, but she was more autonomous and self-confident. Interactions between Mrs. Smith and Miss Jones tended to be relaxed and free flowing. When Mrs. Smith gave advice, Miss Jones believed enough in her own capabilities to accept or reject the suggestions and explain why.

During the post observation conference, Mrs. Smith decided, she would probably be very nondirective with Mr. Miller. After presenting the data and an overview of the patterns of behavior she had perceived, she would concentrate on listening to Mr. Miller's reactions and reflect his feelings back to him. This would not only make him feel less threatened, Mrs. Smith thought, it would also force him to take more responsibility for planning the next lesson. She did not want Mr. Miller to become dependent on her for emotional support or for creative ideas. She wanted him to draw on his own intelligence and motivation to develop a style of teaching that was uniquely his own.

Introduction

To fully appreciate Goldhammer's work, one must remember that he wrote his book, *Clinical Supervision* (1969), in the late 1960s and that his model of supervision reflects the optimism, idealism, and limitless energy of that turbulent decade. The book is more than simply a description of a technique for improving instruction. It is also an indictment of the public education system. While raising serious questions about what and how children are taught in schools, a tone is maintained throughout that might be described as playfully irreverent. At times the book reads like a declaration of independence for students and educators, and in a real sense Goldhammer may have had something like that in mind.

The model of supervision that Goldhammer proposes represents a response to his indictment of public schooling in the United States and is an expression of his desire to generate new "images of what school can be like." Goldhammer obviously cherished individual human autonomy and viewed clinical supervision as a way of increasing self-sufficiency and freedom for teachers, supervisors, and students.

Supervision, Goldhammer suggests, ought to increase teachers' willingness and ability to supervise themselves and their colleagues. The relationship between teacher and supervisor, therefore, should be characterized by empathy and supportiveness for the purpose of promoting self awareness and independence in schools, along with "a community of spirit and of enterprise" with others.

Goldhammer's Clinical Model

The term "clinical," according to Goldhammer, is intended "to convey an image of face-to-face relationships between supervisors and teachers," as opposed to the supervision of curriculum development or instructional program committees (p. 54). Goldhammer suggests that certain forms of teaching and ego counseling are somewhat similar to clinical supervision, though clinical supervision may involve teachers and supervisors working together in groups. The critical element is that teachers and supervisors should work "up close" in trying to improve classroom practice.

The term clinical also implies for Goldhammer a focus on behavior, what the teacher actually does in the classroom. The behavior recorded during a classroom observation is important because it later serves as the basis for an analysis conducted by the teacher and supervisor of what occurred during the lesson. The purpose of this interaction is "to develop categories of analysis after teaching has been observed, rather than beforehand" (1969, p. 54).

What is most easily and most often remembered about Robert Goldhammer's ground-breaking book is the five stage sequence consisting of:

Stage 1:   Preobservation conference
Stage 2:   Observation
Stage 3:   Analysis and strategy
Stage 4:   Supervision conference
Stage 5:   Post-conference analysis

A description of the rationale and procedures for each of the five stages follows.

Stage 1: The Preobservation Conference

The first stage of clinical supervision as described by Goldhammer requires an open, informal, and relaxed relationship between the teacher and supervisor. The supervisor's purpose is to understand and help refine the teacher's plans for the lesson that will be observed at a later time. This stage was intended to occur several days before the actual teaching of the lesson. The teacher would use the intervening time for further planning.

A certain degree of trust is necessary, according to Goldhammer, to minimize anticipatory anxieties and problems of mutual adjustment. The preobservation conference also requires a certain familiarity or "fluency" from both parties concerning the teacher's plans for the lesson to be observed. The supervisor must develop an understanding of the teacher's frame of reference in order to help the teacher function more effectively. The preobservation conference is therefore an opportunity for the supervisor to learn just what the teacher has in mind for the lesson.

The preobservation conference also provides an opportunity, Goldhammer notes, for the teacher to mentally rehearse his or her teaching before enacting it. Informal role playing, with the supervisor taking the part of students, is one way of helping teachers anticipate ways of dealing with unexpected student behaviors or reactions. Such role playing can also be helpful as a means of clarifying directions or improving questions that teachers will be using in the lesson.

The possibility of the supervisor introducing concepts from his or her own frame of reference during the preconference is not entirely ruled out. However, any ideas that the supervisor introduces ought to make sense within the teacher's existing conceptual framework, Goldhammer suggests, rather than from the supervisor's perspective alone. The supervisor should generally avoid questions, objections, and suggestions that might remove ownership of the lesson from the teacher.

The preobservation conference also ought to include a contract negotiated between the teacher and supervisor, Goldhammer advises, that specifies roles, goals, and ground rules governing the relationship of the teacher and supervisor to one another. The contract clarifies communication and makes expectations explicit. The teacher should understand, for example, that the supervisor will be making a written record of the class and be aware of anything in particular on which the supervisor may be focusing.

Contractual understandings between the teacher and supervisor should be reviewed regularly and frequently to make them explicit and understood by both parties. Revisions should be made, according to Goldhammer, only if mutually agreed upon. It is a good idea for the supervisor to always summarize what each has agreed to do, he believes, at the end of the preconference.

The primary purpose at this point is to identify specific problems that the teacher is actually grappling with. Therefore, teachers should be asked whether they feel the upcoming observation and remaining stages make sense for them. If a teacher sees no practical reason for the sequence to unfold at this time, Goldhammer believes, the supervisory experience will almost certainly deteriorate into ritualism or a polite social exchange despite the supervisor's best efforts.

Procedures for the Preobservation Conference

- Asking the teacher for his or her judgments and perceptions is usually a good way to begin a preobservation conference. The supervisor tries to understand as completely as possible what the teacher wants to do during the lesson that is to be observed.

- If the teacher is uncertain or feels that more planning is needed, the supervisor can ask straightforward questions such as:
  1. "What, exactly, is the sequence of instruction that you intend to follow?"
  2. "What key questions do you intend to ask?"
  3. "Will you give the directions before you distribute the materials or afterwards?"

- The supervisor should consciously control his or her own language and nonverbal behavior to avoid inadvertently encouraging passivity and dependency in the teacher.

- The supervisor should reserve personal concerns for the feedback conference (Stage 4) to avoid confusing or undermining the teacher's equilibrium.

- Just prior to the observation (Stage 2), a brief "courtesy call" is appropriate to let the teacher know that the supervisor is ready. This visit is intended to reduce any discomfort the teacher may be feeling about the observation and to determine whether any additional work is needed. The supervisor can simply ask the question: "What can we do right now that would be helpful?"

Stage 2: Observation

The supervisor observes the lesson to provide the teacher with another pair of eyes. An objective, accurate, and complete representation of classroom events is recorded during Stage 2 to establish a firm foundation for the planning of teaching in the future. Goldhammer recommends that the supervisor should record in writing as much as possible of what is said by the teacher and students during the lesson, along with objective descriptions of teacher and student nonverbal behavior.

Data collected during the observation allow the supervisor to intuitively propose the existence of patterns that are "problematic" and worthy of further attention. A "problem," for Goldhammer, is not necessarily a weakness on the teacher's part. A problem may be any complex issue, including strengths the teacher already exhibits. How to firmly establish in the teacher's repertoire some practice that has been effective or to better understand how and when to use it are examples of problems that are worthy of attention. Problems may have been identified earlier in Stage 1 or may emerge from the data during later analysis. In either case, a true representation of reality is needed.

According to Goldhammer, the major purposes of providing descriptive data on the teacher's performance in the classroom are as follows:

a) to help teachers test their own perceptions and judgments concerning events in their classrooms;

b) to increase teachers' autonomy and decrease their dependency on the supervisor for evaluating whether their teaching is "good" or "bad;"

c) to help teachers become more aware of their own behavior by modeling careful and attentive observation of teaching;

d) to demonstrate to teachers the supervisor's commitment to the clinical supervision process; and

e) to develop close and frequent proximity to the classroom so that other types of assistance that teachers may need can be provided.

Procedures for the Observation

- The supervisor's responsibility during Stage 2 is to concentrate on recording the behaviors and events seen and heard in the classroom.

- Written verbatim observation notes are preferred because a written record can be quickly and easily analyzed. Underlining, circling, or rearranging sections of a transcript, Goldhammer suggests, can simply and effectively highlight important patterns of teaching.

- Supervisors can employ abbreviations for frequently repeated words or invent personalized shorthand techniques like skipping vowels to increase speed. An accurate and complete account of short specific episodes is preferable to an inaccurate and incomplete account of an entire lesson.

- It helps to occasionally make note of the time so that the sequence of events can later be established. Coding a seating chart so that individual students and their contributions can be identified is also helpful for purposes of analysis, as well as keeping a running tally of teacher-student verbal interactions.

- Nonverbal behavior should be described as objectively as possible with a minimum of interpretation by the supervisor.

- The supervisor's impressions, feelings, and judgments can be noted marginally for later reference, but the observation data are limited to a descriptive record of events and behaviors enacted by the teacher and students.

- When a specific category of teacher behavior such as questioning or direction giving has been identified during the preobservation stage as an area to receive special attention, the supervisor must refrain from introducing unrelated issues and record only what was agreed upon in advance. If an unanticipated problem appears, Goldhammer advises that the supervisor should stick with the original contract. If the problem is serious, it will undoubtedly recur and can be addressed at a later time.

- During an observation the supervisor should be positioned as unobtrusively as possible and avoid interrupting or interfering with the class in any way. In most cases, leaving at the end of a lesson is good practice so as not to disrupt the lesson's flow and to get all the data available.

- If a lesson is absolutely catastrophic or the teacher must stop to contend with a major discipline problem, Goldhammer advises that the supervisor should tactfully withdraw from the classroom to allow the teacher to reestablish control.

Stage 3: Analysis and Strategy

Supervision can be improved both technically and in the perceptions of teachers, according to Goldhammer, only if it becomes more rational than has been true in the past. Its methods must be based on logic and explicit analysis. The mystery, vagueness, and punishment frequently associated with supervision can thus be overcome so that teachers feel less helpless, defensive, and dependent. Making supervision more rational will also make it more valuable to teachers, Goldhammer argues, especially if teachers are trained to participate in the process of self-analysis.

Stage 3 of the clinical supervision sequence actually involves two distinct phases. In "analysis," the first step, some sense is made of the observational data. In "strategy," the second step, a plan for managing the supervision conference is developed – issues, goals, roles, and tactics are decided upon.

Analysis

The control that teachers exercise over their own teaching can be increased, Goldhammer reasons, by better understanding present classroom reality. Supervisors can contribute to this understanding by engaging teachers in critical analyses of data, thereby promoting rational decisions based upon interpretations and inferences about events that influence instruction. In a truly open dialogue, teachers can legitimately question or dispute the supervisor's reasoning and conclusions.

Teaching behavior, like all human behavior, is both repetitive and patterned. These repeated behavior patterns are expressions of the teacher's professional identity, Goldhammer observes, and over time are likely to have a strong cumulative effect on students. Incidental and unintended learnings, not all of which are desirable, are also passed along in this way. The object of clinical supervision is to reinforce, modify, or extinguish the patterns which constitute a teacher's unique performance.

Data collected during an observation can be used to identify patterns that are unique to each teacher. The supervisor should strive for a process of discovery during analysis, according to Goldhammer, extrapolating meaning from the data by formulating categories of observed teacher behavior instead of imposing meaning beforehand. This invention of categories through analysis places considerable responsibility on the supervisor, who cannot take refuge in the safety of rating scales and check lists.

Strategy

Goldhammer offers several reasons for supervisors to develop a strategy as the second phase of Stage 3:

1) The planned pursuit of preselected goals, he suggests, is preferable to random processes. Strategy may sometimes involve, however, a decision based on analysis of data to conduct an open conference with no formal agenda determined in advance. Or, the supervisor may decide that the conference will consist of a collaborative analysis of the data with the teacher.

2) The emotional importance of supervision for the teacher makes it imperative for the supervisor to exercise what Goldhammer calls reasoned control over his or her own behavior. The issue is not only humane and ethical, he observes, but it is also practical. Teachers are unlikely to find worthwhile supervision that hurts them. By planning carefully in advance, the supervisor minimizes this possibility.

3) Strategy also helps maintain continuity, in that long-term developmental issues can be addressed repeatedly from one conference to another.

Procedures for Analysis

During analysis, raw data collected during the observation (Stage 2) are condensed through a process of sorting and collating to arrive at a streamlined version of what happened in the classroom. The result is a representation that is both concise and true to life. Essentially, according to Goldhammer's description, analysis is comprised of the following procedures:

• Scan the transcripts for easily identifiable patterns of behavior such as frequency and quantity of teacher talk or frequently repeated phrases.

• Give closer scrutiny to the content or substance of what the teacher says, while looking for patterns involving such things as value statements, encouragement to students, or inconsistencies. As one reads the data it is important to continually ask: "What is happening at this point?"

- Examine one's own value judgments as a supervisor concerning each of the patterns identified and ask whether the pattern is real or simply a reflection of personal biases.

- Focus on the likely consequences of the teacher's behavior for students and decide if the consequences are worth doing something about. This essentially involves imagining what meaning a particular behavior might have for students in that class if the behavior were repeated throughout the year.

- Ask whether the observed teacher behavior patterns facilitated or hindered accomplishment of the teacher's goals for the lesson. Simply stated, did the teacher get from the lesson what he or she wanted?

- Pose the question whether the patterns fall into some hierarchical order of importance. The frequency with which a pattern appears, its inclusiveness as an umbrella for other patterns, its relevance to teacher goals, and its relevance to students' experiences are all possible criteria for identifying a hierarchy.

- Once patterns of behavior are discovered and determined to be important enough to address, categories of teaching into which they logically fit should be identified. Behaviors may fit into more than one category. Labelling patterns as categories in this way facilitates the transition to theoretical understanding and discussion.

- The consequences of a pattern should be evident in the data, and hypotheses relative to the pattern should be supported by some psychological, social, or learning theory. Although patterns may be isolated on the basis of hunches, Goldhammer observes that intuition is less satisfactory and less likely to be convincing to the teacher. Analysis must shift back and forth between theory and specific reality of the situation at hand. Categories and implied solutions that make sense theoretically, but do not fit the reality of the classroom under study should not be imposed.

Procedures for Strategy

Goldhammer notes that a formal plan for the conference is not always needed when working with a teacher who is highly experienced in clinical supervision. In most cases, however, the supervisor should at least consider the "what" and "how" of the conference - what content to discuss, what goals to pursue, and how to best accomplish these ends. Goldhammer suggests that three principles be applied when selecting specific patterns of teacher behavior for study and treatment: 1) saliency, 2) accessibility, and 3) fewness.

The most *salient* patterns of behavior are those that appear to have the greatest impact on students, are most relevant to the teacher, or facilitate recognition by the teacher of how minor patterns relate to more prominent ones or to overall teaching style. However, the issues addressed in a conference must also be intellectually and emotionally *accessible* to a teacher or the conference will be wasted. Finally, due to the limited time available in a conference and the limited capacity of humans to assimilate information, only a *few* issues can be fully discussed from the universe of patterns that may be identifiable from the data. A brief summary of Goldhammer's discussion of saliency, accessibility, and fewness follows.

Saliency
When planning strategy, a supervisor must decide whether a pattern of behavior evidenced by the teacher is worthy of attention. Several questions can help the supervisor in this regard:
   a) How frequently does the behavior pattern appear?
   b) Is the behavior pattern consistent with an accepted theory of practice?
   c) How does this teacher's behavior compare to teaching behaviors commonly found among other teachers in the department or grade level?
   d) Does the teacher feel that this behavior pattern is important?
   e) Does one pattern supersede others in that it defines the teacher's overall style (e.g., teacher centeredness) or undermine other effective patterns (e.g., making transitions from one activity to another)?

Accessibility

Another issue in planning strategy involves deciding which patterns of teaching the teacher and supervisor are intellectually and emotionally prepared to address. Again, several questions are useful for the supervisor to consider:

a) Which issue from among several identified by the supervisor does the teacher feel most comfortable addressing?

b) At what level is the teacher intellectually prepared to deal with the pattern or set of patterns that are involved?

c) Is the issue too emotionally laden for the teacher to handle successfully? Will the issue, in other words, produce too much anxiety?

d) Is the issue one that the teacher will find gratifying, from which he or she will receive emotional benefit?

e) What are the supervisor's own feelings and motives?

f) If the supervisor decides to introduce an emotionally "hot" topic for discussion, is he or she prepared to provide the needed emotional support?

Fewness

Once patterns of teaching are identified as salient and treatable, the supervisor must focus on one or two in order to avoid overloading the teacher intellectually. Goldhammer recommends the following principles as useful for making such selections:

a) Does the clarity and abundance of data make certain patterns more efficient targets for change?

b) Which patterns can be addressed from both a general focus, such as style, and a specific instance of behavior?

c) Can patterns be grouped into broad categories, such as classroom management, according to their sameness or difference?

d) What degree of emotional investment does a teacher have in a topic and is confrontation needed for professional growth?

e) Is time available to deal with a pattern of behavior in sufficient depth and how can time be best used?

f) Do the teacher and supervisor have sufficient levels of energy to tackle complex and emotional issues?

g) Can data be sequenced so that the conference flows logically with easy transitions from topic to topic rather than as a random hodgepodge of issues?

How Much Data to Present?

When presenting data to the teacher, Goldhammer suggests, a certain balance must be achieved. Too little information may fail to make the point and confuse, while too much data may result in overkill and be experienced as humiliating. Several rules of thumb should be considered, according to Goldhammer, within the context of previous experience with the teacher:

- Have more data available than is needed.
- Focus on the clearest examples.
- Select well-defined patterns.
- When in doubt ask the teacher to summarize or role play.

Ideally, the conference should end when technical and process goals are met, but unexpected contingencies and time constraints often prevent this. Working on complex, emotional, or ambiguous issues first is usually a good idea, according to Goldhammer, so that enough time is available. If the teacher is to raise concerns, supervisors should be sure to allow time for the teacher to do so at the beginning. It is also a good idea to provide time at the end of a conference for making a transition to the next step (preobservation or observation) or to bring closure to a discussion. Goldhammer recommends always ending a conference on a positive note, while teachers are feeling successful or good about themselves and their teaching.

Stage 4: The Supervision Conference

The post observation conference, according to Goldhammer, is the most essential stage of clinical supervision and should never be omitted. The supervisor, he suggests, owes the teacher a report on what was observed and recorded. The teacher can otherwise only fantasize about the supervisor's perceptions, which is likely to increase the teacher's dependency on the supervisor for approval.

The conference is the one time when the supervisor becomes vulnerable, Goldhammer notes, because supervisory processes are made visible to the teacher. Once exposed in this way, the teacher can respond to the supervisor's thinking and products, and can aggressively take hold of his or her own destiny.

The post observation conference is also a time for reviewing and renegotiating the supervisory contract. Earlier problems and issues can be returned to, or new issues and concerns identified. Care should be taken, however, that conferences do not overemphasize analysis of teaching that has passed.

The supervision conference should be a time for the teacher and supervisor to plan teaching collaboratively. At least a rough plan for the next day's lesson should be developed so that the teacher comes away from the conference with a tangible product. It is important, however, to avoid creating teacher dependency on the supervisor for lesson plans. When some teachers feel that a plan is being imposed upon them, Goldhammer cautions, they may purposely subvert the next day's lesson to demonstrate that the supervisor's suggestions were untenable.

The supervisor's behavioral strategy, Goldhammer advises, should emerge from an awareness that the supervisory process employed is likely to affect not only the quality and substance of the teacher's technical knowledge, but also the teacher's ideas and feelings about himself or herself, his or her teaching, the supervisor, and supervision generally. An overemphasis on technique, Goldhammer warns, may cause the supervisor to overlook the emotional investment that teachers make in their teaching. To be effective, supervision has to go beyond treating superficial behaviors and trading one symptom for another. The teacher's underlying identity must be addressed for truly significant change to take place, Goldhammer believes, because teaching is so much a part of the teacher. Patterns of behavior may be so closely tied to a teachers' definition of themselves, however, that it may be difficult for them to deal with behaviors in an objective fashion.

Process goals relate to learning outcomes that empower teachers to think independently and analytically about their teaching. Process goals require the supervisor to plan with an awareness of the effects the conference will have on the teacher. Stating both technical and process goals behaviorally is strongly advocated by Goldhammer because outcomes may not otherwise materialize. Behavioral goals are useful as well for focusing efforts, marking progress, and defining tasks to be accomplished.

In most cases, Goldhammer suggests, it is best to begin clinical supervision with an emphasis on process goals because the initial interaction between teacher and supervisor essentially determines the direction of the teacher's subsequent development. Supervisors should especially keep a close eye on their own motives because it is easy to rationalize displays of power. Being decent and secure in one's interactions with teachers from the very beginning is more difficult, Goldhammer notes, than turning liberal only after teachers have displayed the proper deference to one's position and authority.

While it is tempting for supervisors to begin their work with teachers didactically by focusing on technical goals, the teacher's dependency is thus quickly established. If teachers are to develop the capacity and motivation to initiate inquiry or the skills to analyze their own teaching independently, Goldhammer believes, they need practice in doing so from the very start. Although the supervisor must provide some structure from the beginning, teachers should not become too reliant upon it.

During the first few cycles of clinical supervision, Goldhammer observes, the supervisor cannot structure the conferences very much simply because the supervisor has little knowledge about the teacher's functioning and they share no history together. It is better at first to concentrate on building trust by being supportive and watching for cues from the teacher to indicate which direction to take.

A common trap for supervisors to avoid, Goldhammer cautions, is stereotyping individual teachers on the basis of initial impressions. The supervisor should strive to become an attentive student of each teacher's teaching. Prematurely categorizing teachers in terms of their strengths and weaknesses, their relative autonomy, aggressiveness, or rationality, he believes, is unwise.

Procedures for the Supervision Conference

The supervisor must make some important decisions concerning the post observation conference. For instance:
- Should the conference approach be didactic or inductive?
- Who will interpret the data, perform the analysis, and develop strategies?
- Should the supervisor or the teacher initiate the issues to be addressed?

Goldhammer expresses uneasiness about describing the supervisory method too specifically because he fears that students may follow his guidelines mechanistically at the expense of developing sensitive and creative responses to individual teachers. He warns that sticking too closely to the strategic plan with no allowance for deviation once set in motion ought to be avoided. Speaking from his own experience, Goldhammer reports that no two conferences are ever alike. What works one day, even with the same teacher, he notes, may not work well the next. The methods he puts forth are suggestions rather than formulas for success.

To illustrate conferencing procedures, Goldhammer presents three case studies of teachers who differ considerably in their levels of competence and self-confidence. Teacher #1 is described as "basically autonomous, professionally sophisticated, experienced in the ways of clinical supervision, and highly motivated to make use of supervisory consultation." Teacher #2 is characterized as "more average ...but has not had much supervisory experience and...tends to be relatively dependent in his professional relationships." Teacher #3 is depicted as "frightened, technically weak, and highly defensive in relation not only to supervision but to his professional role and professional relationships generally." The suggestions for working with stronger, average, and less effective teachers that follow are based on Goldhammer's critique of these three case studies. A summary is presented in *Figure 1-1* below.

Working with Stronger Teachers

Clinical supervision always aims toward *collaborative* analysis, according to Goldhammer, which is characterized by a freeflowing, give-and-take interaction between the supervisor and teacher. Collaborative analysis is possible almost immediately with teachers who are experienced, self-confident, and intellectually open. Such autonomy is exemplified by behavior that suggests that the teacher is neither overly defensive (closed) nor overly uncertain and vulnerable (dependent).

Ordinarily the supervisor should avoid value judgments about teaching that has been observed, so as not to reinforce the teacher's dependency. With a teacher who is clearly an autonomous professional, Goldhammer suggests, this general rule can occasionally be relaxed. While the supervisor should certainly be a source of praise for exceptional performance, teachers should never come to feel that what is "good" or "bad" in their teaching depends upon the supervisor's feelings in the matter.

Similarly, giving advice is not desirable as the principal supervisory

	Stronger Teachers	Average Teachers	Less Effective Teachers
Characteristics	Experienced, autonomous, self-confident, highly motivated, intellectually open.	Intelligent, motivated, capable and resilient.	Uncertain, passive, vulnerable, closed-minded.
Appropriate Supervisory Stance	Collaborative stance characterized by free-flowing give-and-take interaction between teacher and supervisor	Variety of styles ranging from didactic to inductive, essentially authentic and honest, sensitive to teacher's anxieties yet willing to tackle problems.	Inductive and non-authoritative, communicating support and general acceptance of the teacher as a person and a professional.
Supervisor's Goals	To clarify thinking. To order ideas logically. To introduce relevant new information. To expand the teacher's frame of reference. To differentiate events more closely. To reinforce existing strengths.	To clarify ambiguities of meaning and understanding. To specify generalities. To help the teacher decide whether he or she is doing well or poorly.	To exhibit humane sensitivity. To respond to the teacher's emotions. To encourage confidence.
Recommended Language and Behavior	Directive, giving advice and offering suggestions, occasionally confronting and evaluative.	Tentative, making carefully reasoned suggestions, clarifying responses, sensitive to teacher's anxieties.	Nondirective, active listening, reflecting feelings, clarifying responses.
Rationale	Successful, highly autonomous teachers are likely to trust their own perceptions and are less likely to become dependent on the supervisor for approval. They are likely to view a nondirective or inductive approach as a manipulative ploy.	Most teachers possess sufficient integrity, intelligence, resiliency, and strength to confront their own faults and make an effort to improve. They are willing to listen to sound advice and are also capable of engaging in collaborative problem solving.	Less effective teachers are likely to respond to a didactic and directive approach by becoming passive and dependent or defensive and closed-minded. An inductive, non-authoritative approach provides the emotional support needed before they can engage in rational analysis.

Figure 1-1
GOLDHAMMER'S THREE LEVELS OF SUPERVISION

technique because it implies hierarchy and also generates dependency. However, Goldhammer asserts, highly autonomous, self-assured teachers are more likely to trust their own perceptions and are less likely to become dependent on the supervisor for approval. Giving advice and suggestions, therefore, can be precisely what is needed when a very competent teacher and supervisor are collaborating as colleagues.

A nondirective stance is *less* likely to be successful with experienced and self-confident teachers, Goldhammer believes, than more direct approaches. He argues that an inductive style will probably be viewed by competent, intelligent, and autonomous teachers as a manipulative ploy or even throw suspicion on the supervisor's understanding of the issues at hand.

On the other hand, the supervisor should never attempt to impose his or her ideas and thought processes on the teacher. Goldhammer views such behavior as unethical and counterproductive to the fundamental purposes of clinical supervision. More practically, any positive changes in the teacher that are accomplished in this manner, he suggests, usually do not last.

In clinical supervision, as described by Goldhammer, a supervisor builds upon the teacher's existing conceptual framework by adding to it gradually rather than by substituting the supervisor's ideas and preferences for the teacher's. Gradual shifts in teachers' thinking and behavior are preferably accomplished through hard work. Though it takes time to incubate ideas and make them one's own, such long-term cumulative effects of the supervisor's behavior are considered most potent.

Three approaches are especially useful, according to Goldhammer, when working with teachers who are both self-confident and intellectually open:

1) Help the teacher expand the frame of reference in which specific questions about classroom practices are considered. The supervisor can do this by introducing findings from psychological research, for example, or ideas from the education literature.

2) Try to get the teacher to more finely differentiate global perspectives about students, teaching, and events in the classroom. Collaborative analysis can be very beneficial here.

3) Identify and reinforce the teacher's existing strengths (such as using student's ideas) in order to stabilize and consolidate sound practice.

Working with Teachers of Average Ability

Success is far more likely when working with teachers of average intelligence and ability, Goldhammer suggests, if the supervisor exhibits a range of behaviors and a variety of styles. The supervisor should function authentically and honestly with the teacher, being neither punitive nor unwilling to raise important issues. While sensitivity to a teacher's anxieties is important, the supervisor cannot overlook serious faults. According to Goldhammer, supervisors can usually assume that most teachers possess sufficient integrity, resiliency, and strength that confrontation is both possible and useful.

At times it is most appropriate to allow the teacher to identify patterns in the data, Goldhammer notes, but relying on an inductive approach exclusively is missing the point. A direct didactic approach often saves time and will not be interpreted as beating around the bush. On the other hand, while a didactic approach may seem efficient, it is entirely a waste of time if the teacher is not listening.

The supervisor must be very tentative in his or her analysis and strategy in order to adequately and objectively represent the reality of the classroom when working with teachers of average ability. The supervisor tries to clarify ambiguities and specify generalities, but whether the teacher did well or poorly is left up to the teacher to decide. Value judgments, when made by the supervisor, should be carefully reasoned out. The teacher deserves a rationale for the supervisor's judgments, Goldhammer argues, that is based on data, theory, and logic, not on flattery, fantasy, or personal preference.

Another reason the supervisor should explain his or her rationale and reasoning explicitly instead of trying to conceal motives and veil intentions is to avoid the playing of "games." Simply asking leading questions may be perceived by a typical teacher as a game of "I've got a secret," or "Guess what I'm thinking." The teacher may simply choose not to "play" until the supervisor states exactly what is on his or her mind.

Fairly long soliloquies by supervisors are difficult to avoid in practice, according to Goldhammer, and may be entirely appropriate when developing a complex issue. Asking the teacher for input or to summarize occasionally to check for clear understanding is very beneficial under such circumstances. However, it is better to extend a lengthy conference to another meeting. Even a positive conference can become tiresome when extended excessively. A simple rule to follow, Goldhammer suggests, is "Quit while you're ahead."

Working with Less Effective Teachers

Instead of trying to save teachers who are professionally marginal, Goldhammer suggests, it makes more sense for the supervisor to concentrate time and energy on teachers who exhibit strength, intelligence, and proficiency. Goldhammer reports, however, that he has personally found an inductive approach to be most successful when working with teachers who are unable to exercise initiative. If the supervisor begins with a directive and didactic stance, he argues, the teacher's incorrect expectations of what supervision is all about are inevitably confirmed. The teacher learns to be either passive or defensive when the supervisor takes control in this way. Although teachers may at first be confused by inductive, nonauthoritative supervision, according to Goldhammer, they quickly become skilled at making sense of data and establishing direction for themselves.

The supervision of poor teaching is always difficult emotionally for both the teacher and the supervisor. Ineffective teachers usually know they are having difficulty, but may begin a conference by denying any concern. If supervision is often experienced as painful or punishing, teachers will find ways to avoid and circumvent it. Teachers frequently exhibit game-like defensive strategies in such cases to fend off a supervisor's attempt to engage in rational problem solving. Over-agreement, consistent disagreement, launching a verbal barrage, raising red herrings, putting the supervisor on the defensive, and self-deprecation can all be used to deflect the discussion away from the issue at hand. Typically, the closer a behavior pattern is to a teacher's personality, Goldhammer notes, the more anxiety and greater resistance it is likely to provoke.

The supervisor must artfully combine technique with human sensitivity in such cases. Modelling flexibility and intuitiveness and above all, exhibiting humane sensitivity are very important when working with teachers who are having difficulty. Supervisors should respond to teachers' emotions and encourage confidence in their own knowledge and strength to proceed, Goldhammer advises. Active listening, reflecting feelings, and clarifying responses should be used a good deal. To avoid imposing one's own thinking and ideas on the teacher, supervisors may present several alternatives and allow the teacher to choose one they will pursue.

It may be necessary for the supervisor to acknowledge that problems with a lesson were evident, Goldhammer observes, in order to lessen the teacher's defensiveness and stress. However, communicating general acceptance of the teacher as a person and a professional earlier in the conference is essential. A climate of crisis is not suitable for rational analysis and a supervisor and teacher may agree to defer discussion temporarily until a later time if emotions run too high.

Usefulness of Open Conferences

An open conference in which the teacher can provide maximum direction is especially useful with either very strong or very anxious teachers. Many teachers quickly surpass the supervisor at analysis and planning, according to Goldhammer, because they are more familiar with themselves and their students. Also, a teacher's ego-involvement in his or her work can result in high commitment to technical competence. The supervisor's role evolves gradually into that of a coach in such situations. The supervisor works toward becoming a "mirror" and collaborator whose function is to assist the teacher however possible in accomplishing his or her own goals.

An open conference is recommended as early in a supervision sequence as possible. The teacher may want to discuss and compare philosophies of education or focus exclusively on the lesson observed. The teacher may want to use the session exclusively for planning, for discussing a particular student, or may cancel the conference entirely. Any of these are legitimate choices that the supervisor should be ready to accept. The most skillful and autonomous teachers, Goldhammer observes, are those who use the supervisor most vigorously and creatively.

Teachers new to clinical supervision may squander a conference by talking about superficial and tangential issues, especially if they are anxious. The supervisor can build in a check in advance by first suggesting frequent pauses for mutual examination of success and progress. When working with teachers who are anxious, Goldhammer suggests, it may be helpful to gradually build more direction into the conference by making suggestions to train the teacher in the skills of analysis and planning until an open conference can be tried again.

An occasional open conference is also useful for relaxing the intensity of clinical supervision. A moratorium is useful as an opportunity to consolidate the teacher's thinking, Goldhammer suggests, especially when considering a difficult problem. If a teacher requests that clinical supervision be put on hold for awhile, the supervisor should respect the request but explain that he or she is available at any time. Sometimes it is necessary for teachers to confirm that the supervisor is not imposing supervision on them. The supervisor should keep communication open so that the teacher's ambivalence or fear of clinical supervision can be addressed.

The supervisor can best determine a teacher's level of development, according to Goldhammer, by relaxing his or her own behavior occasionally and observing how well the teacher responds. Goldhammer suggests, however, that teachers are the best judges of their own developmental pace. Open conferences allow teachers to determine their own stride. Supervisors may learn that teachers are more capable than believed, or may recognize omissions, biases, and value judgments in themselves. An occasional open conference also allows for discussion of residual questions and issues that remain unresolved from earlier sequences. Subsequent conferences can be scheduled according to the teacher's strengths and needs as they are spontaneously displayed.

Stage 5: The Post-conference Analysis

In the final stage of clinical supervision the supervisor's own practice is critically examined. Goldhammer describes the post-conference analysis as the "conscience" of clinical supervision in that it promotes consciousness and control over the supervisor's professional behavior. The post-conference analysis helps to determine if supervision is actually being effective. As strengths and weaknesses are identified, needed adjustments to supervisory practices can be made. The supervisor's values, goals, techniques, and feelings can and should be explored as well. The post-conference analysis convinces teachers of the supervisor's commitment to the process of self-analysis and serves as an opportunity for the supervisor to model that virtue.

Supervisors should be aware of their own behavior, according to Goldhammer, and be ready and willing to analytically examine its effect on the teacher. Supervisors also need to recognize when games are being played and to end them. This requires that clinical supervisors possess sufficient courage to engage in what Goldhammer calls "reflexive analysis" of their own practice. Careful self examination and analysis of process represent a model of professionalism for teachers to emulate. While the supervisor can expose his or her own dilemmas and problems to the teacher for mutual analysis, the teacher should never come to feel responsible for providing support to the supervisor.

The idea for supervisory "postmortems" originally developed, according to Goldhammer, during group supervision situations where colleagues critiqued one another's work. Ideally, he suggests, the post-conference analysis is conducted with another supervisor. Typically, however, supervisors have to supervise themselves. When done alone, the supervisor must rely on notes and audio tapes as sources of feedback. Teachers and supervisors can acquire insight into their relationship by listening to tapes together. Notes can be taken, of course, as a tape is played back. Writing memos to oneself immediately afterward is especially helpful to supervisors for tracing their own longterm development. The decision whether or not to tape a conference, of course, should be made with the teacher well in advance of the actual event.

A principal difficulty of the post-conference analysis, according to Goldhammer, is being objective about one's own behavior. A useful device is to look for repetitive verbal patterns in tape recordings of conferences with teachers. Goldhammer favors focusing especially on episodes that generate particularly strong positive or negative reactions.

A teacher's responses to the supervisor's behavior is also a good focus. It may be helpful to ask teachers for clarification of their reactions in a particular episode. Listening closely to "flat" or "gray" dialogue where nothing of consequence seems to be happening is especially important to determine what is really going on (e.g., avoidance? defensiveness?) that may be blocking progress.

Performing the post-conference analysis at regularly specified intervals works best. According to Goldhammer, every fourth or fifth sequence of supervision is about right. Too much analysis leads to diminishing returns, too little to avoidance. Another possibility is to do a postmortem at the end of a series of cycles, concentrating especially on earlier sequences to trace the supervisor's development.

Sometimes a teacher can be involved, playing the role of the supervisor. Such role reversal is likely to relieve anxieties related to hierarchical distinctions and enhance the teacher's feelings of dignity. The postmortem, Goldhammer cautions, should by no means become a ritual of penance and absolution for the supervisor. At all times it should be aimed at the supervisor's professional development.

Procedures for the Post Conference Analysis

Some questions that should constantly guide the supervisor's analysis of his or her own behavior include:

- What may the teacher be learning at any given moment in the conference as a result of my behavior?
- Who initiates analytical inquiry, the teacher or the supervisor?
- What kinds of reinforcements are provided?
- How many and what kinds of questions do the supervisor and teacher ask one another?
- Who lays out the plans for future teaching and data collection?
- Is anyone's behavior stereotyped rather than authentic?
- Are rationales and reasons for value judgments and for decisions affecting future work explicitly stated?
- Is agreement or disagreement real or simply based on semantic confusion or ambiguous language?
- Were the goals for the conference accomplished?
- What were the outcomes of the conference?

Summary

Goldhammer's five-stage sequence is the earliest extensive description of the clinical supervision process. Its stated purpose is to increase self awareness and professional autonomy among teachers.

In Stage 1, the preobservation conference, the teacher verbally rehearses the lesson to be taught while the supervisor concentrates on understanding the teacher's conceptual framework. A contract between the teacher and supervisor is agreed upon that describes goals, mutual expectations, and the data to be collected.

During the observation, Stage 2 of Goldhammer's sequence, the supervisor records a written account of behaviors enacted and words spoken in the classroom by both teachers and students as objectively, accurately, and completely as possible. Detailed data are needed in order to develop valid and meaningful categories of analysis *after* teaching is observed, rather than beforehand.

Stage 3 of Goldhammer's model of clinical supervision involves two distinct steps – analysis and strategy. The supervisor first scans the raw data to identify patterns of teacher behavior that promote or hinder learning for students. The supervisor next selects specific patterns to discuss with the teacher.

The supervision conference, Stage 4 of the model, includes both a critical dialogue between the teacher and supervisor concerning the lesson that was observed, and a collaboratively developed plan for the teacher's next class. The supervisor's task is to help clarify and build upon the teacher's understanding of events in the classroom. Goldhammer recommends that supervisors use a range of behaviors and a variety of styles when working with most teachers. For exceptionally competent, autonomous, and intellectually open teachers, however, a direct and didactic supervisory approach is suggested. With teachers who are technically weak, dependent, and defensive, in contrast, an indirect and inductive approach is recommended.

During the final stage of Goldhammer's model, the post conference analysis, the supervisor critically examines his or her own supervisory effectiveness. This can be done alone, with the teacher's involvement, or with another supervisor. The supervisor acquires insights into his or her own practice through analysis of audio-taped conferences, thus ensuring continued personal growth.

References

Goldhammer, R. (1969). *Clinical supervision: Special methods for the supervision of teachers*. New York: Holt, Rinehart, & Winston.

Goldhammer, R. (1992). *The Robert Goldhammer papers*. Stephenville, TX: Council of Professors of Instructional Supervision.

Goldhammer, R., Anderson, R., & Krajewski, R. (1980). *Clinical supervision: Special methods for the supervision of teachers*. 2nd edition. New York: Holt, Rinehart, & Winston.

Goldhammer, R., Anderson, R., & Krajewski, R. (in press). *Clinical supervision: Special methods for the supervision of teachers*. 3rd edition. New York: Holt, Rinehart, & Winston.

Chapter 2

Ralph Mosher and David Purpel's Ego Counseling Model

The Model at Work

Mrs. Smith is examining a video camcorder that she obtained from the school media center as she prepares for an observation of Miss Jones' classroom. Miss Jones is a bright, confident, and highly motivated first year teacher. Checking to be sure the video camera's battery is fully charged, Mrs. Smith thinks about yesterday's planning conference.

Although planning conferences take time away from other duties, Mrs. Smith actively helped Miss Jones select the objectives, materials, and strategies for the upcoming lesson. Together, they made predictions about the effects on students of the subject matter and teaching methods. They paid especially close attention to the content of the lesson, including the appropriateness of the objectives, the suitability of the content for the students, Miss Jones' grasp of the facts to be covered, and the logical sequence of topics. They also noted alternative strategies to anticipate and avoid common pitfalls.

Sometimes Mrs. Smith takes verbatim notes during an observation, but she prefers making a videotape like she will this time because it allows for "stop-action" and "instant replays" during the analysis. Later, she and Miss Jones will view the tape together to identify categories of behavior for analysis. They will examine student behaviors first, looking for evidence of learning. Next, they will look at Miss Jones' behaviors to see whether and how it contributed to student learning. Finally, they will decide whether the predictions they made during the planning conference were accurate.

Several days after the observation, Mrs. Smith will meet with Miss Jones to share with her data that suggest recurrent patterns and relationships among the content, teacher behavior, and student behavior in the videotaped lesson. Mrs. Smith will make suggestions for improving patterns that can be changed, but she is especially interested in helping new teachers like Miss Jones develop an individual style. She will use praise liberally to reinforce and build upon Miss Jones' existing strengths.

Mrs. Smith is very aware of the stress that beginning teachers experience as they try to acquire their professional role. They struggle with conflicting personal expectations, job requirements, and their actual performance, which may not measure up to their own or others' standards. Mrs. Smith will try to help Miss Jones deal with these conflicts on a conscious level by confronting and developing rational solutions to problems that arise.

Miss Jones is capable and confident enough, Mrs. Smith believes, to be introduced very soon to one of her supervision groups. These groups, which are comprised of six to ten teachers, meet every two weeks for about ninety minutes to view and critique videotapes of one another's lessons. They then collectively help plan the next lesson, sharing ideas, insights, and materials. Mrs. Smith functions as a facilitator at these meetings, keeping communication channels open. Frequent classroom observation, along with cooperative critiques and planning sessions, Mrs. Smith is convinced, will create an atmosphere in the school that encourages self awareness, acceptance of multiple perspectives, and willingness to change and grow professionally.

Introduction

The subtitle of Mosher and Purpel's book, *Supervision: The Reluctant Profession* (1972), is drawn in part from the authors' conviction that supervision in education is an elusive concept. Supervision has been variously defined, they note, in terms of improvement of instruction, teacher development, curriculum leadership, and school administration. Practicing educators, by and large, are often themselves confused in their understanding of supervision, Mosher and Purpel suggest, and are ambivalent in their feelings about it at best.

In simplest terms, according to Mosher and Purpel, a supervisor is someone who is charged with making certain that another person does a good job. School supervisors have such diverse and conflicting roles, however, that it is difficult to define exactly what they do. In an attempt to resolve this lack of clarity, the authors offer what they term an operational definition of supervision:

> Teaching teachers how to teach (in which working with teachers as people is a significant subfunction), and professional leadership in reformulating public education – more specifically, its curriculum, its teaching and its forms. (1972, p. 3)

Having defined supervision as a form of teaching, Mosher and Purpel define a teacher (or supervisor) as "someone who deliberately tries to persuade someone else to change his thinking or behavior in a specific direction." (p. 6) The process of teaching (or supervising), in turn, is defined as "a social process involving (mainly) talk and interaction between at least two people, a teacher and a student." The latter definition is the premise for the authors' argument that supervisors need to work with teachers as people.

Supervision, for Mosher and Purpel, is a special kind of teaching wherein teachers play the part of students and curriculum represents the content. The essential spirit and ethic of supervision, they suggest, is derived from an obligation to provide optimal opportunities for learning to individual children.

The curricula in most schools is static, according to Mosher and Purpel, and teaching remains largely unexamined. A fundamental objective of supervision, they believe, should be curricular and instructional leadership. The accomplishment of this objective requires that the supervisor perform several roles, including teacher of teachers, educational leader, and social leader.

Mosher and Purpel's Clinical Supervision

Improving instruction is the primary objective of clinical supervision, in the view of Mosher and Purpel. The focus should be on the *what* and *how* of teaching as it occurs. The supervisor's immediate objective is improving the materials and method of instruction directly at the point where the teacher interacts with students.

The purpose of clinical supervision with respect to the teacher is entirely different from that of evaluation. According to Mosher and Purpel, the goal of clinical supervision is that "of developing *in beginners and in experienced teachers a conviction and a value: that teaching, as an intellectual and social act, is subject to intellectual analysis*" (p. 79, emphasis in the original). This analysis should be rigorous, systematic, and ongoing so that each teacher acquires the analytical skills to enable him or her to become a careful critic of his or her own practice. It is the emphasis on direct application and practice that makes clinical supervision "clinical," as compared, for example, to a typical university course or inservice training session which are necessarily more abstract and less focused on immediate practice.

Clinical supervision, according to Mosher and Purpel, is predicated on the supervisor possessing specialized, expert knowledge of content and the curriculum, including curriculum theory, design, and development. Central to this notion is the assumption that there exists "a logic inherent in the content and in how this content is to be communicated" (1972, p. 82). Clinical supervisors are, first, content specialists, they declare, because analysis of teaching effectiveness independent of the content that is taught is simply not feasible.

Assumptions of the Clinical Model

Mosher and Purpel suggest that four assumptions underlie their clinical model of supervision. These include the following underlying principles:

Teaching is behavior.
Teaching, according to this definition, includes the observable behaviors of both teachers and students in the classroom, as well as the effects of the teacher's behavior on what students learn. Teaching performance and its outcomes are considered to be inseparable.

Teaching behavior is patterned.
Behavior in classrooms does not occur randomly. In other words, what a teacher does and says while teaching typically follows certain characteristic patterns.
Behavioral patterns can be classified and studied.
The behaviors that a teacher exhibits in questioning, speaking, or listening to students can be identified and examined in terms of clarity, intellectual stimulation, or emotional supportiveness.
Teaching behavior is subject to understanding and control.
A teacher's behavior should be conscious and rational, according to Mosher and Purpel, so that changes can be made to improve both the teacher's craftsmanship and the student's opportunities for learning.

Three Stage Clinical Model

The version of clinical supervision described by Mosher and Purpel involves the application of rational analysis by the supervisor and the teacher to three distinct, yet related, areas. These include the teacher's plans for instruction, the teacher's behaviors in the classroom, and the outcomes of the teaching (what students do and learn). Their model, therefore, comprises three stages which correspond to the areas of analysis:

Stage 1: Planning the teaching.
Stage 2: Observation of the teaching.
Stage 3: Evaluation or analysis after the teaching.

Each of the three stages is described briefly below.

Stage 1: Planning the Teaching

In this first stage of the model, the supervisor and teacher review the teacher's intentions as expressed in the plans for the lesson or jointly develop plans before the actual instruction occurs. Mosher and Purpel express a strong preference for the latter approach, while recognizing the time constraints that most supervisors face. They believe that the careful consideration beforehand of the appropriateness of objectives, materials, and pedagogy for the particular curriculum and pupils to be taught is an especially effective use of a supervisor's time.

During their planning together, the teacher and supervisor make hypotheses or predictions about the effects on pupils of the subject matter and method of teaching being considered for a particular lesson. Thinking of a lesson plan as a set of predictions, they note, is very different from how planning for instruction is usually regarded.

"Content," for Mosher and Purpel, refers to the subject matter itself, the materials used in teaching, and the nature of the problems presented to the class. A rational analysis of the content is performed during the planning stage which includes consideration of the following questions:

- How can the objectives for teaching this particular content be justified?
- Is the content suitable to the teacher's purposes?
- Is the content suitable to the intellectual ability of the students?
- Is the teacher's knowledge of the content adequate for conveying it correctly from a factual standpoint?
- What are the motivational characteristics of the content?
- Is the planned sequence of classroom events appropriate for accomplishing the objectives of the lesson?

Usually, issues concerning short- and long-term objectives are addressed during the planning stage as well as the appropriateness of the content to be taught. As a subject matter specialist, however, the supervisor also raises questions relating to the curriculum rationale. Advantages of alternative teaching strategies are considered, and related to predictions about what children will be doing and learning. Contingency plans for students who have not prepared for the lesson and alternative strategies such as group work, readings, and films are also taken into account.

The major purpose of the planning conference is to provide an opportunity for the teacher to think carefully and explicitly about instruction, including its relation to content. This prologue to the lesson helps to reduce pitfalls, randomness, and reliance on intuition. Although Mosher and Purpel assert that teaching cannot be reduced to an exact technology given our present state of knowledge, the process of teaching can be made more rational and systematic, they believe, by specifying in advance behaviors that are hoped will lead to some intended consequences.

Stage 2: Observation of the Teaching

In most schools, Mosher and Purpel note, teaching takes place behind closed doors. In schools where clinical supervision is practiced, however, teaching is regularly observed by the supervisor and other teachers. As the act of teaching becomes public instead of private, the study and modification of its processes and outcomes are made possible.

The supervisor's job during the observation of the teaching is to record in detail what the teacher and students say and do. Although verbatim notes are most often used, Mosher and Purpel prefer and advocate videotaping lessons for later analysis. The completeness of the audio and video record, as well as the capacity for "stop-action" and "instant replay," in their opinion, far outweigh any disadvantages.

In formulating categories of behavior for analysis, Mosher and Purpel recommend that the teacher and supervisor first look closely at what pupils say and do during the lesson, especially in relation to the intentions of the teacher. Student behavior, they suggest, is the most immediate, valid, and direct index of student learning available. The teacher's objectives for the lesson are a good starting point, according to Mosher and Purpel, in that student behavior can be classified in terms of whether or not it furthers or hinders achievement of the objectives. The following questions, attributed to Cogan (1961) are recommended as useful guides to the analysis of student behavior:

- Are students performing the required work?
- Are students initiating reponses independently?
- Are students solving problems?
- Are students learning and using concepts, principles, and generalizations?
- Are students expressing or changing attitudes and appreciations?
- Are students suggesting and relating new problems and new situations to familiar learnings?
- Are students drawing conclusions, voicing opinions, presenting evidence, or challenging the logic of others' conclusions?

Once a clear image of student behavior has been formulated, the teacher and supervisor can shift their attention to teacher behavior and other factors in the classroom that affect learning outcomes. Rather than relying on existing checklists, Mosher and Purpel recommend that the teacher and supervisor use the following six areas of teacher behavior in their analysis of the videotape or transcript:

1. *How well is the teacher able to communicate?*
   This area includes issues such as audibility and coherence of the presentation, how transitions are handled, and the degree of abstraction in the teacher's language.
2. *Is the teaching strategy or method employed logical?*
   The central issue here is the appropriateness and effectiveness of the observed sequence of events for accomplishing the lesson's objectives.
3. *How well does the teacher perform instrumental tasks?*
   Classroom management should be considered, including the teacher's efficiency in tasks such as distributing papers, having materials readily available, and arranging seating for students that is conducive to the activities in which they are engaged.
4. *What is the motivational effect of the lesson?*
   Attention should be given to how imaginative and stimulating the teacher's presentation appears to be.
5. *What is the quality of the personal relationships established between the teacher and students?*
   Data relevant to this area include feelings that students express about the teacher during the lesson, the predictability of the teacher's interactions with students, the types of rewards or punishments employed in the classroom, and the teacher's comments about student behavior.
6. *Was the content communicated?*
   The teacher and supervisor here determine whether or not the predictions they made during planning were supported. The suitability of the content for the objectives and the students taught, whether the content was communicated correctly, and to what extent students found it motivating are again considered in light of the evidence.

Stage 3: Evaluation or Analysis After the Teaching

Mosher and Purpel consider the third stage, the conference following the teaching, to be crucial. They suggest postponing the conference briefly, however, to allow the supervisor time to think and plan, and for the teacher to distance himself or herself emotionally from the lesson. This temporary delay helps to ensure, they believe, that the conference is more objective, rationally organized, and productive.

The advantages and disadvantages of three types of analysis are discussed. The first type of analysis involves the identification by the supervisor of events that occurred during the lesson, along with tentative explanations of cause-and-effect relationships. A drawback to this method, according to Mosher and Purpel, is that it is essentially descriptive and minimally analytic.

A second type of analysis is focused on what are termed "critical incidents," or important turning points in the lesson. Although often interesting, according to Mosher and Purpel, discussion of critical events only skims the surface of the data without probing deeply for meanings or developing understandings.   A third type of analysis is most strongly favored by Mosher and Purpel and involves the identification of recurrent patterns of behavior in the classroom. They suggest that this process is similar to the reading and thought that go into textual analysis. They propose that recurrent patterns are evident in what is taught, how it is taught, and in students' responses to the teaching.

In the post-teaching conference the supervisor should draw extensively on evidence to focus the discussion on recurring patterns of behavior and on the possible interrelationships among content, teacher behavior, and student behavior in the lesson that was observed. Mosher and Purpel recommend that the supervisor select those patterns that can be changed and offer suggestions for more effective teaching. They also advocate liberal use of praise on the grounds that change must be built upon success. The supervisor thus capitalizes on the teacher's strengths by reinforcing positive aspects of his or her existing abilities, preferences, and perceptions of what constitutes good teaching. Ineffective teaching is expected to extinguish simply through lack of reinforcement.

Mosher and Purpel emphasize, however, that the teacher should have freedom and be urged to develop an individual teaching style within very broad limits of competence defined by the supervisor. Current research, they believe, fails to justify any single model of teaching effectiveness. They view as most effective teaching that reflects an authentic, disciplined, personal expression of behaviors acquired over a long period of time. The supervisor should respect the teacher's personal and professional autonomy and steer clear of addressing personality factors. The focus should always remain on improving teaching performance by changing behaviors only.

A number of other suggestions for the post-teaching analysis session are offered to supervisors by Mosher and Purpel. These include:

- plan a strategy in advance of each conference;
- limit major points or interpretations of teaching to two or three areas at most;
- reinforce the effective aspects of teaching with praise;
- avoid making moral judgments or the implication that the teaching observed was somehow "good" or "bad;"
- keep the discussion focused on whether observed behaviors were functional or appropriate;
- remember that clinical supervision is an instructional process that is unrelated to personnel evaluation.

A variation of the post-teaching conference (Stage 3) that Mosher and Purpel favor is a group analysis session in which a number of teachers participate by sharing perceptions and analyses of a videotape recording of the teaching of a colleague. This meeting is moderated by the supervisor. Based on the results of the pooled analysis, the next lesson is planned by the entire group. The individual's skill and personal teaching style are taken into consideration, but the emphasis remains on improvement based on feedback.

Although Mosher and Purpel insist repeatedly on the distinction between clinical supervision and personnel evaluation, they view clinical supervision as an effective way of ensuring quality control over the curriculum. Part of this quality control comes from the opening up of isolated classrooms to regular and frequent observation, thus making public processes that were formerly hidden from view.

Central to the perspective of Mosher and Purpel, however, is the notion of the clinical supervisor as a subject matter specialist who engages the teacher in discussion concerning *what* is taught as well as *how* it is taught. Mosher and Purpel are clearly not concerned with the application of effective teaching practices. They even suggest that general principles of effectiveness can never be identified because of the complexity of the teaching act.

Instead, Mosher and Purpel believe that the supervisor should work toward developing in each teacher a "high order of clinical judgment" that is built upon "experience-based learning or wisdom concerning problematic curriculum and instructional issues" (1972, p. 112).

Working With Beginning Teachers

Mosher and Purpel are especially concerned about the development of beginning teachers, specifically, how beginners acquire knowledge and behavior appropriate to the role of teacher, and how they differentiate the professional role from their personal identities. Mosher and Purpel describe at considerable length a supervisory strategy derived from counseling that they believe is particularly effective in working with novices.

Learning to teach, according to Mosher and Purpel, requires changing what one is. A change in personal philosophy, a new emotional understanding of children, and success in acquiring teaching skill, they note, all depend on the ability to change one's self in some way. Few people are born teachers, Mosher and Purpel suggest, most teachers are shaped into their role by their experiences.

Traditionally, Mosher and Purpel observe, the field of supervision has steered clear of involvement with the teacher's personal self. They argue that this tendency may be unwise because what teachers and their students do in classrooms is directly affected by what teachers are like as people. Therefore, they suggest, supervision ought to broaden its scope by being more responsive to the teacher as a person. In the view of Mosher and Purpel, supervisors should use the clinical supervision process to help teachers *think* themselves into new ways of acting. The change process should be made conscious, in other words, and result in increased understanding and control over personal and professional problems related to teaching, followed by an improvement in the quality of teaching itself.

The Development of a Professional Identity

According to Mosher and Purpel, a beginning teacher goes through several distinct phases as they acquire the professional identity of a teacher. Beginning to teach requires that individuals begin seeing, thinking, and behaving in new ways. These are summarized below:

Phase 1: Job Expectations.
The initial phase of developing a professional identity, according to Mosher and Purpel, involves concern about what others expect one to

be and *do* as a teacher. Mosher and Purpel identify three issues as especially salient in this regard:

  a) What do others (colleagues, administrators, supervisors) expect of me as a teacher?
  b) What attributes are expected of me as a teacher?
  c) What am I supposed to be doing in terms of curriculum and instruction?

Phase 2: Personal Concerns.
The next phase in professional development for beginning teachers, as described by Mosher and Purpel, involves clarifying and formulating plans about what one personally wants to achieve as a teacher. Early experiences, educational background, and personal values all come into play at this point. Previously undetected inconsistencies and contradictions in what one actually believes may surface. Also, conflict may develop between what the norms of the school dictate in terms of academic content and process and what the new teacher prefers. Most disconcerting, however, is the emotional impact of the challenge to one's abilities presented by the students themselves. Often, the requirements of simultaneously teaching and disciplining students exceeds the novice's capabilities. Questions that confront beginning teachers at this point include the following:

  a) What objectives do I want to achieve as a teacher?
  b) What do I want my teaching to be like?
  c) How interested and committed am I to accomplishing what I want as a teacher?

During this second phase, beginning teachers can experience considerable stress arising from the gap between job requirements and personal expectations, and between personal expectations and actual performance in the classroom. The relationship among these is depicted in *Figure 2-1*. Although too much stress and anxiety can lead to rigidity and failure, Mosher and Purpel note that a moderate amount of stress can motivate beginning teachers toward positive growth.

Phase 3: Personal Role Definition.
The supervisor's main task during this third phase of teacher development is to help the teacher realign his or her objectives by considering new attitudes, beliefs, and ways of responding in the classroom. The anxiety experienced during the previous phase of professional development, according to Mosher and Purpel, can lead initially to a variety

of unproductive coping mechanisms that avoid confronting reality. These include, for example:

- intellectualization – addressing problems on an abstract level only;
- reaction formation – stating the direct opposite of one's true feelings and beliefs;
- suppression or denial – pretending that problems do not exist;
- rationalization – explaining problems away through logic without solving them;
- projection – blaming other people or things;
- regression or dependency – asking other people to solve problems instead of assuming responsibility and taking initiative oneself.

Fortunately, Mosher and Purpel suggest, beginning teachers who are confronted by the stress of developing a professional identity also tend to be particularly open to self-analysis and discussion concerning their attitudes and teaching behavior. Essentially, beginning teachers are helped to synthesize the many personal and job-related factors they are confronting into a unique, individual, and consistent definition of a personal and professional identity.

The effective teacher not only adapts to the expectations of others, according to Mosher and Purpel, he or she also finds ways of expressing

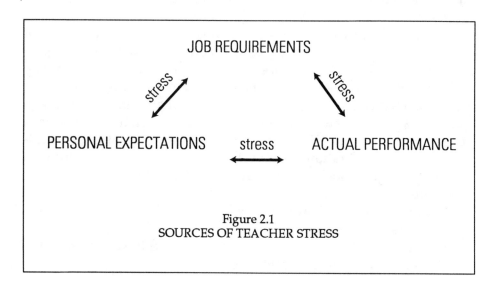

Figure 2.1
SOURCES OF TEACHER STRESS

important personal motives and needs on the job. Thus, the individual is not only involved with becoming a teacher, he or she is actually profoundly changed by the process of developing a professional identity.

Ego Counseling and Supervision

Mosher and Purpel believe that supervisors can best help new teachers overcome the obstacles to achieving a professional identity by drawing on the techniques of counseling, specifically a technique referred to as "ego counseling." They suggest that the procedures and objectives of clinical supervision are similar to those of counseling, although with supervision there is obviously less of an attempt to alter the basic personality of the teacher. Beginning teachers can and do experience considerable stress, as has been noted, and so the line between counseling and supervision is not always entirely clear when supervisors help new teachers cope with job related anxieties. Also, self-evaluation and self-knowledge are sought as outcomes by both counseling and supervision, although the primary focus is mainly personal in one case and professional in the other.

Ego counseling, according to Mosher and Purpel, is based on the proposition that the behavior of normal individuals is organized by the ego, which is comprised of values, attitudes, assumptions, and personal traits along with ego functions such as perceiving, thinking, planning, and taking action. The focus of ego counseling is on problems that exist for the individual in reality.

A feature that distinguishes ego counseling from other forms of counseling, Mosher and Purpel assert, is its emphasis on what psychologists term "secondary process" thinking, namely, logic, planning, and problem solving. Although unconscious motives and feelings are acknowledged as real, they are not the focus of attention. Rather, ego counseling concentrates on intellectual analysis of the individual's personal condition, clarification of problems, revision of understandings, planning, and rational action. This focus is also very reminiscent of Dewey's logic of social inquiry. In essence, ego counseling involves four steps:

1) the teacher carefully appraises himself or herself in terms of the current situation;
2) the connection between present action and the achievement of desired outcomes is examined;

3) personal and situational obstacles to accomplishing one's aims as a teacher are considered;

4) new ways of thinking and acting as a teacher are developed.

A central tenet of Mosher and Purpel's application of ego counseling to clinical supervision is the idea that the teacher is a more active and significant participant in the analysis of teaching than the supervisor. The teacher is encouraged to analyze his or her own teaching, to develop personal understandings and meanings about the role and realities of teaching, and to control his or her own professional behavior. The supervisor can be especially helpful to beginning teachers by helping them to think more abstractly and objectively about their teaching, and to make personal, curricular, and instructional sense out of their experiences. However, the teacher's own thinking is the major impetus for change, not the relationship to the supervisor.

Working With Experienced Teachers

Clinical supervision combined with ego counseling is especially important for beginning teachers, according to Mosher and Purpel, because early experiences contribute significantly to a teacher's effectiveness and often shape the direction of their subsequent development. However, they claim that the same techniques can be productively employed with more experienced teachers, even though the personal and professional problems that experienced teachers face are usually quite different, and experienced teachers may not be as willing initially to talk openly about problems they are having.

The following suggestions are offered by Mosher and Purpel when applying the process of ego counseling in the supervision of more seasoned professionals:

- listen more and talk less;
- rely more on the teacher's perceptions of instructional problems;
- help the teacher to recognize patterns of teaching, then let the teacher decide which are effective and which are not;
- as a basis for discussion, record data from two or more observations and then compare them;
- recognize and be willing to deal with one's own anxieties as a supervisor about talking with teachers in an open and personal manner.

Supervising Teachers in Groups

As noted earlier, a distinctive feature of Mosher and Purpel's version of clinical supervision is the emphasis they place on working as a supervisor with groups of teachers. Although reponsibility for making sense of classroom events ultimately lies with the individual teacher, exposure to the views of colleagues opens opportunities for discovering new perspectives that can be integrated into one's personal style of teaching.

When working with a group of teachers the supervisor functions as more of a catalyst and resource, taking care not to exert influence too early. Mosher and Purpel caution that a group of teachers will usually try to force a supervisor to play a traditional role as an expert in all matters of content and method. Supervisors ought to avoid this trap by intentionally being nondirective at first. Otherwise, the group will become dependent on the supervisor for all the answers. The supervisor should become more direct in interpreting and confronting issues raised by group members, according to Mosher and Purpel, only after the group develops trust and confidence in its own objectives and judgments.

The supervisor should actively invite teachers to learn, however, rather than simply hoping that a learning context in which teachers communicate openly and honestly with one another will emerge spontaneously. This can be accomplished by modeling careful listening, giving teachers opportunities to pursue issues that they care about, and encouraging decision making through consensus.

Learning in a group, Mosher and Purpel note, involves both cognitive and emotional elements. In the process of group learning teachers develop personal resources and competence in using them. Specifically, teachers become aware of multiple perspectives and a variety of approaches to solving any one problem. Teachers can also compare issues that are of personal importance with issues that are centrally important to colleagues, understand conflicts better, and reassess their own assumptions, attitudes, and beliefs. Recognizing the availability of multiple perspectives and approaches provides teachers with a more extensive repertoire of responses, and reduces the risk that teachers will fall into safe, unexamined, routinized methods of teaching that restrict creativity for themselves and their students.

Although the focus of group learning is on resolving concerns and problems of practice, according to Mosher and Purpel, learning for the individual teacher is very personal. At times, therefore, the focus of a learning group shifts to issues of personal competence, self awareness, and self consciousness. When this experience is accepted as a legitimate part of the growth process, a context of mutual support through sharing gets created that affirms the teacher's sense of self. Knowing that one can be open and share the experience of trying something new with a group of colleagues, Mosher and Purpel suggest, gives teachers courage to take risks that they otherwise might not take.

Issues in Group Supervision

Mosher and Purpel compare the informal adjustments and agreements made by the members of a group to a complex and flexible unwritten contract. A variety of factors, they note, influence the specific nature of this contract. The following issues, they suggest, should be carefully considered:

Source of Intiative. Discussion groups are most successful when the intiative to form them comes from the teachers themselves. If the intiative for group discussion comes from elsewhere, a good procedure is to present the general idea to teachers with an invitation opened to those who wish to participate.

Group Size. A group comprised of from six to ten members is recommended as optimal by Mosher and Purpel. Fewer than six makes self disclosure more difficult, while more than ten begins to infringe on the time available for each member to speak when he or she has something to say. Too large a group can result in chaotic agendas that can lead to frustration and even hostility among members.

Duration of Meetings. Although this may vary from group to group, Mosher and Purpel recommend that a session of around 90 minutes works best. Less than that does not allow sufficient opportunity for raising and analyzing issues carefully and in detail. A minimum of eight meetings is recommended, but fewer can sometimes be productive.

Composition of the Group. A group comprised of representatives from diverse content fields can be useful in helping to focus discussion directly on the teacher-learner relationship and away from subject related issues. A balance of male and female, as well as younger and older teachers can also widen the spectrum of perspectives and experiences available to the group.

Community Participation. Mosher and Purpel recommend including student service staff like counselors and school nurses within a group of teachers. Although discussion groups comprised solely of administrators can be beneficial, Mosher and Purpel strongly advise against including teachers and administrators in the same group. They report that the presence of administrators tends to stifle discussion among teachers of the very issues that lie at the heart of effective teaching.

The Art of Facilitating Groups

As noted earlier, Mosher and Purpel strongly advise against a supervisor providing much direction to groups of teachers during their initial meetings because behaviors learned early in a group's existence quickly become expectations that govern future interactions. A supervisor can inadvertently structure an initial meeting, they warn, simply by calling on teachers to speak, giving praise for certain types of responses to questions, saving questions until the end, or summarizing important points at the conclusion of a meeting. Such procedures subtly establish the supervisor as the leader, which may discourage participation and openness from the teachers.

At the very start, Mosher and Purpel suggest, the supervisor should emphasize to the group a respect for the processes of discovery and change through open communication that is based on trust and mutual support. The supervisor should invite teachers to share their feelings and thoughts, and then model careful listening and a sincere interest in understanding the perspectives of others.

It may be helpful during the first few meetings, according to Mosher and Purpel, to use videotapes or transcripts of classroom situations as a common focus. As teachers begin to see that a single event can be interpreted in as many ways as there are group members, they become more careful about listening attentively and develop a broader repertoire of personal responses to situations.

Data from case studies also provide a point to which group members can constantly refer, thus preventing a discussion from becoming too generalized and diffuse. Beginning with the same data and proceeding forward through discussion as a group also gives the group a sense of history and intimacy as personal experiences are shared and individuals come to know one another.

A supervisor may initially have difficulty facilitating a group in a supportive and nondirective manner. The key is to establish expectations which open opportunities for communication and participation to others. After viewing a videotape, for example, a supervisor might ask the group an open-ended question such as: "What stands out for you in the lesson we just watched?" Next, the supervisor should listen as well as possible to the responses, without suggesting that he or she possesses any superior insights into the matter under discussion.

Sometimes uncomfortably long pauses punctuate a group discussion. Often such periods of silence indicate that participants are gathering their thoughts. Mosher and Purpel advise that the supervisor should resist the temptation to break the silence and give teachers time to reflect, reconsider attitudes, and choose their words before responding. An attitude of respectful attention and concern is most highly valued under these circumstances.

Group Communication and Consensus

As individuals begin to speak, the supervisor should concentrate carefully on understanding what they are saying without being judgmental or evaluative. Seeking clarification through questions or paraphrasing opens communication channels still further. Eventually, after group members come to view the supervisor as a resource instead of an authority figure, the supervisor can begin to participate more actively, sharing his or her own perceptions and speculations concerning issues as they arise.

After the initial sessions, teachers may be invited to bring in videotaped recordings of their own teaching. This can be threatening at first, but Mosher and Purpel report that groups usually react to tapes of their colleagues with sensitivity. Often, simply videotaping a teaching episode gives a teacher the objectivity needed to develop new insight which he or she can share with the group.

Consensus should not be pursued as an end in itself. Supervisors may want to verbally acknowledge a consensus when it appears to have emerged, but open exploration of attitudes and beliefs concerning teaching and learning should remain the primary goal of the group.

Anxiety in Groups

Anxiety is inevitable, especially in the early meetings of a group when apprehension over uncertainty or feelings of inadequacy may surface. Mosher and Purpel recommend that supervisors acknowledge the presence of anxiety and encourage group members to talk about their feelings, otherwise anxieties tend to grow worse. When they are acknowledged as appropriate and typical, however, anxieties can become vehicles for learning. By carefully examining our own anxieties, Mosher and Purpel suggest, we often discover value conflicts that can lead to profound personal insights into our behavior. Learning to deal with feelings of anxiety, fear, and helplessness can help us become better teachers as we come to grips with our feelings more honestly and productively.

At times the members of a group may feel that they have reached the limits of their personal and collective growth, especially after a significant breakthrough has been achieved. The supervisor needs to be aware of this occasional feeling of having reached a limit of insight and understanding. Again, acknowledging this feeling is the first step toward urging the group on to face further challenges and professional development by suggesting new directions or perspectives.

Outcomes of Group Supervision

The greatest value for teachers in sharing openly with their colleagues, according to Mosher and Purpel, is that teachers continue an internal dialogue long after the group experience has ended. Teachers are apt to consider and to continue discovering multiple perspectives as they engage in an imagined conversation with others in the group.

Teachers also learn from the group experience that sharing and communicating with colleagues is a rewarding and professionally enriching experience and they are more likely to share and communicate in other contexts. Finally, Mosher and Purpel report that teachers who have been exposed to the reality of multiple perspectives in a group, tend to more readily accept alternative viewpoints and are more willing to try new methods when suggested by a supervisor in individual conferences.

Summary

Mosher and Purpel's version of clinical supervision combines a three stage sequence with elements of ego counseling. The supervisor serves primarily as a content specialist, with expertise in curriculum theory, design, and development. Teaching effectiveness is considered unfeasible without consideration of the subject matter, along with its inherent logic, materials, and special problems.

During the first stage of Mosher and Purpel's model, planning the teaching, the supervisor actively participates in helping the teacher to think through the appropriateness of objectives, materials, and methods for the particular content and students to be taught. Possible effects on pupils are hypothesized and alternative contingencies are considered.

During the second stage, the observation of the teaching, the supervisor videotapes the lesson or takes verbatim notes. The supervisor records both student and teacher behavior, especially as they contribute or detract from achievement of the teacher's objectives for the lesson.

In stage three, evaluation or analysis after the teaching, the supervisor and teacher identify recurrent patterns of behavior evidenced in the classroom and propose possible relationships among the content, teacher behavior, and student behavior. As a content specialist, the supervisor engages the teacher in discussion about *what* is taught as well as *how* it is taught.

According to Mosher and Purpel, beginning teachers need help with the overwhelming task of establishing a positive and consistent professional identity. They recommend that supervisors use principles of ego counseling to help novice teachers deal with stress arising from discrepancies and conflicts among job requirements, personal expectations, and actual performance. Experienced teachers may benefit from ego counseling too as they polish their individual teaching styles, but they need less guidance in analyzing personal and professional issues. Also, they should assume more initiative.

Mosher and Purpel strongly advocate supervision with groups because it exposes teachers to the views of colleagues and opens opportunities for discovering a wide range of perspectives. Supervisors should act more as catalysts than as leaders in group situations, they suggest, to encourage open communication and discovery among the group participants. Although the group may analyze a videotaped lesson and participate in planning, the individual teacher retains ultimate responsibility in this version of clinical supervision for making sense of classroom events.

References

Cogan, M. L. (1961). *Supervision at the Harvard-Newton summer school."* Mimeographed. Harvard Graduate School of Education.

Mosher, R. L. & Purpel, D. E. (1972). *Supervision: The reluctant profession.* Boston: Houghton-Mifflin.

Chapter 3

Morris Cogan's Rationale for Clinical Supervision

The Model at Work

Looking back, Mrs. Smith was somewhat surprised at the amount of preparation that had preceded the lesson that Mr. Davis was beginning to teach. She thought about the end of last summer when she had led a two-week long workshop that introduced Mr. Davis and other teachers on the faculty to the philosophy, objectives, processes, and techniques of clinical supervision. The workshop included simulations, practice, and planning. Considerable time was spent reviewing research, literature, and various instruments, and discussing the criteria of competent teaching. The teachers then planned together in small groups, observed one another teach, and role played aspects of the clinical supervision cycle.

At the very end of the training session Mrs. Smith met with Mr. Davis, who was an experienced and successful teacher, to discuss his unique strengths, interests, and professional needs. They then identified some objectives for improvement and selected several to focus on during the clinical supervision cycle that would follow.

Several weeks after school began, Mrs. Smith and Mr. Davis met again to cooperatively plan the best lesson they could imagine. Mr. Davis recognized that he had fallen into a comfortable and predictable routine in his classrooms, and wanted to try something different. Together, he and Mrs. Smith developed a written lesson plan that involved students in a cooperative learning activity. Mr. Davis noted that the lesson was more innovative than anything he had tried recently. At one point, he said that he was beginning to have some doubts about the wisdom of taking risks when things were already working very well. Mrs. Smith listened attentively and admitted that this whole thing was new and risky for her too. Once these feelings were acknowledged, they finished planning the lesson.

The lesson plan they completed included clear objectives and a motivational device at the beginning to arouse student curiosity. Mrs. Smith and Mr. Davis decided to test the hypothesis that student interest, as indicated by the number and kinds of questions asked, would be strong if Mr. Davis took time to explain how the lesson related to what had been learned previously and to the cooperative activity that would follow.

With the lesson plan finished, Mrs. Smith asked Mr. Davis what aspect of the lesson he wanted to know more about. He answered that he was most concerned about the level of student interest. They discussed several possible data gathering strategies that might be appropriate, including an interaction matrix, but finally agreed that Mrs. Smith would make a verbatim transcript of students' questions and comments, both before and during the cooperative learning activity.

Mrs. Smith was sure that the lesson would go well and already anticipated how best to handle the data analysis. She felt that Mr. Davis had enough self-confidence and insight into his teaching, so they could analyze the data together as soon after the lesson as possible. But she thought that she would lead their discussion this first time as they identified teaching patterns, possible relationships to student outcomes, and patterns worthy of further attention. After Mr. Davis went through this process once, she would shift to a less didactic, nondirective approach. He was a teacher, she thought, who was already open to assistance from others and on his way to being self-directing.

Introduction

The history of public education in the United States, Cogan (1973) observes, can be viewed as a long series of recurring crises followed by unsuccessful attempts at reform. Many of these reform efforts have included valuable ideas and elements which might actually have improved instruction, he believes if only they had been properly incorporated into the schools. Misunderstanding of the reforms, inadequate resources, and faulty implementation, he suggests, often resulted in the abandonment of fundamentally sound ideas before they received a fair chance of success.

According to Cogan, superintendents and school boards have preferred to buy into popular educational fads without critically evaluating the worth and appropriateness of the innovations for their districts. More resources seem to be devoted to promoting and defending an innovation once selected, he suggests, than in seeing to it that sufficient materials and training are available to teachers for its successful implementation.

The result of these haphazard and half-hearted efforts has been that teaching as a profession and education generally have not demonstrated much progress. The promise of new technologies, curricula, teaching methods, and organizational patterns has failed to materialize largely due to the absence of adequate support for teachers in schools and classrooms. Cogan argues that if innovations are to have any chance of surviving and succeeding in schools, a corps of well-trained clinical supervisors is needed to both disseminate and nurture new ideas. It is at the classroom level where new ideas are most likely to break down and fail, Cogan notes, partly because psychological and institutional factors contribute to a tendency among teachers to quickly revert to traditional and comfortable patterns of behavior. Experienced teachers often have great difficulty changing because they must first unlearn safe and successful ways of behaving before trying new ones. Teachers who are naturally innovative and creative, on the other hand, are faced with having to independently reinvent instructional methods and ways of relating to students. What all teachers need, therefore, is systematic, sustained, expert assistance to help them reach their potential. Teachers especially need assistance in the form of "in-class support" when they experiment with new methods. Clinical supervision, according to Cogan, can provide this assistance.

The Framework

Cogan distinguishes *clinical* supervision from what he calls *general* supervision. The latter relates to curriculum development, the preparation of system-wide instructional units and materials, and evaluation of the entire instructional program. Clinical supervision, in contrast, is concerned specifically with improving the instruction of individual teachers in the classroom. The term "clinical" implies for Cogan the direct observation, analysis, and treatment of actual cases and concrete problems with a focus on the in-class behavior of teachers and students. A foundation of clinical supervision, according to Cogan, is the identification and analysis of behavior patterns as a way of giving meaning to classroom events recorded in observation data.

The phases of the clinical supervision cycle as described by Cogan are as follows:

Phase 1.   Establishing the teacher/supervisor relationship

Phase 2.   Planning with the teacher

Phase 3.   Planning the structure of observation

Phase 4.   Observing instruction

Phase 5.   Analyzing the teaching/learning processes

Phase 6.   Planning the structure of the conference

Phase 7.   The conference

Phase 8.   Renewed planning

A major purpose of clinical supervision as envisioned by Cogan is the development of a professionally responsible teacher who is capable of analyzing his or her own performance, who is open to assistance from others, and who is above all self-directing. As a teacher gains experience and familiarity with clinical supervision and as the relationship between the supervisor and teacher develops, Cogan suggests that some phases can be condensed or omitted entirely. The cycle should not be abbreviated, he cautions, until the teacher possesses the appropriate knowledge and skills and has developed the motivation and self confidence to create new strategies and initiate improvements independently.

All teachers continue to need the assistance that clinical supervision provides though at varying intervals. How often a teacher needs this support, according to Cogan, depends on several characteristics of the teacher, including:

a) the teacher's skill in objectively analyzing classroom events and his or her own behavior;

b) the teacher's competence in developing a program of self-improvement;

c) the teacher's motivation for working autonomously; and

d) the progress the teacher actually accomplishes when working alone.

Phase 1: Establishing the Teacher/Supervisor Relationship

The first phase of clinical supervision involves the introduction of the teacher to the philosophy, objectives, processes, and techniques of clinical supervision and the induction of the teacher into the role of colleague. Teachers should have a clear understanding of their relationship to the supervisor and the supervisor's relationship to others in the organization.

During this first phase, the teacher learns about the roles and responsibilities of teachers and supervisors in clinical supervision without actually experiencing them. The supervisor introduces the teacher to the model gradually through a carefully planned program lasting two-to-six weeks that includes general orientation, group training, simulations, discussion, practice, and planning.

Cogan advises that the criteria of competent teaching should be explicitly clarified and understood through discussion. Discussion may begin in a group, but should become more specific between individual teachers and supervisors. Local observation instruments, research, and literature on innovations can be sources of relevant information. During their time together, the teacher and supervisor gain knowledge of both methods and each other. If agreement on some common ground is not possible, Cogan recommends that a new supervisor should work with that teacher.

According to Cogan, groups can provide teachers with the security, motivation, and ongoing reinforcement needed to embark on the clinical supervision process. Teachers can share responsibilities for tasks, clarify understandings of values and philosophies, enhance and maintain one another's morale, and relate to other elements and processes in the school. Groups are especially important, Cogan notes, for avoiding preoccupation solely with clinical problems to the exclusion of more general concerns. Small group work is also useful as a transition to new roles that require accepting and sharing responsibilities with others. Teachers can plan together, observe each other in class, and role play aspects of the clinical supervision cycle.

Encounter groups can be useful, Cogan suggests, for improving communication skills, increasing mutual trust, and lessening defensiveness and rigidity. Developing interpersonal sensitivities, personal insights, and skills are helpful to the clinical supervision process and have applicability in the classroom as well.

An intended outcome of Phase 1 is for each teacher to accept responsibility for improving instruction in the classroom through clinical supervision. Several steps are recommended for this preliminary planning as the teacher/supervisor relationship is established:

1) Teachers and supervisors meet in pairs to develop a plan for each teacher that is congruent with his or her unique strengths, interests, objectives, and needs.
2) After a discussion of these, priorities are tentatively established and objectives formulated for an initial clinical supervision cycle.
3) A record is kept of decisions made and goals agreed upon. This record gives direction to the cycle and is useful when assessing progress.

The teacher and supervisor must be careful, Cogan advises, that the initiative exerted by the supervisor in these early steps does not cause passivity in the teacher. They should share their feelings about the process as it develops to ensure that responsibility does not gravitate to one or the other exclusively. Cogan suggests that it is a good idea to share responsibility for tasks during this early phase and agree upon who will do what to prepare for the next meeting.

Although this elaborate procedure of preparation is both expensive and time-consuming, Cogan emphasizes that it is absolutely necessary for the purpose of restructuring the traditional teacher/supervisor relationship. Once firmly established, this first phase need not be repeated with the same teacher or teachers. The clinical cycle itself is expected to reinforce trust and productive working relationships.

Assumptions About Establishing the Teacher/Supervisor Relationship

Clinical Supervision is not Remediation. Clinical supervision contributes to the maintenance and development of professional competence of teachers, but is not intended to remediate deficiencies.
Clinical Supervision can Help to Overcome Professional Isolation and Loneliness. The isolation of teachers from other adult professionals normally makes them suspicious about visitors to their classes and resistant to supervision. Involvement in clinical supervision can help to alleviate professional isolation and loneliness.
Success Depends on the Quality of the Relationship Established Between the Teacher and Supervisor. The total process that teachers and supervisors develop together is paramount, not the care with which they enact isolated components of the model.

Phase 2: Planning with the Teacher

Planning lessons requires time, Cogan observes, especially early in the implementation of clinical supervision as the teacher and supervisor are establishing a sound working relationship. After an introductory two to six week summer program, Cogan recommends that teachers need at least three planning periods per week of forty-five minutes to one hour in length during the academic year.

Planning together marks the actual beginning of working toward the improvement of instruction in the classroom. The teacher and supervisor in Cogan's model cooperatively plan the best lesson that they can. Each practices the part of colleague as they jointly attempt to solve a concrete professional problem that is important to the teacher.

Cogan advises that the teacher and supervisor should begin with simple plans and progress toward greater complexity. Plans should be neither so specific and detailed that they stifle creativity and flexibility, nor so general that the activities and outcomes are unclear. While planning, the teacher and supervisor should develop hypotheses regarding the likely outcomes of the decisions they make. The lesson, then, becomes the test of those hypotheses.

Teachers are likely to experience considerable uncertainty and anxiety upon first being introduced to clinical supervision, Cogan notes, especially as new roles and behaviors are being tried. The best way to handle such a situation is for the supervisor to first listen to the teacher's concerns. This strategy allows the ventilation of feelings which may otherwise get in the way of rational analysis and also gives the supervisor additional information about the teacher which may provide useful insights.

As the teacher and supervisor plan together, they share information about students and available resources. If the teacher refuses to use a written plan because it inhibits spontaneity and opportunities for student input, Cogan suggests that the supervisor can ask the teacher to simply take notes as they discuss objectives and strategies. By viewing planning as predictions and tentative hypotheses, teaching becomes something of an informal experiment. The teacher should learn not only how to change, but also why change is desirable.

Cogan makes some very specific suggestions for what a lesson plan should include, such as:

- *Written objectives are desirable to help reduce ambiguity and instability of classroom events.* Behavioral objectives can help teachers establish priorities and know when success has been achieved. Objectives should be compatible with one another and with the methods by which they are achieved.
- *The daily lesson should relate both to what has been covered previously and to what is yet to come.* Cogan suggests that it is helpful to include a statement early in the lesson, explaining to students the relevance of what they are about to learn. Previous learning can be reviewed or future learning anticipated. Each lesson should possess integrity and meaning and relate as well in a meaningful way to other learnings over time.
- *Motivational devices at the beginning of a lesson are useful for arousing student curiosity and illustrating the general nature of the problems they will be studying.* Motivational introductions work better, according to Cogan, than simply informing students of the objectives and activities of a lesson. Introductory activities should establish continuity and introduce the general nature of the content. The supervisor can help a teacher select introductory activities that are appropriate for students' interests and evaluate their success.

Assumptions About Planning with the Teacher

Learning to Teach Well is not Easy. Beginning teachers often model styles of teaching to which they were exposed as students, although these styles are not necessarily desirable. Experienced teachers, on the other hand, rely upon comfortable routines that let them get by without taking risks. Both novices and veterans first have to *unlearn* these ingrained patterns before they can learn new ones and incorporate both into a consciously selected personal repertoire.

The Supervisor Should Avoid Probing too Deeply into the Teacher's Psyche or Personal Problems. When a teacher needs help outside the domain of supervision, Cogan cautions, the supervisor's duty is to refer the teacher to specialists who are competent to meet those needs. Clinical supervisors should limit their work to the domain of instructional improvement.

Clinical Supervisors Should Exhibit a Combination of Task and Relationship-oriented Behavior. Cogan reports that in his experience, most teachers are unable to wholeheartedly commit themselves to the challenge of professional improvement until they feel personally secure with the supervisor. At the beginning of the teacher-supervisor relationship teachers inevitably need psychological reassurance, he believes, before turning attention to changing themselves professionally. A strong emphasis on person-oriented behaviors in the initial phases of the relationship is necessary, according to Cogan, followed by appropriate integration of both task and relation-oriented behavior in the later phases.

Uncertainty Concerning Tasks and Outcomes is Inevitable for Supervisors. Information about teaching and learning is often too incomplete, Cogan believes, to make a definite choice, decision, or recommendation. Success or failure may be difficult to explain or understand at times. Because uncertainty is inevitable, supervisors must learn to live with it productively.

Phase 3: Planning the Structure of Observation

A major purpose of clinical supervision is for the teacher to develop a personal style in the classroom. The supervisor helps the teacher select behaviors that are congruent with existing talents by building on the teacher's strengths. Beyond technical mastery, Cogan advises, new behaviors must be consistent with the teacher's personality and style if they are to persist and be effective. The supervisor learns about the teacher through repeated and ongoing cycles of clinical supervision while trying to minimize the possibility of failure by lending support during the difficult process of change.

Another intention of clinical supervision is to increase teachers' knowledge of themselves and their teaching behavior, especially with regard to behavioral patterns exhibited within the classroom. Interpersonal relationships with students, patterns of reinforcement, and feedback between teachers and students are all open to analysis.

Involving teachers in planning the observation, Cogan maintains, encourages them to accept responsibility for analyzing and critiquing their own teaching. After planning the lesson (Phase 2), a good approach is for the supervisor to ask what aspect of the lesson in particular the teacher wants to know more about (e.g., questioning, transitions, etc.). This helps the teacher to focus objectively on his or her own behavior and the behavior of students.

Cooperative planning changes the fundamental meaning of supervision. Instead of a bureaucratic process done to teachers, the involvement of teachers makes the success of a lesson the professional responsibility of both. As the teacher and supervisor rehearse a lesson while they plan, potential problems are identified and strategies refined. The focus shifts from the person of the teacher to behaviors. Because failure and success are shared by the supervisor and teacher together, the roles of teacher and supervisor become redefined.

Cogan advises the supervisor to be cautious that the teacher maintains primary ownership of the lesson. He observes that a teacher can quickly become dependent on the supervisor for ideas and assume a passive stance. On the other hand, if things go poorly, the supervisor is too convenient a scapegoat. Both must remember that the purpose of the observation is to examine and focus upon behaviors and not to locate blame.

Incompatible expectations held by the teacher, the supervisor, and administrators can cause difficulty when choosing objectives for the teacher to pursue. In large part, teachers prefer to determine their own objectives. However, legitimate departmental, school, or district-wide objectives usually exist as well. Cogan suggests that supervisors can help to bridge competing extremes. The supervisor and teacher may develop mutual objectives, for example, on the basis of common ground such as the perceived needs of students. For the supervisor, a key is to know his or her own values and preferences, and to develop flexibility and skills to address multiple expectations simultaneously.

The teacher and supervisor must learn to work as a team, which necessarily means occasional disagreement. They must share common understandings which requires openness and full participation from both. The usefulness of clinical supervision, furthermore, must be demonstrated to the teacher through achievement of real success. Realistic goals help to avoid early failures. Goals that are selected initially, Cogan advises, must be neither trivial nor overly ambitious.

Clinical supervision should be "developmental," Cogan suggests, part of a larger and ongoing strategy to facilitate change in teacher behavior. Experiences to which teachers are exposed should be logically sequenced and responsive to their needs. The pace set by the supervisor must necessarily accommodate the teacher's current capacities and level of skill. Teachers learn and grow not only from the conference which follows the observation, Cogan emphasizes, but from experiencing new professional relationships, by enacting new roles, by planning and analyzing collaboratively, and by experimenting.

Assumptions About Planning the Structure of Observation

Supervisors Should Recognize that Multiple Models of Good Teaching are Possible and Desirable. The temptation to recreate the world in one's own image, making all teachers conform to one's own (ideal) way of doing things, Cogan believes, should be avoided at all cost. Teachers ought to be helped to become the best that they can become by developing a congruent and unique style. According to Cogan, there are likely to be as many different ways to teach as the number of teachers one supervises.

Supervisors Should Know the Teachers with Whom They Work as well as Possible. A supervisor should be familiar with each teacher's professional training and experiences. Getting to know and understand teachers' perceptions of themselves as professionals, their aspirations, their beliefs about education, and preferences regarding practice is essential.

The Hierarchical Distinction Between Supervisors and Teachers in School Organizations Diminishes Teachers Psychologically, Erodes Professional Accountability, and Increases Teacher Dependency. A clinical supervisory relationship in Cogan's view, is ideally a partnership in which responsibility is equally shared. Teachers should fully understand why they are trying to change, should want to change, and should experience satisfaction from success in doing so.

Phase 4: *Observing Instruction*

Cogan defines *observation* as "those operations by which individuals make careful, systematic scrutiny of the events and interactions occurring during classroom instruction." Classroom observation, he suggests, should be used as a tool for improving instruction, rather than a way of evaluating or identifying weaknesses in a teacher.

If a record of events in a classroom does not exist, Cogan notes, it is virtually impossible for a teacher and supervisor to agree on a verbal reconstruction of events. Objective and stable data (e.g. verbatim transcripts or videotapes) are therefore needed to minimize differences of perception and recall between the teacher and supervisor.

Data collected through observation of the teacher's behavior, students' behavior, and other events that occur in the classroom can be used to formulate hypotheses about the teacher's instruction. Deciding what type of data to record depends upon the needs identified and objectives planned by the teacher and supervisor. Data also provide a baseline or benchmark against which progress can be measured.

An informal experiment may be attempted, Cogan elaborates, with the teacher trying to influence student participation, for example, by changing the seating in a classroom or by practicing better listening skills. Types of statements made and whether they originated with the teacher or with students, as well as nonverbal behavior can then be recorded and compared to data collected earlier.

Data collected should always be detailed enough to allow a systematic analysis which can point to specific behaviors, events and instances rather than generalities. Teacher behavior, the context in which it appears, and its outcome for students are especially useful information. Such details facilitate later analysis, interpretation, and understanding of the classroom environment as a whole. Advantages and disadvantages of various data collection strategies as noted by Cogan are summarized in *Figure 3.1*.

	Supervisor as Recorder		Electronic Recording Equipment	
	Verbatim Transcript	**Interaction Analysis**	**Video**	**Audio**
Advantages	Useful as an initial overview to assess the general nature of classroom dynamics.	Scope is limited to manageable dimensions. Provide objective feedback to teachers Provide a structure to the analysis of data. Relevance of predetermined categories for a particular classroom can be tested.	Accurate, objective, and capable of total recall. Especially appropriate when classroom interaction is seriously affected by the presence of an observer. Video recordings are especially well-suited for recording and analyzing nonverbal communication.	
Disadvantages	Unlimited scope can be overwhelming and burdensome to teachers and supervisors.	Supervisors may rely too heavily upon existing instruments and their predetermined categories. Focusing on certain behaviors exclusively means that others are inevitably excluded. Complexity of teaching severely limits the chance that a small number of key behaviors can be identified.	Record of events is nonselective. Analysis can be cumbersome.	

Figure 3.1
DATA COLLECTION STRATEGIES

In general, Cogan notes, a well-trained supervisor has many advantages over electronic recording equipment when collecting data. A clinical supervisor knows which events are related to the lesson plan and which data will have greatest utility to the teacher. Besides being able to concentrate attention on what is relevant and truly important, a human observer can also change focus quickly and can sample events at intervals.

The presence of an observer, however, inevitably affects the social dynamics of the classroom. Discussing this problem with the teacher in advance is a good idea, and the teacher may want to explain to the class that the supervisor is a neutral observer. The supervisor should try to avoid interaction with students as a general rule. Involvement of the supervisor in a lesson is possible, but participation of this kind does not really contribute to the clinical supervisory role or function.

Objective data collection strategies such as interaction analysis, according to Cogan, offer a comparatively solid basis from which to proceed. The supposed relationship between certain teacher behaviors and student outcomes can be tested. However, according to Cogan, the assumption that a behavior which is exhibited by some good teachers will somehow turn others into good teachers is fallacious.

Other Types of Data

The focus of observation and analysis becomes narrower as the teacher's needs and interests emerge while the teacher and supervisor work together. Patterns of teacher/student communication might lead to a focus on frequency or types of teacher questions, for example, and then to the specific language used when a teacher phrases questions and students respond. Cogan also advises that supervisors pay close attention to nonverbal behavior, affective responses, and student behavior.

Nonverbal behavior is a potentially valuable data source, but it is ambiguous, difficult to identify, and to interpret. It can either confirm or contradict what is being said and done. Observing and recording nonverbal behavior is worthwhile nonetheless, for purposes of analysis and discussion. Whether students approach their teacher with smiling confidence or deferential caution, Cogan notes, can reveal much about classroom interactions.

Nonverbal behavior is often neglected because of the difficulty of analysis. However, nonverbal behavior can illuminate or amplify what is really happening between the teacher and students in a classroom. A student who is habitually silent, Cogan notes, may be communicating a great deal by not participating. Unfortunately, no formal theory of nonverbal behavior exists. Interpretations are possible, however, so the supervisor should be sensitive to it.

A related dimension of data that is frequently overlooked involves the *affective responses* of teachers and students to one another. Usually these can be secured only indirectly. Students may be asked to fill out attitude surveys, or to signal their reactions in some nonverbal way while a lesson is actually in progress.

Cogan notes that supervisors generally tend to overemphasize the teacher's behavior when recording data. But *student behavior* is important to fully understand learning processes. The teacher and supervisor can consider information relating to how students enter class, their success in accomplishing the teacher's objectives, as well as unanticipated classroom process outcomes.

Relating the behavior of teachers to student learning, however, is no simple matter. Many factors external to the classroom mediate teacher effects, Cogan observes, which complicates the planning of an appropriate course of action. Dependable knowledge about the relationship between teaching behaviors and learning outcomes in the classroom is sparse. The link is tenuous at best.

Cogan warns against the tendency of supervisors to comment about the lesson, usually in some judgmental way, as they leave the classroom after an observation. It is in fact difficult not to say something with the teacher waiting expectantly. Anything that is said, however brief, is likely to influence the progress of the conference. The only way to avoid this complication is to anticipate it and explain to the teacher in advance why no discussion of any kind will occur. A simple "goodbye" and confirmation of the conference time will then be sufficient.

Phase 5: Analyzing the Teaching/Learning Process

Three distinct types of analysis are performed during this fifth phase of clinical supervision:
1) analysis performed by the supervisor alone;
2) analysis conducted by the teacher alone; and
3) the analysis done collaboratively by both during the conference.

In the first case the supervisor analyzes data pertaining to events he observes in order to develop hypotheses concerning the relationship between the teacher's behavior and student learning. Cogan implies that teachers should independently perform a parallel analysis of the data to identify structures, form hypotheses about the relationship of their behavior to students' learning, and come up with ideas for their own professional development. The collaborative analysis then follows with both supervisor and teacher actively participating as colleagues.

A number of tasks lay before the supervisor when analyzing classroom events. The common purpose of these tasks is the development of a data base upon which a program of supervision can be established. These tasks are as follows:

An Assessment of the Degree to Which Students Have Achieved the Planned Objectives

A supervisor can assess the degree to which students have achieved objectives through the recorded observation data and other sources. Students' responses to questions and their involvement in planned activities in class are important indicators, Cogan notes, as well as district-wide tests, student records, out-of-class observations and interviews.

The Identification of Unanticipated Process Outcomes

Cogan suggests that cognitive objectives are often emphasized in schools to the point that important process learning and unanticipated outcomes get overlooked. As a direct result of their experiences in class, for example, students develop concepts of themselves as learners, acquire study and work habits, and learn skills and attitudes that are both favorable and unfavorable. Supervisors should pay special attention to these unanticipated learnings by recording as descriptively as possible what students actually do in the classroom. Attitude surveys and interviews may also be helpful.

The Identification of Critical Incidents

Critical incidents are events that may occur in an observed lesson only once or several times, but which appear to have a sizable impact on student behavior or learning. Patterns are behaviors which are repeated often enough to be considered a part of a teacher's style. Both are regarded by Cogan as useful foci for analysis.

Identifying critical incidents is important in the analysis because critical incidents by definition are likely to seriously influence student learning either positively or negatively. A critical incident is something of a watershed in determining subsequent events. The supervisor can help a teacher to recognize such turning points in a lesson and try to understand why an event had certain outcomes. The teacher may want to eliminate or try to incorporate the event into his repertoire.

The Identification of Salient Patterns of Student and Teacher Behavior

Patterns of teaching are behaviors that are consistently repeated to the point of being predictable and a part of the teacher's style. The supervisor tries to identify such patterns as documented by the data. Once identified, a pattern economizes effort by focusing attention onto major elements of teaching style and away from trivial isolated details. Inferences and hypotheses are formed concerning the effect that patterns have on student learning. What do students learn, for example, from teacher behaviors that communicate social distance? Supervisors should try to stay close to the data, using it to support their suppositions.

While reading a classroom transcript, Cogan recommends that the supervisor label or classify each statement as a type of teacher or student behavior. Similarities and connections are then looked for in order to discover patterns. Patterns are identified through sheer frequency or in terms of the significance of their impact during the lesson. Patterns and inferences concerning outcomes for student behavior and learning should be discussed with the teacher and related to the teacher's objectives and students' characteristics.

Pattern analysis gives the supervisor a clearer and better understanding of the realities of classroom life. Teachers begin to recognize how their own behavior contributes to or detracts from student learning, which is inferred from student behavior. The structures, processes, and consequences of teacher behavior become the focus of study and critique, not the teacher as a person. This can alleviate some of the anxiety that teachers feel about supervision.

The Relating of Teacher Behavior to the Lesson Plan

A hunch or tentative generalization about a teacher's classroom behavior and its effects can serve as a working hypothesis. Cogan cautions that the supervisor must guard against making inferences prematurely. Supervisors should look for patterns in behavior, not just the words that a teacher uses. It is also important, Cogan emphasizes, to avoid zeroing in on the latest buzzwords and fads in education.

The interaction of patterns is worthy of special attention. A temptation exists to treat each behavioral pattern in isolation, but they are often related. The teacher's interpersonal style and favorite techniques of instruction, for example, are often closely linked. This complex interaction of patterns determines the teacher's overall teaching style and personal effectiveness. A teacher who relies primarily on lecture may be effective, for example, because he nevertheless communicates warmth to students in other ways and motivates them by setting challenging but attainable objectives.

The supervisor must rely to some extent upon intuition when identifying patterns. This does not mean, however, that interpretations are arrived at without a solid basis in reality. A number of reality checks exist which the supervisor can employ to test the reliability and validity of his interpretations. These include:
- repeating an observation to see if the same patterns of behavior emerge;
- dividing a data set into halves and comparing each with the other;
- asking the teacher to verify one's perceptions;
- comparing the existing data against data from other sources, including other observers or students;
- using alternative media or interaction analysis systems;
- trying to develop alternative patterns and explanations;
- examining closely any data that do not fit existing categories;
- examining one's own biases; and
- varying the usual sequence of the analysis.

Phase 6: Planning the Structure of the Conference

When considering a strategy for the conference, a supervisor may decide to occasionally try an unstructured approach, but in most instances Cogan advises laying out a tentative plan. A number of strategies he recommends are presented below:

a) Following the logical flow of the clinical supervision cycle often makes sense because a clear direction is already established. This is especially helpful when a teacher is not yet familiar with clinical supervision. Usually, the conference involves three steps:
   1. The teacher and supervisor first discuss incidents and patterns identified through analysis.
   2. Choices are made as to which behaviors will receive continued attention as foci for the supervisory program.
   3. Plans are made in preparation for the next clinical cycle.

b) Reviewing through conversation the events which transpired during the lesson is another strategy. This approach is most useful when it makes sense to highlight the sequence of a teacher's behavior. A chronological recounting of events is the easiest way to organize data, but important details may be lost without the focus of a particular incident or pattern.

c) Focusing upon student behavior and likely learning outcomes is another alternative. These are then related to methods employed and materials utilized. How these might contribute to the behavior evidenced by students is pursued in a discussion. The strength of this approach is that it works well with teachers who exhibit inordinate defensiveness or anxiety when their own behavior is examined.

d) A didactic strategy may be employed as a way of initially familiarizing a teacher with the steps involved in clinical supervision. Essentially, the supervisor walks the teacher through the analysis of data, including identification of teaching patterns, suggesting possible relationships to student outcomes, and isolating patterns worthy of further attention. This can be useful with teachers who are unsure of enacting the new roles required of them but could "have devastating consequences" if used with a teacher who is self-confident and ready to actively engage in a program of improvement.

e) A nondirective strategy, encourages the teacher to talk openly about feelings, concerns, and ideas while the supervisor listens. This is useful for establishing trust and building rapport, particularly when the teacher is in need of an emotional release. Using a Socratic method is not advised because most teachers find it time consuming and manipulative in the sense that they are placed in the position of having to guess what the supervisor has in mind.

f) Role playing as a strategy requires skill and interest on the part of both supervisor and teacher in order to succeed. It is most powerful for helping people to understand the point of view of others. Although role playing works best in groups, the teacher and supervisor can try it with one or the other playing the role of student.

An important part of the conference should be a commitment by the teacher to actually make the changes agreed upon. Rather than requiring the teacher to promise verbally or in writing, which Cogan finds to be counterproductive, the supervisor can ask the teacher to review orally the decisions and plans that have been developed. This recapitulation at the end of the conference usually is sufficient affirmation.

An occasional final component of the conference should be a professional assessment by the teacher and supervisor of the processes and achievements of their work together. This evaluation is not necessary every time and should be omitted if the teacher and supervisor are fatigued or if emotions have been especially intense. If things are going generally well, this review can be repeated more regularly. This assessment can examine the success and virtues of general processes and events, the exercise and sharing of leadership, the cognitive level of discourse, the functions of analysis and learning, interpersonal relationships, the process of evaluation, and the value of outcomes and products.

If the supervisor and teacher simply cannot resolve an issue because of honest professional differences, the supervisor should be willing to back off. The teacher is responsible for what occurs in the classroom, not the supervisor. They should begin planning the next class session, giving special care to collect data that will shed light on the disputed issue. The climate should be one of problem solving rather than proving who is right. The clinical supervision process, in effect, becomes the arbiter of truth.

The conference should end with a confirmation by the supervisor that the teacher is professionally competent. This should never be left uncertain or inconclusive. When the teacher is undergoing change or is facing some legitimate doubts, the supervisor should assure the teacher that as much support as is available will be provided until the crisis is passed.

Suggestions for Planning the Conference

Flexibility and Adaptability are Needed Once a Conference Strategy has been Decided Upon. The supervisor should have a range of choices available to combine strategies or change course quickly if need be.

Only Manifest Teacher Behavior is Addressed, not Deep-seated Causes. The target is the teacher's behavior, in other words, not the teacher. Behavior changes can ultimately lead to changes in personality, but altering the personal values, beliefs, and attitudes of teachers is a secondary concern. The teacher, in Cogan's model, is never the object of supervision. *The Role of Summative Evaluator or Rater is Fundamentally Incompatible with Clinical Supervision.* Even formative evaluation (feedback) can raise anxiety for teachers which supervisors should openly address and deal with. Typically, however, formative and summative evaluation coexist and influence the teacher/supervisor relationship. The problem for the clinical supervisor is how to be nonthreatening to the teacher under such conditions.

Phase 7: The Conference

The conference is an integral part of the entire clinical supervision sequence. It does not represent a culmination, in Cogan's rationale, nor is it more important than other phases. Every contact with the teacher he notes, should be carefully attended to. Nevertheless, the importance of the conference to the teacher and the teacher/supervisor relationship does warrant special consideration.

A time and place convenient to both the teacher and supervisor should be agreed upon. Conferences may last as long as two hours initially, with one hour eventually being typical. Privacy is absolutely necessary and any equipment needed for reviewing data should be available. The teacher's classroom is both physically and psychologically suitable.

Although the supervisor must be well prepared for the conference, Cogan warns against overdetermining its direction in advance. No standard format or strategy exists, except that the interaction should allow for mutual participation and shared exploration. The processes involved generally include: a search for meaning in the data, an interpretation or diagnosis, and a selection of one or more strategies for improving instruction.

The teacher prepares for the conference throughout the clinical supervision sequence. Just prior to the conference itself, however, the teacher should prepare by thinking about his or her own instruction, developing some tentative hypotheses about what occurred in the lesson that was observed, generating some questions, and identifying some possible strategies for his or her own improvement.

Cogan provides a list of six conference objectives. The first four objectives seem to constitute something of an agenda for the conference.

The last two focus on increasing the teacher's responsibility for clinical supervision and his or her own professional growth. The six objectives are as follows:

1) Listen to the concerns expressed by the teacher and include them in the agenda of the conference.
2) Consider first those patterns that are most closely related to student behavior and learning.
3) Relate the observed student behavior to the intended objectives for the lesson.
4) Identify behavior patterns and critical incidents, and discuss how the teacher's behavior relates to student learning and behavior.
5) Expand the teacher's involvement in enacting the roles required by clinical supervision.
6) Encourage the teacher to assume greater responsibility for formulating and conducting a program of professional self-improvement and self-supervision.

Cogan observes that supervisory practice is often based on the erroneous assumption that teaching can be improved most effectively by identifying and remediating weaknesses. This approach is appropriate, he argues, only when critical incidents or patterns appear which indicate that the teacher's behavior in some way actually hinders student learning or threatens their well being. Cogan suggests that the deficit model is popular because finding professional weaknesses in teachers makes supervisors feel professionally stronger. Supervisors who feel compelled to call attention to the faults of teachers are attempting to demonstrate their personal competence at the expense of the teacher.

Cases where teacher behavior actually poses a serious threat to student learning are comparatively rare. Most teachers, he believes, do a fairly competent job. It is far more effective for the supervisor to concentrate on the patterns of strength that appear in each teacher's behavior. That is not to say that the supervisor should purposely overlook minor deficiencies. Difficulties always exist, but optimal supervisory practice does not focus on deficiencies exclusively.

The supervisor should concentrate on helping teachers to become outstanding with those things that they are already doing well. Asking teachers to improve their existing strengths is a process of building rather than repairing. Supervisors can also help teachers discover how they may undermine or contradict their own professional strengths. Developing existing competencies tends to improve areas of weakness as the teacher's abilities and awareness are expanded. Focusing on the reinforcement of strengths is also likely to be more rewarding psychologically for both the teacher and the supervisor.

Due to the lack of instructional assistance provided to teachers early in their careers, most develop styles of teaching that mainly reflect survival techniques. Because of their survival value, Cogan notes, those patterns are especially resistant to change. By having the teacher focus attention on his or her own style of teaching and building on strengths, appropriate new behaviors can be gradually selected and added. The teacher's existing personal model is thereby defined and then refined.

The supervisor leads an indepth analysis of the data, calling close attention to repeated patterns, critical incidents, and student outcomes. The data should be organized beforehand in a manner that will ease interpretation and discussion during the conference. The supervisor should plan a strategy which takes into consideration the teacher's needs, anticipated behavior, and possible reactions.

Allowing the teacher to talk first in the conference gives him or her the initiative from the very beginning which limits the chances of his lapsing into a passive posture. A problem may develop, however, with teachers who are either overly defensive or self-deprecating. The teacher may introduce a judgment of the lesson that is artificially positive, in the first case, or unnecessarily negative in the latter. If either occurs, the supervisor will have difficulty getting the conversation focused on a realistic interpretation of the data. The supervisor has to rely on professional judgment and knowledge of the teacher in deciding how to begin the conference.

As the conference proceeds, showing a willingness to listen demonstrates the supervisor's interest and concern to the teacher as well as his intention to treat the teacher as a colleague instead of a subordinate. When addressing events in the classroom the supervisor should concentrate on discussing behaviors and their effectiveness rather than the teacher and his work.

Assumptions About the Conference

Most Teachers are Physically, Mentally, and Emotionally Healthy Enough to Embark on a Program of Professional Improvement. The focus of attention should be on each teacher's strengths and resources. In clinical supervision both teacher and supervisor give and receive help. Both grow stronger personally and professionally.

"Colleagueship" is the Most Appropriate Concept for Describing the Teacher/ Supervisor Relationship in Clinical Supervision. The teacher and supervisor work as associates with equal status for the purpose of improving student learning. If either the teacher or supervisor assumes a dominant role productivity quickly deteriorates.

Simply Telling the Teacher What is Wrong and Right with His or Her Instruction is Always a Temptation to be Avoided. Supervisors should resist any urge to display superior knowledge, experience, and insight even though it makes the supervisor feel important, avoids the work of careful analysis, and saves time for everyone involved. Clinical supervisors have to fully understand the reasons collegiality is important, be able to enact it, and be committed to maintaining it.

Phase 8: Renewed Planning

This final phase of Cogan's model of clinical supervision is actually a return to Phase 2 – planning with the teacher – followed by a repetition of the clinical cycle. At this point another lesson is collaboratively planned which incorporates the ideas and findings arrived at in the conference, and another observation is scheduled.

Importance of Self-knowledge

Like all professionals, Cogan observes, supervisors must exercise control over their own judgments and behavior. This requires knowledge of how they view the world, their personal likes and dislikes, fears, predispositions, and prejudices.

Human beings perceive selectively, make interpretations, invent reality, and create meanings. Perception and judgment are commonly influenced by our intentions and preferences. For example, Cogan notes, we often tend to like people who are similar to us. Errors of judgment, perception, and inference may be compounded as the clinical cycle progresses. Supervisors, therefore, need to be open, flexible, and nonjudgmental. They must reserve judgment, and not jump to conclusions too hastily.

As an antidote to these subjectivities of perception and judgment, Cogan prescribes a strong dose of humility. He warns supervisors to be aware of the unconscious tendency to gratify one's own needs to control and exhibit talents. Also, one should be sensitive to the difference between legitimate requests for assistance and those which encourage and intensify immaturity in others.

Inferences and conclusions drawn by the supervisor can and should be "tested" for correctness according to several criteria. These include: outcomes, consistency with other facts or events, consensus, or intuition (affective congruence). Experienced colleagues also can act as sounding boards, and may be the best source of insight into one's own supervisory behavior and of support for continued professional improvement.

New behavior tried by a supervisor has to be congruent with the supervisor's personality. Changes in behavior should be authentic and not do violence to what the supervisor is as a person. New approaches must be tried, however, if the supervisor is to improve skills and grow professionally. Supervisors cannot easily predict whether a new behavior can be assimilated into their repertoire. Being true to oneself, according to Cogan, is most important of all.

Summary

Cogan's rationale for clinical supervision is intended to result in professionally responsible teachers who are self-directing, capable of objectively analyzing their own performance, and open to receiving assistance from others. The purpose of the first phase of Cogan's eight phase sequence is to restructure the traditional supervisor/teacher relationship by making it more collegial. The teacher is introduced to the philosophy, objectives, processes, and techniques of clinical supervision through a carefully planned program of group training, simulations, discussions, and practice lasting from two to six weeks.

During the second phase, the teacher and supervisor cooperatively plan the best lesson that they can. While planning, they develop hypotheses about the likely outcomes of their decisions. In the third phase, the teacher and supervisor plan the structure of the observation. The supervisor asks the teacher what aspects of the lesson he or she would like to know more about. The teacher's concerns become the focus of the data collection. Collaborative planning in the second and third phases helps ensure that the success of the lesson and the clinical cycle become the shared responsibility of both the teacher and supervisor.

Cogan's fourth phase is the observation of instruction. He views observation exclusively as a tool for improving teaching which should not be contaminated by evaluating or identifying weaknesses in teachers. Verbatim transcripts, interaction analysis systems, and audio or video recordings can be used to collect data. Attention should be given to nonverbal behavior and affective responses of teachers and students as well. When analyzing the data, Cogan's fifth phase, the supervisor should consider the degree to which students have achieved the planned objectives and then relate teacher behavior to the lesson plan. In doing so, the supervisor should identify critical incidents, patterns of student and teacher behavior, and unanticipated process outcomes.

Planning the structure of the conference is Cogan's sixth phase. The supervisor may follow the logical flow of the clinical cycle, review the events that occurred in a lesson, or focus on student behavior and likely learning outcomes. Supervisors may be didactic, nondirective, or use role playing as a strategy depending on the circumstances and familiarity of the teacher with the clinical supervision process. The conference should always end, according to Cogan, with a confirmation by the supervisor that the teacher is professionally competent.

No standard format exists for the conference, the seventh phase of Cogan's rationale. A collegial search for meaning in the data, an interpretation or diagnosis, and a selection of strategies for improving instruction, however, are typically included. The emphasis throughout is on reinforcing strengths rather than remediating weaknesses. The eighth phase, renewed planning, may grow directly out of the conference and follow it immediately.

References

Cogan, M. L. (1973). *Clinical supervision*. Boston: Houghton-Mifflin.

Section Two

The Humanistic/Artistic Models

The approaches to classroom supervision described in Section Two depart radically from the step-by-step procedures and traces of behavioralism evident in the original models of clinical supervision. The versions offered by Blumberg and Eisner were not written, however, in response to the original models. Rather, they represent reactions to the narrowly prescriptive, technically mechanical, and bureaucratic supervisory practices prevalent in many schools and districts during the 1970s. Blumberg and Eisner offer alternative ways of appreciating what goes on between students and teachers, and between teachers and supervisors, that are highly consistent with and elaborate on the humane and expressive facets of the earlier clinical models.

Much of the difficulty that supervisors and teachers have in working together, Blumberg believes, stems from behavioral conflicts that originate in the organizational context of schools. This view differs from the traditional clinical models which concentrated almost exclusively on the classroom and virtually ignored organizational factors. Blumberg views the larger social system as a source of differing perceptions, misperceptions, distorted signals, and degenerative communication cycles that often result in cynicism about supervision. Supervisors need to rely more on personal credibility and interpersonal influence, he suggests, instead of trying to exercise control over teachers.

Goldhammer, Mosher and Purpel, and Cogan were very concerned about the quality of relationships between teachers and supervisors, but Blumberg raises the social-emotional dimension of interpersonal relations to pre-eminence. He advises supervisors to concentrate on resolving the psychological barriers that exist between them and teachers by attending to issues of trust, affection, and influence. Otherwise, the rational structures that logically should improve teaching simply will not work.

Teachers actually control the effectiveness of supervision, Blumberg argues, because of the autonomy that schools allow them. Supervisors have little choice, therefore, but to treat teachers like adults and serve as integrating agents who help find ways to make teachers' goals and the goals of the school congruent.

Eisner proposes aesthetic sensitivity as an alternative to technical rationality, which he sees as dominating educational practice. An aesthetic view is another way of understanding reality that is less prescriptive, mechanistic, and stifling of personal and professional growth than technical rationality. It admits the possibility that multiple perspectives of reality exist. By relying on personal sensitivities and experience, Eisner proposes, a supervisor can become the major instrument through which the classroom and its context are perceived and understood. He views supervisors ideally as "connoisseurs" who perceive what is important yet subtle in classroom behavior, and who can eloquently describe its expressive nature.

An artistic approach to supervision acknowledges the holistic nature and unpredictable qualities of teaching, Eisner suggests, and recognizes teaching as an "art" rather than a "science." He argues strongly and convincingly against uniform enforcement by supervisors of any single approach to instruction. He is especially critical of perspectives that invoke research and science to legitimize the fragmentation and trivialization of teaching. However, the characteristics that Eisner attributes to teaching as art — playfulness, experimentation, surprise, discovery of rules and parameters — sound much like science at its best.

Eisner states that he dislikes the term "supervision," because it connotes hierarchical relationships like those found in offices and factories. He favors a consultative relationship in which teachers reserve initiative and are free to accept or reject a supervisor's recommendations. On the whole, however, he appears to be less concerned about improving interpersonal relationships than with nurturing and legitimizing the expressive dimensions of teaching and supervision. His artistic approach is considerably more supervisor-centered than the earlier clinical models, in that it does not provide for the teacher's involvement in analysis and interpretation. Although he addresses the issue of validity, Eisner does not comment on the possibility that a heavy reliance on the subjective impressions of supervisors may be abused in the real world.

Blumberg and Eisner differ substantially in their views on curriculum and evaluation with respect to supervision. Blumberg contends that many supervisors are overly preoccupied with matters related to instructional technique and curriculum. Supervisors ought to be more concerned, he advises, with how they work with teachers than with *what* they do with teachers — meaning that nothing can be accomplished in a climate of distrust and defensiveness. Accordingly, Blumberg devotes great attention to interpersonal relations between supervisors and teachers, and between teachers and students, and says comparatively little about instruction or curriculum.

On the other hand, curriculum is the central focus of Eisner's book. He believes that the essence of teaching is the transformation of curriculum into action. Supervisors, therefore, should focus on both the how and the what of teaching and supervision. How well a lesson is taught, Eisner observes, matters little if the content is trivial, invalid, or biased. Like Mosher and Purpel, he suggests that a supervisor's expertise in the subject area being observed is an advantage in appreciating what is happening in the classroom. The artistic approach to supervision that Eisner favors aims to contribute to the development of each teacher's individual style. The discovery and nurturance of personal teaching styles, of course, is also a major emphasis of the original clinical supervision models.

Blumberg asserts that evaluation simply has no place in the interpersonal intervention approach that he favors. Supervisors should treat teachers as colleagues, he suggests, providing them with data about behaviors and events in their classrooms, discussing it with them, and letting them deal with it. Blumberg urges supervisors to openly confront with teachers the inherent conflict between helping and evaluating, though he admits that to do so is difficult and risky. He proposes that experienced teachers should take responsibility for socializing new teachers into the profession and that schools should become "centers of inquiry" where teachers, administrators, and supervisors assume responsibility for their own continuous learning.

Eisner questions the usefulness of quantitative measures for evaluation and introduces the alternative concept of educational "criticism." The term criticism is not meant to imply a negative appraisal, he explains, but rather the ability to perceive work more deeply and comprehensively. Criticism relies on the sensitivity, appreciation, and expressive language of the connoisseur to perceive and record the complexity, subtlety, and importance of what happens in classrooms. The connoisseur looks for variety in teaching rather than conformity, and for the presence of multiple visual, auditory, and kinaesthetic dimensions.

Eisner considers both connoisseurship and criticism to be forms of inquiry that are qualitative in nature and employ social science concepts for interpreting data. Criticism differs from connoisseurship, however, in that it involves public disclosure of the supervisor's findings. Eisner cautions that the validity of educational criticism requires (a) a coherent, holistic, and persuasive representation of the rules governing classroom events, and (b) repeated observations over extended periods of time to ensure accuracy. Unavoidable disagreements among critics, he suggests, can provide a basis for professional dialogue.

Chapter 4

Arthur Blumberg's Interpersonal Intervention Model

The Model at Work

Mr. James, the district office supervisor of instruction, stepped out of the principal's office, then turned back suddenly to exchange one last quip and bit of laughter. He then stopped briefly at the school secretary's desk to ask about her family, before proceeding down the hall to Mr. Barth's classroom.

Mr. James remembered when Mr. Barth had begun teaching almost seven years ago and thought about how their relationship had developed during that time. Mr. Barth began his career like most new teachers, full of idealism and a sense of professionalism. Many novice teachers quickly lost their enthusiasm and sense of mission, however, when confronted with life in schools. Supervisors sometimes contributed to the problem, Mr. James believed, by treating new teachers as if they were children who needed to be told what to do, or by avoiding frank discussions with them about sensitive issues like evaluation and tenure.

The first time they met, as Mr. Barth was unpacking his supplies, Mr. James stopped by to introduce himself and asked, "What can I do to help?" Together, they began cataloguing textbooks as Mr. Barth described the kind of interpersonal relationships he wanted to establish with his students.

After a month or so, Mr. James asked to visit Mr. Barth's class and offered to take notes on how students interacted with each other and their teacher. During the feedback conference, Mr. James described the patterns of communication he had observed. He noticed, however, that Mr. Barth seemed less willing to talk openly about his class than before, even though the lesson had gone very well.

Mr. James guessed that Mr. Barth's detachment may have been due to concern about whether this classroom visit was really a formal evaluation of his teaching. Mr. James explained that his duties included both helping and evaluating teachers but that he tried to keep the two processes separate. Right then he was there to help, but he told Mr. Barth that he frankly hoped they could identify some performance objectives that might serve as a basis for evaluation later in the year. He then asked Mr. Barth how he felt about that arrangement.

In subsequent interactions, Mr. James tried to build and maintain trust by treating Mr. Barth as a competent professional. He was supportive and listened attentively to Mr. Barth's concerns, but expressed his own opinions and made suggestions freely. He viewed their purpose as one of solving problems together.

After Mr. Barth was awarded tenure, they talked about the implications of that event for their relationship and the responsibility that professionals have to continue their development. Mr. James decided to model that ethic by tape recording one of their conferences and asking Mr. Barth to help analyze it and make suggestions for improvement.

Lately, Mr. James had been thinking about the possibility of groups of teachers meeting regularly to discuss common problems, and then plan and test solutions together. He hoped to formalize the informal network of support that he noticed already existed among some of the teachers in each school. Mr. Barth was waiting at his classroom door. As they shook hands in greeting, Mr. James said, "I need your help." "Come on in," Mr. Barth responded, "What can I do?"

Introduction

The nature and quality of human relationships that develop between supervisors and teachers as they work together is the primary focus of Blumberg's writing in supervision (1974; 1980). He points out that low trust, defensiveness, secrecy, and a preoccupation with winning, unfortunately, often characterize interactions between teachers and supervisors in schools. This results in unproductive relationships wherein supervisors view teachers as being uncooperative, while teachers view supervisors as being ineffective and insincere.

Blumberg proposes that a change of direction is needed in schools, away from relations between supervisors and teachers that are closed and defensive, and toward relations that are more open and supportive. Instead of "Who will win?," the concern for both should be, "Can we solve this problem together?" Although practitioners commonly attribute differences between supervisors and teachers to personality conflicts, Blumberg suggests that most problems are actually caused by behavioral conflicts, and that these are related to the norms and role requirements of schools as organizations. His stated purpose is to help supervisors overcome these sources of conflict and misunderstanding, so that they can work more effectively with teachers.

Blumberg is reluctant to attach a label to his work or to prescribe specific procedures that supervisors should follow. Once an idea is labelled, classified, and institutionalized, he warns, it is likely to lose its potency. According to Blumberg, supervisors ought not concern themselves with conforming to a model or following a series of stages or phases when working with teachers. Rather, supervisors should concentrate on issues of process, how things are done, rather than structure. Blumberg says he is more interested in helping supervisors understand the effect of their behavior on others, along with the types of relationships with teachers that their behavior may bring about.

What Is Supervision and What Makes It Work?

Blumberg defines supervision as giving and receiving help in performing some task or in resolving a problem. Fundamentally, he states, supervision in schools is supposed to do two things, namely, improve instruction and promote the personal and professional growth of teachers. For supervision to succeed at these purposes, however, three conditions must be met:

1) The teacher must want help.
2) The supervisor must have the resources to provide the help required or know where the needed resources can be found.
3) The interpersonal relationship between the teacher and supervisor must enable both to give and receive in a mutually satisfactory way. (This last condition, Blumberg believes, is most important to successful supervision).

Rational solutions to problems simply will not work, Blumberg maintains, if the emotional dimensions of interpersonal relationships are ignored. A teacher who does not feel a need for help or who views receiving help as degrading, for example, is unlikely to be receptive to help if it is offered. Supervisors should therefore recognize that their interactions with teachers include emotional as well as rational content, and they should be prepared to deal with both.

Sources of Conflict Within the System

According to Blumberg, the consensus among a majority of teachers is that supervision is ritualistic and generally a waste of their time. Supervisors are frequently viewed by these teachers as uncaring, uninvolved, or domineering. Supervisors may view such teachers, in turn, as secretive and overly defensive. Social distance between the two groups increases under such conditions and a degenerative communication cycle results which Blumberg compares to a "cold war." The causes of such cynicism, he suggests, are multiple and arise largely from the organizational environment in which supervision is conducted. These include the traditional autonomy of teachers and schools, teacher tenure, norms against seeking help, distorted perceptions, and the inordinate influence that teachers exercise over the supervisory process. Each of these obstacles is discussed briefly below.

Autonomy of Teachers and Schools

The traditional autonomy that teachers enjoy in their classrooms presents something of an obstacle to supervisors who want to influence what happens in those classrooms. Blumberg suggests that relationships between teachers and principals, and between schools and the central office, are analogous to relationships between feudal barons. He observes that principals will usually leave teachers alone as long as the teacher is loyal to the school and runs his or her classroom with few complaints.

A similar arrangement holds between the principal of a school and the district office. The common practice of dividing supervisory responsibilities between schools and the district level, however, can lead to disputes which divide teachers' loyalties. The autonomy of each school also encourages and perpetuates an idiosyncratic culture, Blumberg believes, which may create a barrier between it and the central office. Collusion, distrust, and cyncicism may be heightened, Blumberg notes, as principals and central office supervisors compete for influence and teachers' loyalties. Polite and ritualistic interaction between supervisors and teachers may result without anything useful or meaningful getting accomplished.

Teacher Tenure

Teacher tenure, along with its accompanying presumption of competence, serves as an important protection against whimsical and arbitrary administrative behavior and provides a measure of stability for the organization. The security afforded by tenure may also compensate teachers somewhat for low pay. But the cost to schools, Blumberg observes, is that tenured teachers are difficult to influence because they are insulated from sanctions.

While tenure has the benefit of allowing each teacher to develop an idiosyncratic style, Blumberg notes, tenure also makes the supervisor's job more challenging. Teaching style is usually closely related to a teacher's world view, which is very difficult to alter. Interpersonal influence is more likely to be effective when trying to get tenured teachers to change, Blumberg concludes, than the use of power.

Norms Against Seeking Help

Blumberg notes that most teachers can certainly use a little help, but very few are ever likely to ask for it. The reason that teachers are reluctant to seek assistance is that asking for help in schools is often interpreted as admitting incompetence. A teacher who continuously sends discipline problems to the principal's office, for example, is not likely to be judged well by the principal. Teachers quickly learn, therefore, that not admitting to problems has considerable survival value.

Help to teachers should be offered by supervisors in a way that is neither offensive, Blumberg advises, nor irrelevant to what teachers are trying to accomplish. Instead of asking teachers, "Do you need any help?," supervisors ought to ask, "What can I do to help?" The latter question shifts the focus off the teacher and onto the task of improving instruction. It also demonstrates a willingness by the supervisor to engage actively in problem solving.

Perceptual Screens

At the heart of the cold war between teachers and supervisors, according to Blumberg, are differing perceptions and misperceptions that teachers and supervisors have of themselves and of each other. These perceptual screens interfere with communication by distorting it.

To the extent that assumptions based on such perceptions and misperceptions are untested, clear communication is impossible because suspicions and mistrust inevitably result in increasingly degenerative cycles of interaction. Blumberg suggests, however, that most teachers actually desire closer, warmer relationships with supervisors, and greater accessibility to assistance. He calls for increased concern in supervision for human hopes and fears, instead of strict reliance on rational structures that do not work, although rationally they "should." His advice to supervisors is to test assumptions before acting upon them.

The Classroom As A Closed System

In addition to teacher autonomy, tenure, norms against asking for help, and distorted communication arising from untested assumptions, Blumberg points out that another major constraint for supervisors exists. Specifically, teachers exercise an inordinate influence over the supervisory process. They are easily able to limit both the amount of information accessible to supervisors and the amount of influence supervisors can exert over instruction. The classroom is essentially a closed social system that is run and controlled by the teacher.

Blumberg believes, however, that the major obstacle to successful supervision is not the physical barrier of the classroom door. Rather, supervisors face the less obvious but more difficult challenge of overcoming psychological barriers between themselves and teachers.

Although supervisors in many schools can walk unannounced into a teacher's classroom at any time they please, or impose a cycle of observations and conferences over a teacher's objections, teachers can easily defend themselves against such actions by simply pretending to cooperate. Teachers can effectively neutralize a supervisor's efforts, Blumberg observes, in much the same way that people deal with door-to-door salesmen - by smiling and listening politely without making a commitment. Eventually, the salesman or supervisor goes away without ever being told "no."

Contrary to what other authors imply, Blumberg asserts that it is the teacher who actually controls supervision and not the supervisor. In other words, if teachers do not permit access to their teaching on a social and psychological level, nothing will change in their classrooms. Although teachers can be coerced into going through the motions of classroom observation and conferencing, supervision becomes a game or a ritual in such situations instead of a sincere attempt to improve instruction.

The Supervisor/Teacher System

Blumberg observes that the supervisor must initiate communication with teachers, because teachers can perform their jobs with few external contacts. While such isolation is likely to make teachers less effective than they might be, some teachers actually prefer being left alone.

When teachers and supervisors work productively toward improving instruction they form a miniature social system, rather than functioning as two individuals meeting to solve a problem. This means that issues of power, trust, affection, and influence need to be addressed. Because the supervisor is nominally in control, his or her behavior sets the tone, although the supervisor is by no means responsible for the teacher's behavior.

Gaining Access to the Classroom

To bring about real change, supervisors have to first establish interpersonal credibility with teachers so that they will grant supervisors access to their classrooms. Blumberg believes that teachers want supervisors to listen to them and to try to understand their concerns. Teachers also want to be treated as competent professionals and to work collaboratively with competent supervisors. According to Blumberg, teachers are more likely to permit supervisors to influence their behavior under the following circumstances:

- when supervisors give teachers immediate, nonpunitive feedback about their teaching;
- when supervisors use a collaborative approach for solving problems;
- when teachers are treated as experts on teaching;
- when supervisors are genuine in their relationships with teachers;
- when supervisors make teachers feel intelligent;
- when teachers feel that supervisors are available to provide assistance;
- when teachers feel that supervisors are listening to them;
- when supervisors are open about what they know or do not know;
- when teachers feel that supervisors are interested in them as people;
- when supervisors attend to the problems that teachers are interested in solving; and
- when supervisors are perceived as having competence and expertise.

Individual Needs and Organizational Objectives

Blumberg points out that teachers have psychological needs that they seek to satisfy in their work environment. Prominent among these are needs for ministration, maturation, and mastery (Levinson, 1968). These may be defined as follows:

- *ministration* - the need for closeness to others, support, guidance, and protection;

- *maturation* - the need for opportunities to grow and develop;
- *mastery* - the need to control one's environment.

The organization also has certain objectives that it expects teachers to work toward. However, teachers may not be strongly committed to these objectives, especially early in their careers. Successful supervisors function, in Blumberg's words, as integrating agents who bring teachers' individual goals into conformity with the objectives of the larger system.

Essentially, three paths of action are available to supervisors in seeking to integrate the teacher's goals with the organization's objectives. Blumberg identifies these as the exchange model, the socialization model, and the accommodation model (Barrett, 1970). Each is defined below:

- *Exchange Model* - In schools which apply the exchange model, teachers are rewarded for doing their jobs correctly according to the supervisor's view. Teachers are discouraged from making an excessive commitment of energy either to their jobs or to their relationships with the supervisor.

- *Socialization Model* - With the socialization model, the teacher is persuaded by the supervisor or colleagues to accept the organization's objectives and to strive to attain them. Supervisors and other teachers paternalistically model the behavior and attitudes that are preferred. The teacher receives guidance, support, and acceptance for submitting to the organization's way of doing things.

- *Accommodation Model* - In schools that use the accommodation model, the supervisor first considers the teacher's skills, needs, and aspirations, and then seeks to adjust the system to the teacher's goals while maintaining the organization's standards and objectives. The supervisor acts as a collaborative helper who is interested in the teacher's problems and has the resources to help solve them, but who also represents the interests of the school.

The focus in the accommodation model, which Blumberg seems to prefer, is on problem solving. The supervisor essentially helps teachers to find ways of making their own goals congruent with those of the school.

Supervisory Styles

Supervisory behavior can be classified, Blumberg observes, in terms of direct and indirect categories of behavior. Examples of each category are presented below:

Direct Supervisory Behavior
- Giving opinions about current teaching practices.
- Making specific suggestions.
- Telling a teacher what to do.
- Criticizing a teacher's behavior.

Indirect Supervisory Behavior
- Accepting and clarifying a teacher's ideas and questions.
- Asking a teacher for information.
- Asking a teacher for opinions and suggestions.
- Praising a teacher's performance.
- Discussing with a teacher feelings about communication, productiveness, and threat in the supervisory relationship.

Although direct and indirect behaviors may appear to be polar opposites lying along a single continuum, Blumberg presents evidence which suggests that teachers perceive four distinct supervisory style types. The four styles are depicted in *Figure 4.1.*

Teachers' Perceptions of the Four Styles

In a survey conducted by Blumberg, teachers reported that the four supervisory styles differed appreciably in terms of a number of specific outcomes. The reactions of the teachers to the four styles of supervisory behavior are presented in *Figure 4.2.*

As illustrated in *Figure 4.2,* teachers perceived "Style A" (high direct and high indirect behavior) as most helpful of the four supervisory styles, though "Style A" also made them feel most defensive. Teachers

	High Indirect	Low Indirect
High Direct	Style "A" The *supervisor exhibits both direct and indirect behaviors,* telling and criticizing, but also asking questions and listening.	Style "B" The *supervisor emphasizes direct behaviors,* telling and criticizing, with little asking or listening.
Low Direct	Style "C" The *supervisor emphasizes indirect behaviors,* asking questions, listening, and reflecting back ideas and feelings, with little telling or criticizing.	Style "D" The *supervisor uses neither direct nor indirect behaviors,* is generally passive, and appears uncaring, directionless, and disinterested.

Figure 4.1
FOUR SUPERVISORY STYLES PERCEIVED BY TEACHERS

Positive Outcomes	Ratings of Supervisory Styles				Negative Outcomes
Helpful	<............A	C	B	D.........>	Unhelpful
Satisfying	<............C	A	D	B.........>	Unsatisfying
Supportive	<............C	D	B	A.........>	Defensive
Empathic	<............C	A	D	B.........>	Neutral
Productive	<............C	A	D	B.........>	Unproductive
High Morale	<............C	A	B	D.........>	Low Morale
Problem Solving	<............C	D	A	B.........>	Control
Descriptive	<............D	C	A	B.........>	Evaluation

Figure 4.2
POSITIVE AND NEGATIVE OUTCOMES OF SUPERVISORY STYLES

rated "Style B" (high direct and low indirect behavior) as least satisfying, least empathic, least productive, and most concerned with control and evaluation.

In contrast, teachers viewed "Style C" (low direct and high indirect behavior) as most satisfying, most supportive, most empathic, and highest in eliciting morale. "Style C" was also rated highest in terms of productivity and having a focus on problem solving. Teachers considered "Style D" (low direct and low indirect behaviors) to be least helpful of the four supervisory styles and resulting in the lowest morale, despite the fact that they rated "Style D" highest on description and lowest on evaluation.

On the basis of this evidence, Blumberg observes that a pattern of high indirect supervisory behavior (Styles A and C) is uniformly associated with a higher quality of interpersonal relationship with teachers. A pattern of high direct behavior alone (Style B), in contrast, correlates uniformly with negative reactions from teachers.

Blumberg concludes that supervisors ought to expend a balance of energy on developing positive interpersonal relationships with emphasizing concern for issues relating to the task of improving teaching. The most productive supervisory style, in Blumberg's view, combines a relatively heavy emphasis on questioning, listening, and reflecting the teacher's ideas and feelings, with giving information, making suggestions, and criticizing (Style A). Teachers prefer supervisory relationships in which communication is supportive and free, in other words, but that are productive as well.

Understanding Supervisor-Teacher Interaction

Understanding one's own behavior and the impact of that behavior on teachers, Blumberg asserts, is essential for supervisory effectiveness. He proposes a framework for analyzing conference interactions that provides a variety of useful information.

Blumberg offers an interaction analysis system that is comprised of fifteen categories of behavior, and closely follows the Flanders model for analyzing classroom interaction. Ten of Blumberg's categories describe the behavior of the supervisor, four focus on the behavior of the teacher, and one indicates silence or confusion. The fifteen categories are presented below.

Supervisor's Behavior Categories
1. Support-inducing behavior (e.g., encouragement, or accepting feelings).
2. Praise.
3. Accepting or using the teacher's ideas.
4. Asking for information.
5. Giving information.
6. Asking for opinions.
7. Asking for suggestions.
8. Giving opinions.
9. Giving suggestions.
10. Criticism.

Teacher's Behavior Categories
11. Asking for information, opinions, or suggestions.
12. Giving information, opinions, or suggestions.
13. Positive social-emotional behavior (e.g., humor, agreeableness).
14. Negative social-emotional behavior (e.g., defensiveness, sarcasm).
15. Silence or confusion.

Blumberg recommends that supervisors tape-record their conferences with teachers and later use the fifteen categories to analyze the verbal interaction. While listening to the tape, the supervisor is instructed to record the number of the category of behavior that is occurring every three to five seconds. These numbers, which are written in a column, are then paired sequentially and transferred as tallies onto a 15 x 15 cell grid. By totalling the tallies in columns and rows, a supervisor can determine the percentage of time during a conference that is spent in various behaviors by the supervisor and teacher, as well as how each reacts to the other.

Gathering Other Data

As noted earlier, Blumberg avoids presenting a series of stages or phases as recommendations for how supervisors should work with teachers. He considers such devices to be artificial, mechanistic, and rationalistic. What truly matters in supervision and what is most likely to make a difference with teachers, he believes, is the manner in which the supervisor thinks about supervision and understands human relations.

Blumberg suggests that a more humane and organic understanding and practice of supervision may be possible by examining the relationships among various sources of information. According to this view, a supervisor needs four kinds of information:

a) data about oneself;
b) data about the teacher;
c) data about the teacher's behavior in the classroom;
d) data about the students' behavior.

Each of these sources of information is discussed separately below.

Data About Oneself

In order to establish productive working relationships with teachers, Blumberg maintains, supervisors should first become more aware of their own interpersonal needs, their personal reactions to the behavior of others, and their ability to recognize and handle conflict situations. Supervisors should also realistically assess their own level of competence.

One important area of self-knowledge for supervisors is their own interpersonal needs. Three especially pertinent dimensions of these needs are: the need for giving and receiving affection, the need for controlling and being controlled by others, and the need for including others and being included (Schutz, 1958). Blumberg suggests that supervisors can gain knowledge about these needs through introspection and self analysis, through interpersonal needs inventories, or by participating in encounter groups.

Supervisors also ought to be aware of their personal reactions to the behavior of other people. Monitoring positive and negative emotional responses when working with teachers, Blumberg proposes, can make supervisors more consciously aware of what they are doing and why. Interpersonal relationships can be more clearly analyzed with such knowledge and more positive outcomes can be achieved.

An awareness of conflict situations and how one handles them is especially important to supervisors. Recognizing when conflict is occurring and knowing that it sometimes results from unresolved issues of trust or power, for example, can help a supervisor deal with conflict more successfully. Also, knowing how one usually reacts to conflict (fight, flight, or pairing) opens up the possibility of conscious choice when working out disagreements.

Finally, a realistic assessment of one's own talents and inabilities is important to ensure that one does not offer help that one cannot provide. Blumberg suggests that a supervisor should seek feedback from teachers about what they perceive to be the supervisor's strengths and deficits.

Data About Teachers

The information about teachers that supervisors need, according to Blumberg, is similar to the information that they ought to know about themselves. Supervisors should be aware of teachers' interpersonal needs, including what pleases and displeases them, how they usually deal with conflict, their need for direction or to control a situation, and their level of competence. Blumberg suggests that supervisors should be alert to such information about teachers as it is manifested in behavior.

Data About Behavior in the Classroom

Before a lesson is observed, Blumberg advises, the supervisor and teacher should establish a common frame of reference. They should agree on what the supervisor will be looking for as well as on the type of feedback to be provided by the supervisor.

Blumberg offers examples of the kinds of things that supervisors can look for in a classroom. Most reflect the concern for interpersonal interaction and group dynamics that pervades his work. Some of these teacher behaviors include:

- How much time does the teacher spend talking?
- How much time is devoted to lecturing and how much to asking students questions?
- What kinds of questions does the teacher ask?
- How does the teacher deal with problems of control?
- What, if anything, does the teacher do about students who are uninvolved?
- Does the teacher enhance or devalue students' self esteem?
- Does it appear that the teacher is having fun?

In providing feedback to teachers about such matters, Blumberg cautions, supervisors should use language that is descriptive and nonjudgmental. Labelling behaviors and interpreting motives should be avoided, he advises, so as not to undermine the teacher-supervisor relationship.

Data About Students' Behavior and Attitudes

The concern that Blumberg has for the quality of interpersonal relationships extends beyond the teacher and supervisor, and into the classroom. He believes that supervisors ought to pay close attention to how students as well as teachers behave during a classroom observation. Some of the behaviors of students that he thinks are especially important include:

- Do students interact with one another or only with their teacher?
- Do students speak only when asked or do they contribute to the class discussion spontaneously?
- Does discussion flow easily or do students' responses seem forced?
- Are some students involved while others remain detached?
- Do students build on each other's comments or are they competitive?
- Are students able and willing to disagree with the teacher's ideas?
- Do the students appear to be having fun?

Another strategy suggested by Blumberg that a supervisor might employ is a pencil and paper survey that asks students to describe their feelings and perceptions about their classroom. An alternative might be to interview a group of students about their feelings toward classroom activities and the teacher's style.

Helper or Evaluator?

The conflict between the supervisor's dual role as helper and evaluator, Blumberg observes, distorts the relationship between a teacher and a supervisor even before it gets underway. Supervisors are expected, on the one hand, to promote professional growth among teachers and to assist those who need help. On the other hand, supervisors are frequently expected to make decisions about a teacher's fitness for continued employment on the basis of classroom observations and conferences. Whenever a supervisor visits a teacher's classroom, therefore, both parties are acutely aware that the supervisor is making judgments about the teacher's capabilities. Teachers who are interested in keeping their jobs, consequently, maintain an image of self confidence and competence whenever they interact with their supervisors. They also never ask for help, so as not to be viewed as weak.

Blumberg suggests that the only way out of this dilemma is to confront it openly. Otherwise, classroom observations and conferences will inevitably be tainted by a degree of dishonesty and deception. Resolving the conflict between helping and evaluating can be confronted as follows:

a. both the teacher and supervisor should understand and accept the existence of the supervisor's conflicting responsibilites as helper and evaluator;

b. both the teacher and the supervisor should accept ownership of the problem and discuss their feelings about it. The teacher and supervisor should also reach agreement on a range of objectives that are important to the teacher personally, yet are consistent with the goals of the school and district;

c. the teacher and supervisor should decide what data are necessary to evaluate the teacher's performance and how soon the data will be made available to the teacher after an observation;

d. the supervisor and teacher next determine whether the performance objectives have been met; and,

e. finally, follow-up activities are collaboratively planned.

The procedure outlined above, Blumberg notes, requires that the inherent conflict between helping and evaluating be addressed on the district and school levels as well as between individual teachers and supervisors. The essence of his proposal is that teachers should be free to define their own objectives regardless of style, within broad limits defined by the organization. The success of such a program depends on how helpful teachers find the process to be.

Socializing Beginning Teachers

The supervisor's work with novice teachers primarily involves the socialization or induction of the beginners into the professional culture and the culture of the school. Socialization, according to Blumberg, involves the acquisition of knowledge, values, and skills that are needed to function in a particular role.

Adult socialization is viewed as involving the creation of new arrangements of what an individual has learned previously, in addition to the acquisition of new material. That is to say, what is learned in a new role is strongly influenced by what was learned in earlier roles. Thus, a new teacher's behavior is likely to reflect his or her earlier experiences in the classroom as a student. It may be necessary for the teacher, therefore, to first unlearn prior learnings before new learning is possible.

The following questions, according to Blumberg, represent important issues in socializing beginning teachers:

- Are the attitudes, knowledge, and skills needed for successful teaching presented to the teacher in an effective manner?
- Are opportunities made available to the teacher for gaining practice in applying the relevant knowledge and skills?
- Are rewards provided when effective performance is evidenced?
- Is the teacher capable of learning what is required for teaching effectively?
- Is the teacher motivated to learn new attitudes, knowledge, and skills, and put them into practice?
- Is the teacher able to put new ideas and skills into practice appropriately?

Obstacles to Professionalism

Problems of adjustment exist for beginning teachers, Blumberg points out, because professional expertise and organizational rules and expectations are often incompatible. Colleges of education view their mission as that of preparing professionals, but many new teachers begin to doubt the value of what they learned at the university when faced with the more prescriptive expectations of schools. Professional skills and attitudes acquired during professional training are, therefore, often put on hold early in a teacher's career as bureaucratic norms and expectations are learned. The problem is that the professional attitude is often lost and forgotten before teachers are able to gain the autonomy needed to apply professional principles.

A way to ensure that professional issues are addressed, according to Blumberg, is to facilitate informal interaction among teachers concerning issues of instructional effectiveness and how teaching performance in the classroom can be improved. Making it easier for new teachers to communicate with more experienced colleagues may help develop a norm of collegiality and induce professional growth. By observing one another's classrooms, teachers can discuss similarities and differences, strengths and weaknesses, and advantages and disadvantages of how they teach.

When working with teachers, Blumberg suggests, supervisors often rely on the adult-child pattern of interaction they learned as teachers. Many teachers, in turn, too readily respond with a child-like dependency. By providing teachers with opportunities to interact as adults, he believes, supervision and teaching can become more professional as teachers develop responsibility for socializing their colleagues into the professional culture. The involvement of experienced, tenured teachers increases the chances that long-range issues that are important to the organization are considered as well.

Working With Tenured Teachers

Working with tenured teachers to improve their classroom performance is one of the most difficult problems facing supervisors, Blumberg believes. The reason for the difficulty is that tenure severely restricts the types of influence that are available for the supervisor to draw upon.

The granting of tenure to a teacher, Blumberg notes, is an expression of confidence in the teacher's competence and ability. It also implies an expectation that the teacher will continue to grow professionally and develop new skills. Unfortunately, some teachers feel little responsibility to improve further, and mistakenly interpret professional autonomy as a right to be left alone.

Supervisors cannot easily coerce tenured teachers because their ability to reward and punish is severely restricted. Poor evaluations of performance in the classroom, for example, are much less threatening to teachers once tenure is awarded. Consequently, supervisors have to rely on their own expertise and their ability to get teachers to accept them as role models if they are to have any influence at all.

Blumberg offers two alternatives for working with tenured teachers. The first approach is to concentrate attention on those teachers who are open to new ideas and who are interested in skill improvement and professional growth. Eventually, Blumberg suggests, those teachers who were initially reluctant will want to become involved as the supervisor establishes credibility and trust.

The second suggestion is to confront the issue head-on by openly discussing in a group meeting the nature of the relationships that exist between supervisors and tenured teachers and the perceptions that each group has of the other. Communication channels may open up once major barriers are uncovered in this way, but Blumberg admits that this latter method is potentially risky.

Supervision As Interpersonal Intervention

Blumberg proposes a reconceptualization of supervision in terms of interpersonal intervention. The outcomes of supervision, he suggests, ought to go beyond improving instruction to include the personal and professional development of both teachers and supervisors.

Because teaching occurs in an interpersonal and group environment and many obstacles to student learning have roots in interpersonal and group problems, Blumberg proposes that supervisors should help teachers deal with these problems so that their teaching skills can be more fully applied.

The field of supervision in education, according to Blumberg, tends to be overly preoccupied with issues relating to instructional technique, methodology, and curriculum. Before progress can be made in these areas, he believes, open communication, trust, and minimal levels of defensiveness between teachers and supervisors are necessary.

Blumberg believes that relationships between supervisors and teachers need to be viewed as significant and authentic by both parties. The focus for supervision, he suggests, should at times include noninstructional issues such as:

- situations that cause teachers to feel anxiety in the classroom, and how they deal with it;

- the behavior of teachers and supervisors as they interact with each other; and
- personal and professional growth problems experienced by the teacher.

In order to achieve success in such areas, however, Blumberg argues that supervisors have to begin acknowledging and accepting teachers as adults. This involves presenting appropriate data to them and then letting them make decisions for themselves. Supervisors should stop acting like parents, he asserts, who know what is best for their children.

Citing work by Argyris (1970), Blumberg identifies three basic elements of interpersonal intervention. These are:

- collaborative data gathering with respect to interpersonal aspects of the classroom and the teacher-supervisor relationship (especially related to behavior and emotions).
- free choice by the teacher to accept responsibility for actions based on the data; and
- internal commitment by the teacher to problem solving and by the supervisor to helping.

The teacher and superisor must both engage in feedback and self disclosure under such circumstances. Blumberg notes that evaluation of teachers has no place in the interpersonal intervention model.

Schools As Centers of Inquiry

Obviously, Blumberg considers the interpersonal interaction between teachers and supervisors to be the most problematic and most central issue in supervisory practice. He focuses attention on that interaction as the key to improving supervision in schools as they currently exist. But he argues as well that schools are limited in how good they can actually get, given their traditional structure and operating procedures. If schools are to improve substantially, according to Blumberg, then new ways of thinking about and organizing both schools and supervision are needed.

The one-to-one supervision that is most prevalent in schools, Blumberg believes, is both inefficient and ineffective. In place of working with individual teachers, or even small groups, he proposes that supervisors should begin thinking of schools as normative, organic, organizational systems.

Blumberg recommends that schools move away from merely dispensing information, skills, and attitudes. Instead, he believes, they should become "centers of inquiry" where everyone – teachers, administrators, and supervisors included – has the responsibility to learn (Schaefer, 1967). Only by systematically studying teaching can instruction be improved, Blumberg believes. The role of supervisors in such schools would be to manage the process of inquiry while they also learn.

Teachers tend to rely on other teachers as their primary resource, Blumberg notes, when seeking assistance in solving instructional problems. In contrast, teachers rarely go to their principals to discuss issues relating to instruction or curriculum. He suggests, therefore, building upon the informal network of assistance that already exists in schools as a way of working toward a school becoming a center of inquiry. By formalizing the informal network, assistance can become less chancy and possibly more productive. A wider range of expertise can also be brought to bear on problems.

The uncertainty of the technology of teaching suggests to Blumberg that collaborative problem solving could be a workable focus for peer supervision. Earlier attempts at changing the way schools operate, however, suggest that simply implementing a program of peer supervision will result in superficial adoption followed by eventual abandonment.

What is needed, Blumberg believes, is normative change. Essentially, educators have to stop thinking of schools simply as places where information is dispensed and begin thinking about schools as places where people actively study the processes of teaching and learning. Teacher isolation has to be replaced with opportunities to talk with other teachers about instruction and to try out new ideas with colleagues. Because teachers usually have not had an opportunity to work together, Blumberg suggests that they will need some training in how to do so successfully.

Once again, Blumberg points out that no universal "shoulds" are available to be followed as a formula, but a range of possible alternatives exists. To succeed in changing a school into a center of inquiry, principals and supervisors have to model and reinforce certain norms and expectations. Blumberg provides the following advice for principals and supervisors:

- begin *thinking* of the school as a "center of inquiry;"

- demonstrate an active interest and concern about what teachers are doing in their classrooms and how teachers relate to each other;
- model and emphasize the value of open communication and collaboration;
- seek feedback on your own behavior;
- emphasize that solutions to problems in education are never certain, they must be tested;
- acknowledge both failures and successes;
- let people know that seeking help from others is "all right."

Summary

Blumberg's model of supervision focuses on the nature and quality of the human relationship that develops between a supervisor and teacher as they work together. Supervisors have the primary responsibility, according to Blumberg, for ensuring that their relationship with teachers is both positive and productive. However, the autonomy of teachers and schools, teacher tenure, norms against seeking help, perceptual screens, and the closed nature of the classroom present obstacles to open communication and supervisory effectiveness.

Because teachers are able to perform their jobs with few external contacts, Blumberg observes, supervisors have to establish interpersonal credibility with teachers so that they will grant supervisors access to their classrooms. Supervisors must therefore be open and honest with teachers and treat them as colleagues. Part of the job of the supervisor is to accomodate teachers' individual goals within the broader objectives of the school through a process of collaborative problem solving.

Blumberg identifies four supervisory styles which represent various combinations of direct and indirect behavior, and offers a system for analyzing conferences that supervisors can use to improve their own effectiveness. Other types of data that he considers important include information about oneself as a person, information about the teacher, information about the teacher's behavior in the classroom, and information about students' behavior and attitudes.

Supervision at its best, according to Blumberg, involves interpersonal intervention. Because classrooms and schools are mainly places where human beings interact with one another, supervisors should model openness and authenticity in their own behavior, and be skilled at helping teachers resolve interpersonal problems that they face with students. The necessity of teacher evaluation complicates the supervisor's ability to act as a helper, but Blumberg believes that this problem can be overcome by confronting it directly and involving teachers as active participants in the evaluation process.

Finally, Blumberg envisions schools becoming "centers of inquiry" where groups of teachers would engage in collaborative problem solving. The supervisor in such a school would facilitate informal interaction among teachers concerning issues of instructional effectiveness and how teaching performance in the classroom can be improved. This would require that supervisors stop thinking of schools simply as places that dispense information and begin thinking of schools as places where adults share responsibility for studying and improving the process of teaching.

References

Argyris, C. (1970). *Intervention theory and method*. Reading, MA: Addison-Wesley.

Barrett, J. (1970). *Individual goals and organizational objectives*. Ann Arbor, MI: University of Michigan, Institute for Social Research.

Blumberg, A. (1974). *Supervisors & teachers: A private cold war*. Berkeley, CA: McCutchan Publishing Corporation.

Blumberg, A. (1980). *Supervisors & teachers: A private cold war*, 2nd edition. Berkeley, CA: McCutchan Publishing Corporation.

Blumberg, A. & Jonas, R. S. (1987). Permitting access: The teacher's control over supervision. *Educational Leadership*, 44(8), pp. 58-62.

Levinson, H (1968). *The exceptional executive*. Cambridge, MA: Harvard University Press.

Schaefer, R. J. (1967). *The school as a center of inquiry*. New York: Harper & Row.

Schutz, W. (1958). *FIRO*. New York: Holt, Rinehart, Winston.

Chapter 5

Elliot Eisner's Artistic Approach

The Model at Work

Ms. Hawthorne was a classroom teacher for seven years and has been a director of curriculum and instruction for seven more. She considers herself a student and "connoisseur" of good teaching and strives to learn something new about it each day.

When she observes a lesson, Ms. Hawthorne carefully records all the sights and sounds that come to her attention in an attempt to capture the richness and complexity of that classroom's life. Often, during an observation, Ms. Hawthorne's mouth is slightly open as if she is about to speak. The teachers joke that she is trying to "get a taste" of every classroom in the district. She smiles back at them and says that good teaching, like fine wine, must be savored with all one's senses.

Teaching, Ms. Hawthorne believes, has much in common with the performing arts and athletics. They all require qualities like creativity, spontaneity, and ingenuity that cannot be quantified or *measured with a checklist or rating scale.*

Upon entering the classroom of Mr. Oates, a middle school science teacher, Ms. Hawthorne pauses and snaps a photograph with the camera she often carries. The room is a collage of natural wonders. Birds' nests, hornets' nests, turtle shells, dried flowers and weeds seem to be everywhere. All sorts of creatures live in aquariums, terrariums, and small cages that are carefully arranged to simulate each animal's natural habitat.

Although she has visited Mr. Oates' room many times, Ms. Hawthorne is always tempted to explore every nook and corner because she knows that she will find something new and interesting. She writes "exploration" in her notebook and then underlines the word. It seems to nicely express the quality of the teaching and learning that take place in this classroom. As students begin working, she takes more photos and adds many more words to her notebook.

In her office afterward, Ms. Hawthorne reviews the detailed notes she took during the lesson. She decides that "exploration" is indeed an image that aptly describes the experience of being in Mr. Oates' class, but realizes that the lesson involved much more than that. Ms. Hawthorne begins to recognize three distinct phases in her notes as the lesson unfolded – first mystery, then exploration, and finally discovery. She can easily imagine Mr. Oates wearing a pith helmet while leading a group of wide-eyed 11-year-olds through a South American rainforest.

Ms. Hawthorne next focuses her attention more critically in assessing the educational significance of the lesson. Were the students actually learning something, or were they just having a good time? She looks again at her notes, this time considering how the curriculum and student outcomes were related to Mr. Oates' lesson. She realizes that the lesson included elements of both the inquiry and discovery methods of teaching.

As she writes a narrative description of what she observed to share with Mr. Oates, Ms. Hawthorne chooses her words carefully and precisely as if weaving a tapestry depicting important aspects of the lesson. She wants to be sure to vividly portray and highlight the many fine things she saw and heard. Mr. Oates has an original and creative teaching style that she wants to encourage. It reflects his personal interests and sense of wonder, she thinks. Ms. Hawthorne decides at that moment to have slides made of the photographs she took in Mr. Oates' classroom and to include them, with his permission, in a presentation she will make next month before the school board on the district's instructional program.

Introduction

Elliot Eisner does not care for the term "supervision" and uses it infrequently because of several connotations commonly associated with it. His main objection is that supervision implies hierarchical relationships that are more typically found in factories and offices than in professional work settings. A "supervisory" relationship also implies that a superordinate can prescribe to someone in a subordinate role how a job should be done. Finally, according to Eisner, the word supervision seems to eliminate the possibility for exchange and dialogue between colleagues.

Eisner proposes an alternative – an artistic approach to supervision – in which the supervisor relies upon personal sensitivities and experience for direction, and becomes the major instrument through which the classroom situation and its context are perceived and understood. He believes that supervisors should ideally behave more like consultants when working with teachers. Consultants are invited into a setting, are talked to, and offer views for a client to consider. In a consultative relationship the intitiative remains with the client, who can freely accept or reject the consultant's recommendations. The artistic approach requires supervisors to be connoisseurs of education, according to Eisner, possessing the ability to see what is important yet subtle in classrooms and schools.

Supervisors who use the artistic approach do not simply note the presence and count the number of behavioral events that they observe in a classroom. They pay closer attention to the expressive nature of classroom behavior, the meaning that events have for the teachers and students who experience them. The unique contributions of an individual teacher to the educational development of students can be fully appreciated, Eisner argues, only when meaning attached to behavioral events is seriously considered.

During classroom observation, supervisors who follow Eisner's model use richly descriptive language to record the classroom context and the events that occur in an effort to capture the expressive and subtle qualities of the experience as fully as possible. An eloquent description is important in order to communicate what was seen and heard in a way that preserves the complexity of classroom reality and enables the teacher and others to view it from a different perspective.

The artistic approach requires repeated observations of classroom life over extended periods of time. Repeated observations place events in a temporal context, Eisner suggests, which enables the supervisor to recognize their significance. An extended period of interactions between the teacher and supervisor also provides an opportunity to develop rapport and trust so that open dialogue can occur between them.

Essentially, according to Eisner, the artistic approach involves four elements:

1. Supervisors must first be able to see and grasp the important aspects of the situation they are observing. In other words, they must be "connoisseurs" of classroom life.
2. Next, supervisors must be able to describe what they see and hear in language that vividly captures the expressive essence of the experience.
3. The third element involves interpretation, where the supervisor applies appropriate theories, models, and concepts to explain the dynamics of that specific classroom.
4. The final phase of the model involves appraising or assessing the educational significance of what has been described and interpreted.

Errors of "Scientific" Supervision

Eisner explains the artistic approach to supervision by contrasting it with what he calls "scientific" approaches to supervision. Supervision is most often practiced, Eisner suggests, as if teaching can be studied with the objectivity usually associated with physics or chemistry. The assumptions and methods of physical science, he contends, are inadequate for capturing and appreciating the richness and complexity of classroom life.

Eisner has little regard for views of teaching and supervision that adopt the trappings of science and the methods of scientific management. Eisner points to a number of fallacies that he believes make these perspectives inappropriate for understanding events in classrooms:

- First, the presence or absence of a particular teacher behavior has nothing to do with the quality of the lesson. A brilliant lecture should not be judged inadequate, Eisner observes, because the teacher failed to have students work in groups.
- Second, good teaching is not a matter of being able to do all things well. A teacher's performance in the classroom may be superb in some respects, yet lacking in others. Eisner argues that it is better to emphasize and build on teachers' strengths than to concentrate on remediating deficiencies.
- Third, focusing exclusively on behaviors that occur in a classroom misses the more important question of what those behaviors mean to the teacher and students. A supervisor who only records the number of questions that a teacher asks during a lesson, for example, overlooks the crucial issue of whether the questions had any meaning for the students.
- Fourth, teaching techniques that have been found effective under certain conditions may not be successful in other situations. Classroom strategies that correlate with higher achievement in mathematics among low-ability elementary children, for instance, may not be relevant to the teaching of high school physics.
- Fifth, a preoccupation with validity and unanimity among observers can lead to the neglect of important qualities in a lesson. Supervisors who vary in their training, interests, and professional experience, may each see something different but nevertheless valuable to understanding a classroom's dynamics. This uniqueness of perspective, Eisner notes, is unfortunately often treated as if it were a vice.
- Sixth, words and numbers cannot always adequately convey the essence of an event that occurs in a classroom. Photographs, videotapes, or artifacts representing student work can communicate dimensions of reality that a verbal or numerical account miss entirely.
- Finally, a "scientific" orientation to the study of teaching and the practice of supervision places an undue emphasis on control and predictability. Novelty, surprise, creativity, personal expression, ingenuity, and unforeseen outcomes, Eisner observes, are equally important to the quality of life in classrooms. Highly prescriptive methods of teaching and models of supervision are likely to diminish teachers' pride and satisfaction, Eisner believes, as well as students' interest in learning.

Teaching vs. Instruction

Although the terms teaching and instruction are often used inter-changeably, Eisner argues that important differences exist in the images that the two terms conjure up. Instruction is more concerned with control over the content that students learn and is more appropriately used to refer to the kinds of training that occurs in the church and military. Teaching is more flexible and emergent in its orientation, according to Eisner, and more accurately describes what is typically found in schools. Differences between instruction and teaching as described by Eisner are summarized below:

Characteristics of Instruction	Characteristics of Teaching
mechanical	organic
controlling	flexible
predictable	emergent
bureaucratic	personal
technical	humane

The difference between the terms instruction and teaching is more clear in actual practice. *Individualized instruction*, Eisner notes, typically means that different students are allowed more or less time to achieve predetermined outcomes by completing prespecified workbooks, read-ing materials, and test forms. Teaching, in contrast, is an attempt by one person to communicate with another. *Personalized teaching* may involve altering the content, the methods, or even the goals to suit the unique characteristics of particular students. Prepackaged curricula and in-structional units are no match for the repertoire of choices available to a teacher who wants to communicate with a student. Eisner notes that the following alternatives are among many available to teachers who wish to adapt their teaching to different students:
1. trying a different explanation;
2. asking a variety of questions;
3. giving another example;
4. using various motivational strategies;
5. speaking more loudly or softly;
6. speeding up or slowing down the presentation.

Prepackaged curricula and instructional units that promise effi-ciency often get in the way of good teaching, Eisner contends, by making teachers forget the many alternatives at their disposal.

Eisner also notes that teaching can be defined and thought about as a process (like *running* a race) and as an outcome (like *winning* a race). How one evaluates teaching is determined in part by which view of teaching (process or outcome) one holds. When viewed as a process of trying to foster learning, Eisner suggests, all the activities that a teacher engages in during a lesson may be evaluated regardless of their effects. Whether a lecture is logical, whether an example is vivid, or whether a question is relevant are legitimate questions when teaching is viewed as a process.

In addition to being viewed as a process of trying to foster learning, teaching can also be defined in terms of outcomes or achievement directly related to student learning. Teaching tied to outcomes is assessed by such criteria as student behavior, grades, and test scores. Eisner suggests that it is profitable to view teaching from both perspectives, process and outcome, rather than one or the other.

Teaching as Art

Eisner describes good teaching as sensitive, intelligent, and creative. He considers the practice of good teaching to be an art (rather than a science) that is guided by a teacher's values, personal needs, and beliefs. Teaching can be considered a form of art, Eisner argues, from four different points of view:

a) *The skill and grace of teaching can attain an aesthetic quality.* The manner in which teachers orchestrate activities, ask questions, or deliver lectures can be experienced, described, and understood similarly to performances in the fine arts.

b) *Teachers constantly "read" their students and respond appropriately in order to lead them in certain directions.* Like painters, musicians, actors, and dancers, teachers selectively react to qualities that unfold during their performance and react by adjusting the tempo, climate, or pace of a lesson.

c) *Teachers apply established repertoires or routines to the unpredictable contingencies that arise in their classrooms.* Like artistry, teaching involves a combination and balance of automatic action and inventiveness.

d) *Like art, the ends of teaching may be created in process rather than as preconceived objectives.* Goals are as likely to be emergent as they are to be specified in advance.

Artistry in Teaching

Artistic teaching, according to Eisner, provides a climate that encourages exploration and risk-taking. Artistic teaching encourages students to play with ideas and to experiment with new combinations through fantasy, metaphor, and even constructive foolishness and failure. Eventually, play leads students to discover their own capacities and the limits of their ideas. Students also develop rules that establish parameters for play and guide their subsequent actions. True artistry in teaching, Eisner believes, is an ideal rather than a common occurrence. To achieve artistry, teachers need to feel free to explore, to innovate, and to be playful themselves.

In place of the common view of teaching as assembly line work, Eisner offers another analogy - basketball. Both teaching and basketball, Eisner notes, are activities that are defined by rules and strive toward goals. Also, both teachers and basketball players must watch events closely and understand new configurations as they emerge, both must generate alternative strategies on the spur of the moment to exploit opportunities as they occur, and both need to know how to pace their behavior to speed the action up or to slow it down. Most essentially, both teachers and basketball players require "fluid intelligence" that enables them to improvise within preplanned patterns and create new patterns to exploit unanticipated opportunities.

Artistic teaching may also be thought of as a form of inquiry, Eisner suggests, in which the problems one faces cannot always be predicted or defined. Flexibility, ingenuity, and creativity are essential to such a process. This view of teaching is incongruous, however, with the frequent admonition that the aims of teaching should always be stated clearly and in measurable form. Verbally stating behavioral objectives before teaching begins, Eisner argues, is naive for at least two reasons:

1) Teachers often conceive of their teaching in the form of visual or other sensory images that are not easily articulated. Having teachers specify precisely what they intend to accomplish before a lesson begins, Eisner suggests, can be as absurd as asking architects to specify verbally what they intend to accomplish before they begin a set of blueprints.

2) Teachers often discover new intentions during the process of teaching. Frequently, people figure out what they are doing only after they begin their work. Actions can lead to the invention of goals as easily as goals can lead to actions.

Artistic teaching, however, is not undisciplined and does not eliminate the need for theory. Teaching, according to Eisner, is inevitably influenced by theory. Teachers may not be consciously aware of their beliefs about intelligence, for example, or motivation, or the conditions that foster learning, yet these beliefs influence their actions in the classroom.

Teachers, Eisner believes, should avoid a single view of reality and be able to view the classroom situation from multiple theoretical perspectives. Theory should be neither ignored, nor followed as a prescriptive formula for success. Theoretical frameworks, he believes, serve teaching in two important ways:

1. Theories call our attention to certain aspects of reality. We can use them to focus our efforts in areas that we might otherwise neglect.
2. Theories are tools that can be used to help make sense of reality. They provide general expectations that can guide planning.

In summary, Eisner offers an aesthetic rationale for teaching that allows for playfulness, exploration, surprise, and novelty in the classroom. In this alternative to technical rationality, a teacher may hold and pursue intentions without being able to state them clearly and may allow intentions to emerge from teaching instead of preceding it. Here flexible human intelligence and imagination can prosper.

Teaching and Curriculum

The quality of the curriculum and the quality of teaching, according to Elliot Eisner, are the two most important issues facing schools. The content and the process of teaching are inseparable, he believes, because teaching is a transformation of the curriculum into a course of action. Supervisors should therefore focus their attention on *what* is being taught as well as *how* it is being taught when observing a classroom.

Curriculum and teaching are inseparable issues, Eisner argues, because the quality of learning is determined by both. No matter how excellent the curriculum, it will not be communicated if the lesson is poorly taught. On the other hand, a lesson that is taught extremely well is wasted if the content is not worth the effort. When evaluating a lesson, Eisner suggests, an observer should focus on three major areas: *curriculum, teaching,* and *student outcomes.*

Evaluation of Curriculum

No matter how good teaching may be, according to Eisner, the quality of the curriculum is a key factor in determining student outcomes. It is of little consequence how well a lesson is taught, he argues, if the content is trivial, invalid, or biased. The educational significance of the content, he suggests, depends on the values one holds about what is important. Eisner offers two criteria that he considers especially important when evaluating curricula:

- the intellectual significance of the content and the validity of the concepts presented; and
- the appropriateness of the curriculum for the developmental level and prior experience of the students for whom it is intended.

When evaluating curriculum materials, Eisner emphasizes the importance of having a wide range of possibilities available for expressing ideas and presenting information. Diversity is needed because individuals vary in how they process and express what they know, think, feel, and believe. A third criterion for evaluating curricula, therefore, is:

- the variety and diversity of visual, auditory, and kinesthetic modalities available for presentation and expression.

Evaluation of Teaching

Eisner is opposed to the application of a single set of skills when assessing the quality of a lesson, because various types of teaching require different criteria. Lectures, discussions, small group activities, and individualized counseling are all legitimate forms of teaching, and it is unreasonable to assess the quality of one form with criteria that apply to another.

The criteria for excellence in teaching differ, according to Eisner, depending on the type of teaching taking place. There is no single set of qualities or skills that can be applied universally to all teachers or even to the same teacher in different situations. Furthermore, a teacher can be a highly skilled lecturer, yet be incompetent in relating to individual students. In fact, Eisner goes so far as to say that good teaching does not necessarily require much interaction with students. A teacher can encourage students to discover and learn independently, for example, simply by arranging a set of conditions (e.g., materials, displays, books) and providing a minimum of guidance.

Eisner believes that teaching should provide teachers with an opportunity for expressing individual creativity. Teachers are people, he reminds us, who need room to grow themselves if they are to nurture growth in others. The growth of teachers, he argues, should not be stifled by overly prescriptive and mechanistic models of teaching and school organization.

He also believes that attempts to identify specific qualities of effective teaching have not been fruitful. Eisner characterizes so-called scientific efforts to isolate particular causal relationships between teaching behavior and student learning as reductionistic. He suggests that the following may be more relevant considerations when evaluating teaching:

- What type of relationship does the teacher establish with the class?
- Are the teacher's explanations clear?
- What level of enthusiasm does the teacher display?
- What kinds of questions does the teacher raise?

Evaluation of Student Outcomes

The learning outcomes that are achieved in a classroom, Eisner observes, are often more broad and important than the specific objectives of the lesson. He classifies learning outcomes into three categories that pertain to outcomes related to the content, to the student, and to the teacher.

The most commonly examined learning outcome has to do with the content. Multiple choice tests, for example, tell the teacher how much of the content that was taught has been learned by the students as a group. However, some of the learning related to content, Eisner points out, may lie outside the objectives that the teacher has specified.

An area of outcomes that is less frequently considered is how students individually make sense of what is taught and what occurs in the classroom. Students have personal interests and experiences that they draw upon in organizing new information and ideas. Teaching can be personalized, Eisner suggests, by focusing evaluation on how students go about developing personal meaning and understandings.

Interviews, open-ended essays, and projects that allow for individual expression are needed to gather this type of information.

Another area that is often overlooked in evaluating outcomes relates to what students learn from the personal qualities of the teacher. The experience of working with a truly great teacher, Eisner suggests, can be more important to a student's education than the content of the course. Relevant questions for evaluators to consider along these lines might include:

- What intellectual style does the teacher model?
- What standards does the teacher uphold?
- Is the teacher willing to take risks?
- Does the teacher tolerate nonconformity?
- Does the teacher value precision and punctuality?

Reporting Evaluations Artistically

Eisner says that his artistic approach to supervision is intended primarily "to improve the quality of educational life" for students and teachers. It relies on the supervisor's sensitivities, insights, and knowledge as a means of highlighting important subtleties of classroom reality. The supervisor is the instrument, in other words, through which meaning of events is construed. Poetic, expressive, and metaphorical language are used to communicate or reflect back to teachers and to others what has been observed.

Supervisors who employ the artistic approach, Eisner suggests, must learn to function somewhat like music coaches. They must be able to appreciate the quality of a teacher's classroom performance in its entirety, while simultaneously attending to the parts that comprise the performance. Furthermore, supervisors should recognize that teachers naturally display different styles, and should try to help teachers exploit and further develop their unique talents. Supervisors should be sensitive to the characteristic traits of the teacher, in other words, as well as the overall quality of the lesson observed.

Eisner admits that the limited amount of time available for supervision, and the limited influence of occasional feedback, make the artistic approach difficult to employ effectively. However, he points out that the dual focus of artistic supervision – improving both the teacher's general performance and the teacher's distinctly characteristic style –

makes it particularly potent.

The artistic approach to supervision concentrates on the expressive dimension of behavior in the classroom, the meaning behind the actions. It is not enough for the supervisor to simply record and count behaviors. Supervisors who employ the artistic approach must try to comprehend what behavioral events in that particular classroom mean to the teacher and students who enact them. Sensitivity and appreciation for subtlety are only prerequisites, however, that enable the supervisor to artistically render an account of the experience.

After observing a classroom and noting the expressive qualities of the setting and of interactions between the teacher and students, the supervisor must artistically construct a representation of that experience. This rendering of events should convey to the teacher and others the expressive dimension of life in that classroom. The supervisor typically uses richly expressive language to construct an interpretation in the form of a verbal narrative.

Eisner provides the following illustration to demonstrate how a supervisor can vividly describe a classroom situation in a way that permits the reader to recognize its expressive qualities and some of its implicit values. The supervisor carefully records his perceptions in artfully crafted language, using metaphor, poetic devices, and the tempo of words to convey the tone of the classroom to the reader:

> The room invites me in. It is a large, extended room drawn at the waist: It was once two single rooms that have come together to talk. Surely I could spend a whole childhood here. A wealth of learning materials engulfs me, each piece beckoning me to pick it up. The patchwork rug that hides the floor is soft and fluffy and warm. Some desks have gathered together for serious business. Chairs converse across semicircular tables. At the bookshelf, dozens and dozens of books slouch around, barely in rows, leaning on each other's shoulders. Children's drawings line the walls...
>
> A massive wooden beehive called The Honeycomb, with geodesic cubicles in which to hide yourself. A towering ten-foot dinosaur made of wire and papier-mache, splotched with paint ... blue and red colors crawling up its body. The monster is smiling helplessly - is he not? - because a convoy of tiny people have just been tickling him with their paintbrushes...
>
> Soon I am not alone. The other children are pouring through the door, infusing the room with life, brimming with energy

hankering for release... Lots of Erics and Chrises and Heathers and Lisas. Each seems to be drawn to his own corner of the room, his energy pulling him toward a special task. One moves to the bookshelf and snatches up a book. Several take themselves to the math table. Three crawl in the Honeycomb. One tickles the dinosaur with a paintbrush. Others string pull-tabs or watch a film.

Criticism and Connoisseurship

Both parents and the public are accustomed, Eisner notes, to using grades and standardized test scores for judging the outcomes of schooling. They are, in fact, encouraged to do so because such numerical data are what educators most often report. Eisner suggests that narrative descriptions like the one above could serve as alternatives to grades and test scores that would help parents and others better understand the richness and complexity of what goes on in classrooms and schools.

Eisner calls this alternative to quantitative measures for evaluating educational outcomes "educational criticism." Educational criticism relies heavily on written descriptions and visual images to communicate in vivid detail the experience of participating in a classroom or school. Eisner suggests that parents and others can vicariously relive important events over the course of a semester or an academic year through a richly descriptive narrative, for example, that may be accompanied by photographs or slides. Tape-recorded interviews of students and videotapes of classrooms are other ways of conveying to the public a deeper understanding of what actually happens in schools.

When evaluation is conceived of artistically in this way, according to Eisner, parents and the public may become more appreciative of the elusive nature of schooling. The strengths and weaknesses of the educational program are more evident and understandable when described in a rich manner that relies on a variety of media.

Successful evaluation of educational programs, Eisner points out, requires more than technical or artistic skill. To separate the trivial from the important and to understand the meaning of what is seen requires a normative and historical perspective for making sophisticated interpretations and appraisals. He refers to this sensitivity as "educational connoisseurship."

Educational connoisseurship and educational criticism represent a form of inquiry that Eisner characterizes as qualitative in character, similar to the work done by critics in areas such as literature, dance, film, music, and theater. A critic of the arts is faced with the task of describing the work of an artist in language that helps others to perceive the art work more deeply and comprehensively. By "criticism," Eisner does not mean to imply a negative appraisal. Rather, the critic illuminates certain qualities of art so that an appraisal of its value becomes possible.

Connoisseurship, according to Eisner, is the capacity to see and appreciate the complexity, subtlety, and importance of an object or event. It is essentially a personal and private act. Criticism, on the other hand, involves the public disclosure and judgment of the qualities that are perceived by a connoisseur. Connoisseurship is, thus, a prerequisite of criticism. As with wine tasting or listening to music, Eisner observes, educational connoisseurship requires a range of experiences and a sensory memory that serves as a context for appreciating the qualities of a particular object or event. He cautions, however, that the length of time one has spent in the classroom is not necessarily a good predictor of connoisseurship. Connoisseurship requires more than simply perceiving and recognizing qualities, it necessitates being able to perceive the subtleties that make a particular work of art unique.

Classroom observation forms are inconsistent with educational criticism, according to Eisner, because they predefine what the observer is to look for and prescribe to a high degree what is important. The overreliance on classroom observation forms in many schools prevents observers from seeing important aspects of classroom life by limiting their perspective to only a few categories.

Classroom observation forms, Eisner notes, focus a viewer's attention on things that lessons share in common, but may blind the observer to what is different and significant in a specific case. Connoisseurship requires an observer who is capable of perceiving subtle characteristics as well as recognizing how those characteristics are part of a larger structure of classroom life and the rules that provide order to that structure.

To refine and develop one's capacities for educational connoisseurship, Eisner recommends the following:

  a) focusing in a sensitive and conscious way on the events that occur in classrooms and schools;

  b) comparing one's perceptions with others in order to recognize new events, and to refine, integrate, and appraise what has been seen;

c) developing a descriptive language that is incisively literary and poetic;
d) understanding the context in which an event occurs by acquiring some knowledge about the people involved and the circumstances surrounding and preceding the event; and
e) possessing a working familiarity with the social sciences, theories of education, and the history of education.

Educational Criticism

As noted earlier, Eisner views criticism as the art of publicly disclosing or rendering the significant qualities of an object, event, or situation that is observed. The purpose of the observation determines what the specific focus will be. For example, an education critic might focus on the learning patterns of a single student, the nature of classroom discourse, the visual environment, or the meanings implicit in how time is used.

Eisner contrasts the more traditional approach to research and evaluation with educational criticism. Criticism allows for multiple ways of knowing and provides a variety of modes for expressing what is known. Research and evaluation in education have traditionally accepted only a behavioral definition and an operational mode of expression as valid. Eisner says that he does not want to replace traditional research with aesthetic criticism, he only wishes to augment and enhance the richness and depth of our understanding of what goes on in schools and classrooms.

Rather than using language to classify and categorize events in the classroom, Eisner suggests that the critic should strive for "metaphoric precision" in attempting to bring to consciousness the feeling engendered by the qualities that are observed. Proper and powerful metaphors must be sought to accurately render, disclose, reveal, suggest, and imply truths about nonquantifiable dimensions of a lesson such as how life is led in the classroom or what the person or the teacher represents to students. A person who reads an educational criticism, according to Eisner, should have the sense of vicarious participation in classroom life and an empathetic understanding of events and situations.

An educational critic, Eisner explains, strives to identify and portray the significant qualities of a classroom or school. The focus might be on pervasive qualities like the climate of a school, the style that pervades a classroom, or the tempo of a lesson. The focus can also more narrowly focus on component qualities. For example:

a) the relationships of students with each other;

b) covert messages in the teacher's tone of voice; or

c) the visual quality of the classroom environment.

The critic, in other words, selectively brackets what he or she wishes to attend to instead of writing down everything that is said and done. "Games" being played, unspoken rules, behavioral regularities, and core values are other legitimate and potentially valuable qualities to examine.

The interpretive aspect of criticism employs concepts from the social sciences. It enriches the description by attempting to account for the events observed and predicting their consequences. When making interpretation, an educational critic might examine a particular practice employed by a teacher with such questions as:

• What does this practice mean to the teacher and the students?

• What is the long-term effect of this practice?

• What unintended ancillary learnings are occurring?

• How does this practice affect social relationships?

• How does this practice affect the students' concept of purpose in school?

An educational critic also attempts to apply ideas, concepts, and theories from the social sciences to explain the major features of the observed lesson. The purpose, according to Eisner, is to discover the deep structure or rules that govern events in the classroom. Obviously, one must be familiar with a variety of theories and be able to apply them appropriately.

The evaluative aspect makes educational criticism different from social science. In order to improve education, which is the aim of educational criticism, Eisner observes, questions such as the following should be asked:

• Is student learning being helped or hindered by this form of teaching?

• Does this type of teaching contribute to or hamper further development of students' thinking?

• What is the relative value of the learning occurring in this classroom?

An educational critic should be aware of the values that he or she holds and be able to justify the value choices that are made. The critic should also be aware of values that he or she rejects and should recognize that other value choices are possible. A knowledge of the historical and philosophical foundations of education is essential to making value choices, as well as experience as a teacher.

In summary, educational criticism focuses on educational events and materials. The major purpose of educational criticism is to develop a richer and fuller appreciation of these events and materials. A high level of connoisseurship is necessary to function effectively as a critic. This involves an ability to vividly describe the events observed in a classroom or school, to interpret these events using the concepts, models, and theories of the social sciences, and to assess the educational importance of the events or materials that are described and interpreted.

Other Applications of Criticism

Eisner suggests that educational criticism should look beyond the interactions of students and teachers in classrooms and schools, to include other aspects of the school environment. Textbooks and illustrations that appear in them, for example, can be examined critically, as well as school architecture and furniture. Questions relevant to such artifacts of schooling might include:
- What do they communicate to students?
- What values do they reflect?
- How are the student's image and experience of schooling affected?

Questions pertinent to student work include:
- What is the student's distinctive style of expression?
- What is the quality of the student's writing, art work, or analytic abilities?
- How does the student respond to new ideas and opportunities?
- Is the student sensitive to the feelings of others?
- How is this student's thinking unique?

Subjectivity and Validity

Eisner does not view as a problem the possibility that two educational critics may disagree about the value of the same set of events.

Rather, he believes that such disagreement could improve the quality of dialogue in education. Certain advantages and liabilities can be found in almost every educational practice, policy, form of school organization, and style of teaching. More open discussion about these matters could be beneficial, Eisner believes, by contributing to the appreciation that education is a very complex matter.

Anticipating the argument that his concept of educational criticism is too subjective, Eisner offers two ways of determining its validity: structural corroboration and referential adequacy. Structural corroboration is achieved when the description and interpretation of the events portrayed support one another by forming a coherent and persuasive whole. Referential adequacy requires that the criticism be tested through follow-up observations of the same classroom or school. Educational criticism, in other words, is not quick and easy. Time and repeated observations are needed to ensure its accuracy.

Like orchid growers, wine tasters, cabinet makers, and football fans, educational connoisseurs should acquire the ability to appreciate qualities of which others are not even aware. Educational critics, in other words, must be connoisseurs of classrooms and schools. The practice of educational criticism itself, Eisner believes, refines the perceptions of the critic and enhances the ability to anticipate distinctive qualities. Educational criticism, as conceived by Eisner, is more of a function than a role. Students, teachers, supervisors, administrators, university professors, and school board members can all serve as educational critics in their collective effort to improve education. These people already rely upon their perceptions, sensibilities, and ability to describe what they see and hear, though these dispositions may need refinement. If used in a nonspecialized way, Eisner believes that educational criticism could open communication and contribute to a supportive and humane community in schools that includes all its members.

Meta-criticism

Finally, Eisner describes and advocates a practice of turning the critical process upon the criticism itself. He terms this critical examination of criticism, meta-criticism. It is important to remember, however, that criticisms are likely to be very different from one another in several respects:
- Educational critics rely on their own perceptions and sensibilities and do not follow a standardized format of expression. Each

critic has a unique style of writing that gives expression to his or her own voice.

- Educational critics do not rely upon observation forms with predetermined categories of behavior and events when observing classrooms. Rather, critics use personal categories, criteria, models, frameworks, and interests to identify relevant qualities of a classroom or lesson and then construct coherent patterns that help others understand the meaning of these qualities.
- No standard format for presenting an educational criticism exists. A criticism may be expressed in a literary style, as poetry, through photography, or may be audio- or video-taped. A criticism is credible to the extent that it is coherent and sheds light upon the situation it describes.

The issue of whether the description and interpretation offered by a criticism actually illuminates the observed situation, according to Eisner, is the key to assessing the worth of a criticism. He suggests several other questions that may be asked as well, such as:

- What process does the author follow?
- What type of language is used?
- What are the central metaphors and categories?
- What insights are disclosed?
- How are conclusions supported?
- Are the conclusions credible?

Eisner suggests that educational critics are somewhat better equipped to provide a meaningful appraisal of a lesson if they possess expertise in the subject matter of the lesson being observed. A useful criticism can be developed, however, without this specialized expertise as long as it does not focus on the substance of what is taught.

Summary

Eisner argues that the content and process of teaching are inseparable and that the quality of a lesson is determined by both. He portrays teaching as a transformation of content into action. The *what* and the *how* of teaching, therefore, must be considered simultaneously.

A supervisor employing Eisner's approach must be a connoiseur of teaching who can detect important subtleties of classroom life. This capacity is derived from personal sensitivities and experiences, and is heightened by observing classrooms frequently.

The supervisor serves as the major instrument for perceiving classroom reality and its context. He or she uses vivid, richly descriptive language to preserve the complexity of classroom life and capture its expressive essence. Eisner recommends repeated observations so that supervisors consider the significance of events within the context of an extended period of time. A variety of media can be used besides written notes, including videotapes, photographs, slides, and audiotaped interviews.

After an observation the supervisor interprets the data drawing on theories, models, and concepts from the social sciences as well as poetic imagination. According to Eisner, the supervisor should consider the process and the outcomes of teaching and try to develop metaphors that precisely reveal the expressive qualities of the lesson that cannot be quantified, such as the meanings of classroom events for the teacher and students.

Educational criticism, as conceived by Eisner, relies exclusively on methods of qualitative inquiry. Because of the rich language and metaphors used to describe the objects and events that are observed, the description that results allows the reader to envision and participate vicariously in the experience.

Assessing the educational significance of the lesson is an essential part of Eisner's approach. Here, the supervisor focuses on the curriculum, the teaching, and student outcomes, separately and in relation to one another.

The artistic approach to supervision is closely tied to Eisner's perception of teaching as artistry. Qualities in teachers that should be encouraged include flexibility, creativity, ingenuity, and novelty, among others. The emphasis is on helping teachers exploit and develop their unique talents. While the artistic approach strives to improve each teacher's general performance, the stronger thrust is on improving each teacher's individual style. Eisner believes, therefore, that teachers should ultimately be free to accept or reject the supervisor's recommendations.

References

Barone, T. (1985). Of Scott and Lisa and Other Friends. Reprinted from *The Educational Imagination: On the Design and Evaluation of Educational Programs,* 2nd edition. New York: Macmillan Publishing Co.

Eisner, E. W. (1976). Educational connoisseurship and criticism: Their form and functions in educational evaluation. *The Journal of Aesthetic Education, 10*(3-4), 135-150.

Eisner, E. W. (1977). On the uses of educational connoisseurship and criticism for evaluating classroom life. *Teachers College Record, 78*(3), 345-358.

Eisner, E. W. (1979). *The educational imagination: On the design and evaluation of educational programs.* New York: Macmillan Publishing Co.

Eisner, E. W. (1985). *The educational imagination: On the design and evaluation of educational programs.* 2nd edition. New York: Macmillan Publishing Co.

Eisner, E. W. (1982). An artistic approach to supervision. In Thomas J. Sergiovanni (Ed.), *Supervision of teaching,* 1982 ASCD Yearbook. Alexandria, VA: Association for Supervision and Curriculum Development.

Section Three

Technical/Didactic Models

The approaches to supervision described in Section Three gained considerable popularity, especially among practitioners, during the 1980s. They differ fundamentally from the models of supervision described in earlier chapters in that the technical/didactic models emphasize the *acquisition*, and not the discovery, of teaching behaviors and skills. They are based on the assumption that objective criteria of "good" teaching exist independent of any specific classroom context. Being an effective teacher according to this view means meeting some external ideal standard.

Underlying the technical/didactic models of supervision is an enormous amount of research conducted during the 1970s that attempted to link teacher behaviors with student learning outcomes. Reviewing this body of research to identify "effective" teaching behaviors became a popular pastime for some educators. These and other studies of teaching provided the criteria for practice to which teachers are expected to conform. Although their particular citations may differ, Hunter, Acheson and Gall, and Joyce and Showers, all advocate the general application of research findings to classrooms.

Clinical supervision, according to this perspective, becomes a tool for implementing behaviors, skills, and strategies that are discovered or invented outside the classroom being observed. This requires much less introspection, self analysis, and self direction on the part of the teacher. There is also less room for the discovery or expression of meanings, or the nurturance of a personal style of teaching.

Both the Hunter and the Joyce and Showers approaches begin with an extensive period of staff development involving the introduction and transmission of teaching skills. Observation and feedback are then used to reinforce this staff development effort. "Coaching" for both Hunter and Joyce and Showers is not content neutral, but focuses on specific instructional techniques and innovations. Training of teachers was the first phase of Cogan's model as well, but the focus in that case was on the theory and techniques of clinical supervision. Cogan did consider his rationale for clinical supervision as compatible, however, with the introduction of innovations into classrooms and schools.

According to the technical/didactic view, knowledge is something that is discovered, possessed, and controlled by supervisors or other experts. Teachers assume the role of recipients who consume or apply that knowledge. The original clinical models, and the humanistic/artistic approaches that followed in the 1970s, portrayed teachers and supervisors as the inventors and creators of professional knowledge that had special relevance to particular classrooms. In the earlier approaches, supervisors assisted teachers in the processes of inquiry and discovery.

The view that professional knowledge is objective and in possession of experts precludes the necessity of a pre-observation conference for both Hunter and Joyce and Showers, and diminishes the need for Acheson and Gall. The original models of clinical supervision emphasized the necessity of the supervisor thoroughly understanding the lesson from the teacher's point of view. Hunter argues, in contrast, that a pre-observation conference only biases the observer. Initial goal setting and planning conferences are expected, for Acheson and Gall, to take no longer than twenty or thirty minutes. Joyce and Showers simply ignore the issue of pre-observation. Once one understands the external standard of quality, these authors imply, there is obviously no need for dialogue before the observation.

The type of data recorded during the observation differs for each of the technical/didactic models. Acheson and Gall provide an impressively broad array of strategies for recording behavior that generate both quantitative and qualitative data. Hunter recommends only "script taping," a system of phonetic abbreviations intended to provide as complete a record as possible of what is said and done in the classroom. A system for transcribing classroom dialogue that is almost identical to script taping, interestingly, is described in Goldhammer's 1969 edition. Joyce and Showers recommend the use of rating scales that indicate the degree to which a teacher has successfully enacted the intended behaviors, skills, and outcomes.

Because of the variety of data gathering strategies offered by Acheson and Gall, their analysis phase is also quite diverse. Teachers are encouraged to use data to help close the gap between their real and ideal behaviors in the classroom. Analysis for Hunter and Joyce and Showers involves matching observed behaviors against a preselected pattern.

Unlike the original clinical models, the technical/didactic approaches generally preclude the discovery of behavior patterns and meanings after the fact. Accordingly, feedback to teachers in the technical/didactic models is intended to reinforce predetermined behavior patterns. Data do not serve as a basis for dialogue aimed toward discovery. Cooperative problem solving is also minimized.

Acheson and Gall think it is possible, and Hunter contends desirable, to combine the functions of formative feedback with summative evaluation. Joyce and Showers, however, argue that the two processes should be kept separate and prefer that administrators and formally designated supervisors not be involved in the coaching process.

The quality of interpersonal relations between teachers and supervisors is de-emphasized in the technical/didactic models. Neither Hunter nor Joyce and Showers make mention of emotions or feelings with regard to supervision. Acheson and Gall distance supervisors from teachers by emphasizing neutrality, and transform emotions into the conferencing "technique" of acknowledging and using teachers' feelings. None of the technical/didactic approaches calls for self examination by the supervisor of his or her own values, beliefs, biases, or intentions.

Joyce and Showers' view that teachers are in a better position to provide the kinds of assistance that other teachers need most is consistent with Blumberg's recommendation of involving teachers more directly in the induction and socialization of colleagues. Joyce and Showers' framework for turning schools and districts into "learning laboratories" is also bears some resemblance to Blumberg's notion of schools as "centers of inquiry" and to Mosher and Purpel's use of teacher groups to discuss and solve pedagogical problems.

Obviously, many important differences in both philosophical assumptions and practices exist between the technical/didactic models and earlier approaches to clinical supervision. The influence of the technical/didactic models on schools during the last ten or fifteen years has been tremendous. Although these approaches have been criticized in the literature of supervision at times, the popularity of the technical/ didactic models has been instrumental in initiating much needed discussion among scholars and practitioners about the possibilities, limitations, and ethical dimensions of classroom supervision.

Chapter 6

Acheson and Gall's Technical Model

The Model at Work

Mrs. Whyte paused for a brief moment to glance at her watch as she carefully tallied the data she had recorded earlier that morning. She had observed the sixth grade social studies class of Mr. Morris, a second year teacher who was warm and friendly, but a little frustrating to work with. The two of them had met at the beginning of the year to establish several improvement goals for Mr. Morris to strive toward. When she asked whether he had any concerns about his instruction, Mr. Morris had difficulty specifying them behaviorally, so Mrs. Whyte suggested that she videotape one of his lessons for him to view.

After recording the lesson Mrs. Whyte gave Mr. Morris the tape along with a checklist of effective teaching behaviors to consider. The checklist was developed the year before by a committee of teachers and administrators after consulting the education research literature on effective teaching. These behaviors comprised district-wide standards that all teachers were expected to exhibit during formal evaluations.

When they met for a post observation conference a few days later, Mr. Morris spent some time at first talking about problems he was having with the used car he had bought. Eventually, however, he selected "increasing student involvement" and "time on task" as his major performance goals for the year.

Mr. Morris and Mrs. Whyte met again a few days later for ten minutes to arrange a time for a formal observation. Although he initially tried to engage Mrs. Whyte in unrelated small-talk, she managed to get him to focus on the upcoming lesson. They arranged a time and date, and they discussed the content and purpose of the lesson, and the teaching strategy to be used. Because students were to be working on projects in small groups, Mrs. Whyte recommended an at-task analysis. She would record the behavior of a different student every few seconds on a seating chart, and then tally the behaviors on a table to illustrate the percent of time that students were engaged in various activities.

When students entered the class that Mrs. Whyte observed, they were excitedly discussing a television program on famine in third world countries that had appeared the previous evening. Mr. Morris picked up on the students' conversation, having viewed the program himself, and began to lead a discussion on the distribution of wealth among countries in the world. Mrs. Whyte recognized that he was responding to the students' interest, which was good, but the discussion made the at-task record inappropriate for gathering data. Instead, Mrs. Whyte began to record the number of times that Mr. Morris called on each student and the number of times each student asked or answered a question, data that was relevant to Mr. Morris' performance goal of increasing student involvement.

Mrs. Whyte stood at her desk and stared a moment longer at her analysis of the data as she prepared to meet Mr. Morris in his room for a post observation conference. She saw a very balanced pattern of interaction between Mr. Morris and both boys and girls. Also evident was the fact that two minority students, who were usually silent in the classes of other teachers she observed, had participated in Mr. Morris' discussion several times.

During the feedback conference, Mr. Morris unexpectedly tried to initiate a conversation about global economics with Mrs. Whyte.

She interpreted this as a defensive effort to avoid dealing with the matter at hand, so she introduced the data as tactfully as possible and suggested that they look at it together.

Mr. Morris immediately became very interested in the findings, and said that he felt pleased that his discussion included as many students as it had. He made a deliberate effort to involve the females in that particular class, he explained, because several male students were "real talkers" who readily dominated discussions if given the chance. Although pleased herself, Mrs. Whyte was careful to avoid being judgmental. She listened to and paraphrased Mr. Morris' feelings and comments carefully, asked several questions for clarification, and praised him by pointing out that his efforts indicated progress toward the performance goal of "increasing student involvement."

Introduction

In their book, *Techniques in the Clinical Supervision of Teachers* (1992), Keith Acheson and Meredith Gall point out that supervision in many schools is closely tied to the enforcement of local and state policy. As a result, teachers often feel threatened by supervisors and react negatively to supervision because they equate it with rating scales and evaluation. Acheson and Gall contrast their model of clinical supervision with this common emphasis on enforcing policy.

The primary goal of clinical supervision, according to Acheson and Gall, is the professional development of teachers, with a special focus on performance in the classroom. This version of clinical supervision is based on the premise that teachers will react more positively to supervision that responds to their concerns and aspirations. It focuses on teachers' classroom behavior in order to improve their instructional performance. The clinical method, as described by Acheson and Gall, is intended to be interactive instead of directive, democratic instead of autocratic, and teacher-centered instead of supervisor-centered.

Clinical supervision is described as a recurring three stage cycle. A brief summary of each stage of the Acheson and Gall model follows:

Stage 1:   Planning Conference – During the planning conference the supervisor helps the teacher clarify his or her personal concerns, needs, and aspirations, with a focus on possible discrepancies between the real and ideal situations. New techniques of instruction may be suggested to help attain the ideal. Hypotheses can be proposed for testing against observational data. Finally, a method of collecting data during the classroom observation is cooperatively agreed upon.

Stage 2:   Classroom Observation – During the classroom observation stage the supervisor records data relative to some indicator of performance. The evidence recorded is intended to be objective, instead of being based on subjective value judgments. Data are obtained through either direct or indirect observation.

Stage 3:   Feedback Conference – The data collected during Stage 2 is reviewed and discussed by the teacher and supervisor. The supervisor encourages the teacher to make inferences about his or her own teaching and to identify areas where improvement may be desirable. This discussion often leads to a return to Stage 1, with the teacher and supervisor developing a plan for the next observation or for the teacher's continued improvement. The emphasis of the clinical cycle, according to Acheson and Gall, should be on identifying and reinforcing successful patterns in instruction rather than focusing on weaknesses.

Assumptions and Characteristics

Acheson and Gall describe a number of assumptions and essential characteristics that underly their three-stage model of clinical supervision. They believe, for example, that teachers need to acquire specific intellectual and behavioral skills to improve instruction. Supervisors have the responsibility, they suggest, to help teachers develop these skills. The ability to analyze instruction using systematic data, and the ability to experiment, adapt, and modify the curriculum are viewed as especially useful for teachers.

Supervision, according to Acheson and Gall, should be a dynamic give-and-take process between colleagues who are searching for mutual understanding as they analyze instruction. During conferences supervisors can help teachers select a few important and relevant issues related to their instruction, yet amenable to change. The three stage cycle of planning, observing, and analyzing ought to be continuous, Acheson and Gall believe, and cumulative in its effect.

Supervisors should focus their attention on improving the content and process of teaching, according to Acheson and Gall, instead of trying to change teachers' personalities. Every teacher should feel free to develop a personal style of teaching. This freedom includes responsibility for initiating, analyzing, and improving one's own teaching. Acheson and Gall also believe that supervision can be viewed, analyzed, and improved in much the same way as teaching. In other words, every supervisor should feel free and responsible for analyzing and evaluating his or her own style of supervision.

Goals

Acheson and Gall identify five goals that all relate to the primary aim of improving teachers' classroom instruction. These are as follows:

1) *Furnishing Teachers with Unbiased Feedback Concerning their Instruction.* Acheson and Gall compare this purpose to holding a mirror up for teachers to see themselves in action. Teachers are often surprised at what they see, which can provide stimulation to try to improve.

2) *Diagnosing and Solving Problems Related to Instruction.* Supervisors can use data and conferencing techniques to help teachers locate discrepancies between their actual and ideal classroom performance. The supervisor may have to intervene if the teacher has difficulty diagnosing problems independently.

3) *Helping Teachers Acquire Skill in Applying Instructional Techniques.* According to Acheson and Gall, clinical supervision is more than problem-solving. It is also useful for reinforcing effective teaching strategies that already exist or are newly introduced.

4) *Evaluating Teacher Performance for Making Decisions Concerning Promotion and Tenure.* Although not an intent of clinical supevision as originally conceived, Acheson and Gall suggest that objective, systematically collected data is a sound basis for evaluating

teachers. The "sting" of evaluation can be lessened, they reason, if the supervisor clearly conveys the criteria to be used.

5) *Helping Teachers Acquire Positive Attitudes Related to Ongoing Professional Growth.* Clinical supervision encourages the view among teachers that professional development is a career-long process, Acheson and Gall believe. Supervisors can model this ethic by displaying a willingness to change and improve themselves.

Criteria of Good Teaching

Acheson and Gall define supervision in terms of helping teachers decrease the gap between the behavior that characterizes their current teaching and the teaching they ideally want to achieve. By "ideal" they do not mean to imply "unrealistic," but rather, "effective." They suggest further that setting goals for clinical supervision requires some agreement between the supervisor and teacher concerning what is meant by ideal, good, or effective teaching.

Acheson and Gall believe that four elements should be considered by supervisors when assessing the quality of a teacher's performance:

1. the teacher's behavior in the classroom;
2. student behavior;
3. the teacher's planning; and
4. the teacher's performance outside the classroom (within the school).

Acheson and Gall suggest that the classroom behaviors that characterize good teachers are fairly obvious. They argue against the view that teaching is too complex to analyze behaviorally, and against the view that different criteria should be applied to different teaching situations and individual teachers. As evidence, Acheson and Gall cite several studies from the process/product line of research, adherents of which claim to have identified teacher behaviors (processes) that correlate with student outcomes (products) like achievement and improved attitudes. Several examples of these "effective" behaviors include:

- being warm and understanding;
- acknowledging students' ideas;
- being businesslike and organized;
- structuring classroom time;
- reinforcing the accuracy of student answers;

- checking student progress and adjusting instruction accordingly; and
- using a variety of questioning strategies to stimulate student thinking.

Student behavior can also be an accurate indicator of a teacher's effectiveness, according to Acheson and Gall, even when a supervisor knows nothing about the teacher. Examples of observable student behavior that indicate effective teaching include:
- performing well on tests;
- learning independently;
- displaying positive attitudes toward themselves and others;
- displaying positive attitudes toward the teacher the curriculum, and the school; and
- engaging actively in the task of learning.

The quality of planning is a third perspective from which a teacher's effectiveness can be assessed, according to Acheson and Gall. A supervisor should talk with the teacher and examine written lesson plans in order to understand the rationale for a lesson. This enables the supervisor to judge the appropriateness of the instructional objectives, learning materials, and evaluation strategies used. Acheson and Gall indicate that good planning also includes the consideration of student characteristics and abilities, as well as an ability to adjust classroom plans on the basis of outcomes.

The fourth indicator of teacher effectiveness that Acheson and Gall allude to relates to the teacher's behavior outside the classroom. Some of the behaviors that they suggest are evidence of effective teaching are:
- participating in schoolwide activities;
- cooperating with colleagues;
- serving on curriculum committees;
- engaging in professional growth activities; and
- behaving ethically.

The Goal Setting Conference

Acheson and Gall suggest that a goal setting conference betweeen the teacher and supervisor should precede the implementation of the three-stage clinical cycle. They suggest that teachers who are working on personal growth goals should be allowed to exercise more control over the agenda and outcome of this initial meeting. Supervisors should retain greater control, however, when working with teachers who are overcoming some deficiency through an assistance plan. Data collected and recorded during subsequent cycles of planning, observation, and feedback, may or may not become part of a teacher's personnel record, depending on whether the teacher's performance is being summatively evaluated.

Four specific techniques are recommended by Acheson and Gall for facilitating the goal setting conference – identifying the concerns that the teacher may have about instruction, translating these concerns into observable behaviors, identifying ways of improving instruction, and helping the teacher develop goals for self improvment. Each is described briefly below.

a) *Identifying Concerns that the Teacher may have about Instruction.* The first technique described by Acheson and Gall is intended to get the teacher to talk about his or her concerns regarding instruction. They suggest that the supervisor ask questions such as:
- *How is your teaching going?*
- *Are you more successful in some areas than others?*
- *Is there anything about your teaching that we should take a look at for improvement?*

If the teacher cannot or will not identify any concerns, Acheson and Gall believe that the supervisor should accept the statement, while recognizing that the teacher may feel threatened and be reluctant to disclose a weakness at this point. The supervisor may suggest, however, what Acheson and Gall refer to as a "wide-lens" approach to the observation, such as videotaping. After viewing the recording the teacher may become aware of some shortcomings. Another strategy is to let the teacher review a checklist of effective teaching behaviors or a variety of observation instruments to give them some ideas about areas they might like to focus upon.

Acheson and Gall note that teachers seem to differ in the types of concerns they have at different points in their careers. Beginning teachers, for example, tend to be very concerned about their authority in the school and their ability to control students. Novices are also worried about their ability to master the subject matter, to answer questions, to anticipate problems, to admit ignorance and failure, to make needed changes, and to cope with evaluation. Later in their careers, Acheson and Gall point out, teachers tend to focus more on students. These mature concerns reflect a greater awareness of students' abilities, a desire to specify appropriate objectives for them and to accurately assess their achievement, as well as a willingness to evaluate oneself based upon student outcomes.

b) *Translating the Concerns of the Teacher into Behaviors that can be Observed*. Acheson and Gall consider this to be one of the most important techniques in clinical supervision. Supervisors must listen carefully to what teachers say about their teaching and help them clarify statements that are ambiguous, abstract, or general. Supervisors can ask teachers for further information or to provide specific, concrete examples of what they are talking about. The purpose is to get teachers to describe their concern *behaviorally* so that the supervisor knows what to look for during the observation.

If a teacher is concerned about his or her clarity, Acheson and Gall suggest, the supervisor can observe for behaviors such as these:
- giving examples and explaining them;
- letting pupils ask questions;
- writing major ideas on the chalkboard;
- using ordinary words; and
- asking students questions to check on their understanding.

c) *Identifying Ways of Improving Instruction*. The third technique follows logically from the first and second. After identifying a concern and stating it behaviorally, the teacher can now begin thinking about how to best address that concern. The supervisor participates in this process to some extent by offering encouragement and suggestions.

If a teacher wants to change student behavior in some way, Acheson and Gall recommend asking the following questions:
- What specific behaviors are expected from students?
- What instructional procedures will be used?
- How can the new instructional procedures be practiced or learned?

For example, in answer to the first question, a teacher may decide to try to increase student verbal participation during class discussion. In answer to the next question, the teacher might decide to praise students more frequently when they offer comments that are relevant to the topic being studied. Acheson and Gall note that the response to the last question can be either simple or complex. A simple way of learning and practicing the new procedure, they suggest, could be to write the reminder **"PRAISE!"** on an index card kept in a visible location while teaching. A more complex procedure could be to read about and attend workshops on the use of praise in classrooms.

d) *Helping the Teacher Develop Goals for Self-improvement.* The fourth technique obviously fulfills the purpose of the goal-setting conference. The teacher's personal goal may seem obvious after going through the first three techniques, but Acheson and Gall advise that the teacher or supervisor should state the goal in order to avoid misunderstanding or confusion about the direction of the clinical supervision cycle that will follow. They also recommend that the teacher and supervisor check for agreement at this point, to ensure that their understanding is the same.

Stage 1: The Planning Conference

The first stage of the three-stage clinical supervision sequence is the planning conference. The goal-setting conference described above is a chance for the teacher and supervisor to identify concerns that the teacher may have about his or her instruction. These concerns are then translated into behaviors that can be observed. Important decisions made during the planning conference described below relate to the observation, such as the type of data the supervisor will record.

Acheson and Gall note that success at this point depends upon teachers believing that the supervisor is primarily interested in helping them and that data will not be used against them. Trust can be built between the supervisor and teacher, they suggest, by sharing experiences based on classroom observations over time. Holding planning conferences on neutral ground or in the teacher's classroom is also proposed for putting the teacher at ease.

The planning conference should take no more than five or ten minutes, Acheson and Gall believe, unless it is combined with the goal-setting conference. In that case, they suggest, goal-setting and planning together should take no longer than twenty to thirty minutes. Three techniques are provided that can contribute to the success of the planning conference, namely, arranging a time for the observation, choosing an observation strategy, and clarifying the classroom context. These are as follows:

Arranging a time for the observation.
A mutually convenient time is decided upon for the supervisor to visit the teacher's classroom. Acheson and Gall believe that a teacher should have a feeling of some control as a professional over when the supervisor is likely to to be present. The lesson should be selected beforehand, they suggest, because it provides an appropriate opportunity for the teacher to exhibit his or her attempt to address the instructional concerns identified earlier.

Choosing an observation strategy.
Selecting the behavior to be observed and the instrument the supervisor will use to record data are important decisions made during the planning conference. Data collected during the observation should match the teacher's concerns. For example, that a videotape recording may be most appropriate if a teacher is concerned about nonverbal behavior.

Teachers should select the observation instrument used, according to Acheson and Gall, unless they are unfamiliar with the choices available. Supervisors should emphasize the nonevaluative nature of the observation instruments, and the fact that the teacher can form his or her own opinion about the lesson from the data during the feedback conference. A realistic schedule for the clinical cycle should also be agreed upon.

Clarifying the classroom context.
The supervisor needs to have an understanding of the instructional context, Acheson and Gall note, in order to accurately interpret the behaviors targeted for observation. The context includes, among other things, the content of the lesson, how it related to what students learned previously, what they will learn later, and the instructional strategy that the teacher will use. Asking questions about the lesson also signals to the teacher that the supervisor is interested in his or her perceptions. Asking questions is suggested as a good way to get teachers to accept the supervisor's presence in their classrooms.

The following statements and questions are examples of the kinds that Acheson and Gall suggest can be helpful for encouraging teachers to talk more about the instructional context:
* Tell me about the content of the lesson to be observed.
* Tell me what you think students will learn.

- Describe the techniques and strategy that you plan to use during the lesson.
- What behaviors are students expected to exhibit?
- Do you anticipate any problems during the lesson?
- Can you think of anything else I should know before I observe this lesson?

Stage 2: Classroom Observation

A major strength of Acheson and Gall's book is the number and variety of observation techniques that they provide. They note that supervisors should have a wide variety of these techniques at their disposal. Acheson and Gall describe eight different observation techniques which they classify into four broad categories:
- selective verbatim techniques,
- records based on seating charts,
- wide-lens techniques, and
- checklists and timeline coding.

Selective Verbatim Approach

The *selective verbatim approach* to classroom observation involves the supervisor writing down exactly what is seen and heard in the classroom. The supervisor's notes are selective, in that they are limited to what the teacher has agreed are the kinds of events that will be recorded (e.g., effective teaching behaviors).

Acheson and Gall note a number of advantages and disadvantages to using the selective verbatim approach. One major advantage of this approach is that the resulting data focus attention directly on what the teacher and students say to one another, which may sensitize the teacher to the verbal process of the classroom. Because this approach is "selective" the teacher is able to concentrate on changing one or two behaviors instead of an overwhelming constellation of possibilities. Other advantages of selective verbatim are that the approach is simple to use and that it results in an unbiased and nonjudgmental record of teacher behavior.

Several disadvantages of the selective verbatim approach are also evident. First, teachers may become overly conscious of using the observed behavior, resulting in an artificial classroom performance. Second, the broader context of the classroom may be missed by too narrow an application of this approach. Third, the focus of the observation may be trivial if it is chosen in haste.

The selective verbatim approach also presents a difficulty for some supervisors who cannot keep up with the classroom action. Acheson and Gall believe that recording a few verbal statements exactly as stated is better than paraphrasing. The supervisor also might audiotape the lesson and write a transcript from the recording at a later time. Three techniques are specifically associated with selective verbatim – questions that teachers ask, feedback that teachers provide, and teachers' directions and structuring statements. Each is described below.

Questions that Teachers Ask.
A supervisor using this technique writes down the questions that a teacher asks during a lesson. Instead of tediously writing down every question that is asked during the course of an entire lesson, the observer may want to record a sample of questions for several minutes at the beginning, middle, and end of the lesson. Acheson and Gall recommend writing down anything that is asked in a questioning tone, even if it may not exactly qualify as a question.

Questions that have been recorded provide a wealth of data that can be analyzed in a variety of ways. Supervisors and teachers may want to consider the following five issues:

- At what cognitive level are questions asked? Are students required to think or only remember facts?
- How much information is called for in answering the questions? Are questions open-ended or narrowly focused?
- Are questions redirected? Does the teacher ask several students to answer the same question or settle for one response?
- Are probing questions asked? Does the teacher try to improve a student's first response by asking follow-up questions?
- Are questions multiple and confused, or does the teacher ask questions that are clear and precise?

Feedback that Teachers Provide.
Feedback on one's performance is essential whenever anyone tries to learn a new skill. Praise and criticism, Acheson and Gall remind us, are especially relevant as forms of feedback in the relationship between

teachers and their students. Supervisors can easily record verbal feedback for teachers who are concerned about the amount of praise or criticism they use in the classroom. Observers may also note the student behavior that prompts the feedback as well as the affective tone (e.g., enthusiasm, support, sarcasm, etc.). Obviously, a lesson should be chosen in which there is plenty of verbal interchange.

Teacher feedback can be analyzed in a variety of ways. Acheson and Gall recommend that supervisors and teachers should take note of the following:

- How much feedback does the teacher give to students?
- How frequently does the teacher provide feedback?
- How specific is the feedback that is provided?
- Does the teacher rephrase students' ideas?
- Does the teacher apply students' ideas to the problem being discussed?
- Does the teacher compare students' ideas with ideas expressed by others?
- Does the teacher try to summarize what individuals and groups of students have said?

Teachers' Directions and Structuring Statements.
Acheson and Gall cite evidence suggesting that the directions and statements that a teacher uses to structure a class can contribute to student success. These include statements that provide a preview of what students will learn from a lesson, summaries of what happened during a lesson, indications to students that a transition in the lesson is underway or about to occur, and highlighting important facts and ideas.

Most directions and structuring are evident at the beginning and end of a lesson, according to Acheson and Gall, but understanding the context of the entire lesson is helpful for making interpretations. As with feedback, data can be analyzed in terms of amount, specificity, and variety of directions and structure given.

Records Based on Seating Charts

Records based on seating charts are a second category of observation techniques described by Acheson and Gall, which they refer to by the acronym SCORE (Seating Chart Observational REcords). The advantages of using these techniques to record data include:

- Use and interpretation are easy.
- Much information is condensed on a single page.
- Seating charts can be drawn up immediately and designed for specific purposes.
- SCORE instruments provide important information about both individual students and the entire class.

The major disadvantage in using seating chart observational records, according to Acheson and Gall, is that they can lead to simplistic and superficial observations and analysis.

Three different SCORE techniques are described: at task behavior, verbal flow, and classroom movement patterns. A description of each follows:

At Task Behavior.

The purpose of this observation technique is to provide descriptive data on the amount of "on task" and "off task" behavior exhibited by students. If a teacher is concerned about the amount of time that students spend off task, the supervisor and teacher can create a list of things that students are likely to be doing during a lesson. The behaviors on this list are the categories that the supervisor will use while observing.

A typical list of student behaviors in an elementary classroom might include, for example, "being on task," "talking to friends," and "playing." Acheson and Gall suggest using no more than five categories of behavior to avoid confusion, and say that two categories – "on task" and "off task" – are sufficient for many classrooms. They recommend the following series of steps for gathering at task data:

1) the supervisor should find a place in the classroom from which all the students can be easily seen;
2) a chart is constructed that reflects the seating arrangement in the room;
3) students are identified on the chart by sex, name, or some other characteristic;
4) the supervisor consults the list of student behaviors identified during the planning conference and designates each with a different letter, like so:
     A = On task
     B = Off task
5) the observer scans the room and records on the seating chart the

letter of the behavior that each and every child is seen to exhibit;
6) another scan of behavior is repeated every three or four minutes;
7) the time of each scan is indicated.
The result of scanning the behavior of four students five times would
look something like this:

Robert	Karen	Paula	Alfred
1. A	1 B	1 B	1. B
2. A	2. B	2. B	2. A
3. A	3. A	3. A	3. A
4. A	4. A	4. A	4. B
5. B	5. A	5. A	5. B

Analysis of the data can focus on the behavior exhibited by individual students at different times during the lesson. In the example
above, Robert is on task for most of the lesson except at the very end,
Karen and Paula are off task at first but later get to work, while Alfred
deviates between on and off task behavior.

To gain an understanding of the performance of the class as a whole,
Acheson and Gall suggest summarizing the data in a manner as follows:

BEHAVIOR	Time 1	Time 2	Time 3	Time 4	Time 5	TOTAL	%
A = On task	1	2	4	3	3	13	65%
B = Off task	3	2	0	1	2	7	35%

The chart illustrates that the four students as a group spent 65 percent
of their time on task and 35 percent off task. It appears that most of the
off task behavior occurred at the beginning of the lesson (Time 1 and
Time 2), suggesting that the teacher may want to provide more
structure for students as activities are introduced.

Verbal Flow.
The verbal flow observation technique focuses solely on who is talking
to whom in the classroom and ignores the content of what is being said.
This technique can be very powerful, however, in helping teachers
discover biases in their verbal interactions with students and differences in the amount of participation by various students. The verbal
flow technique is most appropriate for class discussions or question-
and-answer sessions.

The supervisor using this technique begins by selecting a position from which students can be easily observed. Once again, a chart is constructed that reflects the seating arrangement of students. Students are again identified by name or some physical characteristic. When a student interacts with the teacher, an arrow is drawn in the box that represents the seating location of that student. An arrow pointing toward the bottom of the page indicates that the teacher has made a

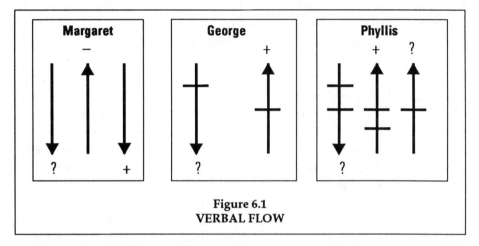

Figure 6.1
VERBAL FLOW

comment to the student. An arrow pointing toward the top of the page indicates that the student has made a comment to the teacher. Examples of data for three hypothetical students follow:

The interaction between a teacher and three students is illustrated in *Figure 6.1*. The teacher interacted with Phyllis more often than with George or Margaret. This is evident from the number of arrows in each box as well as the hash marks on each arrow which represent another interaction of that particular type. An arrow with a question mark (?) at its point indicates that a question was asked. Thus, the teacher asked Phyllis three questions, George two questions, and Margaret one question. Phyllis also asked the teacher questions on two occasions.

An arrow pointing to the top of the page with a plus (+) at its apex indicates that a student gave a correct answer. Phyllis gave three correct answers, as indicated by the arrow with two hash marks, while George gave two correct answers. Margaret's answer to the only question directed to her, however, was incorrect. This is indicated by an arrow pointing to the top of the page with a minus (-) at its apex. The teacher then responded to Margaret with encouragement or a positive comment, which is represented by the arrow pointing to the bottom of the page with a plus (+) at its point.

Analysis of a verbal flow seating chart can demonstrate whether a teacher shows preferences of various sorts. Some teachers unconsciously favor certain locations in the room when they interact with the class, like the front row or middle columns. Some teachers may interact more frequently with certain types of students based on sex, race, or ethnicity. The verbal flow seating chart can also call attention to the types of verbal statements that a teacher uses often. For example, a teacher might be pleased to learn that he or she frequently praises students but rarely makes negative comments.

Classroom Movement Patterns.
This SCORE technique records the movements of the teacher and students in a classroom. Obviously, some degree of movement should be a part of the lesson plan for that class. As with the on task and verbal flow techniques, the observer begins with a seating chart coded with student names. As the teacher and students move around the room, the observer records changes in each individual's seating with arrows and lines connecting different locations. Acheson and Gall recommend that supervisors change colors periodically to indicate sequential time intervals, for example, red for the first five minutes, blue for the second five minutes, and so forth.

Analysis of classroom movement patterns can indicate preferences that teachers may have for certain parts of the room. Analysis can also suggest whether students are progressing with the activity and spending their time as the teacher intends.

Wide-lens Techniques

Wide-lens techniques are a third category of approaches to classroom observation. These include anecdotal records, video and audiotape recordings, and a technique called the global screen technique. As noted earlier, wide-lens techniques are considered useful for helping teachers identify concerns about their instruction by offering them an objective overview of what happens in their classrooms.

Anecdotal Record.
The anecdotal record requires the supervisor to write brief nonevaluative descriptions of the events that unfold in a classroom during a lesson.

This approach is somewhat similar to the intensive direct observations employed by anthropologists when they study cultures.

Acheson and Gall suggest that the supervisor and teacher may decide to focus only on the teacher's behavior, on just one student, on a group of students, or on the entire class. The record itself is usually comprised of a series of brief descriptive sentences which provide an objective account of the events that occur during a lesson as well as the context. In other words, the supervisor tries to record everything that is seen and heard. Evaluative comments should be avoided, according to Acheson and Gall, because teachers will concentrate on these and miss the rest of the description. The emphasis should be on salient events so that the teacher can later get a sense of the temporal flow of the lesson.

Videotape and Audiotape Recordings.
The most objective observation techniques, according to Acheson and Gall, are probably video and audio recordings. Their major advantage is that they miss very little. One disadvantage of recording equipment is that it may intrude and disturb the classroom's normal dynamics by causing anxiety for the teacher or distracting students. Another problem may arise during analysis. Teachers sometimes have difficulty focusing on substantive issues because their attention is absorbed by superficialities like their physical appearance.

Acheson and Gall suggest that a video recording should be no longer than thirty minutes in length. They recommend allowing the teacher to view the entire tape before the feedback conference so that they can offer comments of their own. The supervisor's job is to focus the teacher's attention on significant events and to encourage the teacher to draw inferences about them. The teacher may be given the tape to keep in order to allay anxiety.

Checklists and Timeline Coding

Checklists and timeline coding are the fourth category of observation techniques that Acheson and Gall discuss. These are more structured than the techniques discussed earlier and can be completed by the students who are in a teacher's classroom or by the supervisor. Several checklists, questionnaires, and rating scales are offered that students can complete as a source of feedback to the teacher. These instruments include items that ask students to assess areas of performance such as the teacher's friendliness, knowledge, expectations for students, concern for students, and classroom control.

Acheson and Gall also offer a number of rating scales and checklists for supervisors to use. Different teacher behaviors are included on these forms depending on the type of lesson. For a lesson that they describe as question and answer, a checklist is provided that lists teacher behaviors that are intended to increase student participation and to elicit thoughtful responses.

An instrument combining a checklist and rating scale are presented by Acheson and Gall for evaluating lecture-type lessons. Items on this instrument include behaviors related to the meaningfulness of the content, the degree of student involvement, organization and sequence, and the teacher's skills in delivery.

The original version of Flanders' classroom interaction analysis system which includes categories of direct and indirect teacher behavior and student behavior is discussed. Acheson and Gall also introduce a less well known checklist that attaches the Flanders categories to a timeline.

Stage 3: The Feedback Conference

The feedback conference is the third stage in Acheson and Gall's clinical supervision cycle. The supervisor begins by presenting objective data to the teacher concerning the teacher's performance in the classroom. They analyze the data together and try to reach agreement about what they see happening.

Acheson and Gall believe that teachers rarely set out purposely to do a poor job. They note that most teachers set reasonable goals for themselves and have a range of strategies that they can call upon if they see a need. Nonjudgmental feedback allows teachers to view themselves from a new perspective. Acheson and Gall believe that the supervisor should act collaboratively, as a colleague to the teacher instead of a superior. Insights that teachers develop for themselves from descriptive data are likely to bemore persuasive than admonishments as well as being retained longer and acted upon with more energy and enthusiasm.

Steps in the Feedback Conference

The supervisor's job during the feedback conference is to elicit reactions to the data from the teacher, including both opinions and feelings. The supervisor and teacher next make inferences and consider possible cause and effect relationships. Finally, they make decisions about future courses of action. These actions may include changes in instructional strategies, in objectives for students, or in the teacher's improvement goals. Plans may also be made at this point for the next observation.

In essence, the feedback conference involves the five following actions. The supervisor assumes major responsibility for the first (display) and last (reinforce), with the teacher taking ownership for the remaining three:

1. *display* the data without judgmental comments;
2. *analyze* the data to determine what was happening during the lesson;
3. *interpret* the data by identifying causes and consequences of various behaviors, and discussing their relative desirability;
4. *decide* on alternative instructional strategies to resolve problem areas or to build on strengths;
5. *reinforce* the teacher's announced intentions with encouragement and assistance.

Four Techniques to Encourage Positive Action

Four techniques are discussed for facilitating these steps – providing feedback to the teacher, eliciting opinions, feelings, and inferences, encouraging the teacher to consider alternatives, and providing the teacher with opportunities to practice and compare. Brief descriptions of each follow.

Providing Feedback to the Teacher.

The key to a successful feedback conference is objective, accurate, and relevant data, Acheson and Gall believe, because it minimizes teacher defensiveness and is something that teachers find useful. A good way to begin the feedback conference, they suggest, is to simply say, "Let's take a look at the data." Several steps are involved in this technique:

a) analysis - someone, preferably the teacher, should describe in a nonjudgmental way what the data suggest is happening in the classroom;
b) interpretation - the data are examined further and the teacher

forms hypotheses regarding possible causes and consequences of various behaviors. Alternative behaviors are proposed.

c) decision - the teacher and supervisor decide what changes to make in the future. These may include the nature of the lesson, the learning objectives, the instructional strategy, or student activities. The teacher and supervisor may also decide that further data is needed before an intelligent decision is possible.

Eliciting Opinions, Feelings, and Inferences.
The purpose of this technique is to get the teacher to begin talking about the data that the supervisor has collected. After introducing the data, Acheson and Gall recommend that the supervisor ask the teacher questions such as the following to stimulate a dialogue:
- Which aspects of the data would you like to talk about first?
- After reviewing this data, what would you repeat if you were going to teach this lesson again?
- What aspects of the lesson would you change?
- What would you want changed about the lesson if you were a student in this class?

Acheson and Gall suggest that supervisors should try to keep the conversation with the teacher as close to the data as possible, and to avoid getting entrapped into making value judgments. They also recommend that supervisors should reinforce reasonable inferences and alternatives that the teacher identifies.

Encouraging the Teacher to Consider Alternatives.
A major goal of this clinical supervision model is to develop teachers who are self-critical, who rely on objective data to make decisions, and who are willing to try a broader range of alternative approaches. Teachers should be encouraged from the very beginning of their careers to suggest alternative explanations for why things happen in their classrooms and to provide multiple suggestions on how they might change the situation, the instructional strategy, or the activities. Beginning teachers have a more limited repertoire of alternative choices from which to draw, Acheson and Gall observe, but they learn quickly when given meaningful feedback and adequate support.

Providing the Teacher with Opportunities to Practice and Compare.
Acheson and Gall believe that many benefits can be obtained by inviting teachers to participate in clinical supervision as *observers*. Teachers can

fulfil the role of observer in several ways, they suggest, including: a) observing and recording data on a demonstration lesson that is taught by the supervisor to acquire new instructional strategies; b) observing and recording data on a lesson taught by a colleague to compare styles and pick up new techniques; and c) observing and recording data on themselves with video and audio equipment, through structured student feedback, or with the assistance of an aide.

Many teachers can work independently toward their own improvement, Acheson and Gall believe, with assistance from the supervisor in selecting a central focus and an appropriate source of data. They suggest that beginning teachers should be encouraged to practice various instructional strategies and techniques without direct supervision, and to collect data on their own performance. Conferences with the supervisor can then revolve around the documented progress that the new teacher has achieved and the difficulties with which they are still struggling.

Direct and Indirect Styles

Acheson and Gall distinguish between direct and indirect styles of supervision. They associate a direct style with behaviors that include asserting, leading, expressing, and respecting. They associate an indirect style, in contrast, with behaviors that include caring, guiding, appreciating, and empathizing. While they acknowledge that direct behaviors may be appropriate at times, Acheson and Gall prefer and recommend indirect behaviors. Even supervisors who are directive or self-centered by nature, they claim, can use indirect techniques to improve the quality of their interactions with teachers.

Indirect Techniques

Listening More and Talking Less.
Many times supervisors dominate their conversations with teachers. Acheson and Gall suggest that supervisors who seek to apply the clinical supervision process should refrain from this tendency.

Acknowledging, Paraphrasing, and Using What the Teacher is Saying.
Supervisors should acknowledge what teachers are saying by occasion-

ally using phrases like, "Yes," "Uh huh," or "I understand what you are saying," to show that they are listening. Paraphrasing what the teacher says or using the teacher's ideas demonstrate that the supervisor also understands what the teacher is saying and has internalized it to some degree.

Asking Questions for Clarification.
Sometimes supervisors need to probe a statement that a teacher makes, Acheson and Gall suggest, to help clarify the teacher's thinking. Phrases like the following may be helpful in this regard: "Tell me a little more about that." "Can you give me a specific example?" "I am not sure exactly what you mean."

Giving Teachers Specific Praise for Performance and Growth.
Praise is especially effective in promoting change when it is attached to some specific behavior. It is important to reinforce progress that teachers make toward their stated goals, partly because they receive thanks for their efforts so rarely.

Avoiding Direct Advice.
Acheson and Gall believe that self-discovery is a much more effective and long-lasting way of learning than being told what to do by someone else. They caution that it is better to state one's concerns as a supervisor honestly, however, than to be perceived as playing games of manipulation. The aim is to make teachers responsible for themselves.

Providing Verbal Support.
Acheson and Gall recommend that supervisors should be supportive of teachers when they are facing problems and should openly express some feeling of sympathy or empathy. A statement along the lines of "I know this is difficult, but I am sure you can do it," may be a needed expression of a supervisor's confidence in a teacher's capability.

Sometimes teachers' personal problems overlap with difficulties they may be having in the classroom. For serious psychological or medical afflictions, supervisors are advised to refer teachers to appropriate specialists. If laws or official school policies are being violated, it is necessary for the supervisor to demand that the teacher comply. But if personal problems are not too serious, Acheson and Gall believe that supervisors can effectively apply some client-centered counseling to help teachers identify problems or alternative solutions. Counseling requires some skill, but it may be necessary if personal problems interfere with a teacher's classroom success.

Acheson and Gall note that counseling and curricular support are considered by some experts to be facets of supervision. Beginning teachers may feel anxious about their performance in the classroom and veteran teachers occasionally experience problems in their personal lives that interfere with professional responsibilities. Sometimes teachers ask supervisors about the availability, suitability, and use of alternative curriculum materials, or are uncertain about curriculum topics, coverage, or organization. While Acheson and Gall observe that such teachers are in need of sympathy, support, and reassurance, they do not view counseling and curricular support as part of clinical supervision. In fact, they suggest that teachers sometimes use problems and events outside the classroom as evasive ploys to avoid confronting difficult issues related to their teaching. Clinical supervisors should listen sensitively to teachers' difficulties, they advise, but then tactfully shift the focus back to behavior in the classroom.

Acknowledging and Using the Teacher's Feelings.
Supervisors should recognize that many of the things that teachers say during a conference have emotional as well as intellectual meaning. In fact, feelings are often the most important part of the message being conveyed. Acheson and Gall recommend, therefore, that supervisors should reflect teachers' feelings with statements like: "You sound very angry about that," or "You seemed to be enjoying yourself during the lesson." Acknowledging emotions lets teachers know that supervisors consider what they are feeling to be important.

Teacher Evaluation

Supervisors are often responsible for both formative and summative evaluation of teachers. Acheson and Gall acknowledge that summative evaluation interferes with the collegiality and trust that are necessary for formative (growth) activities, yet they believe that a practical compromise is possible. One way of dealing with the conflicting nature of the formative and summative functions is to assign them to separate roles, they suggest, with colleagues taking responsibility for the former and administrators concentrating on the latter.

A number of components can also be added to the clinical supervision framework, Acheson and Gall contend, to arrive at a workable system of evaluation for tenure, promotion, and dismissal that remains consistent with the tenets of clinical supervision. These components include: district standards for performance, written job descriptions, performance goals, assistance plans, formal evaluations, evaluation conferences, and procedures for fair dismissal.

District standards for performance should be identified, according to Acheson and Gall, by a committee of teachers, administrators, and others. Standards can include behaviors that teachers exhibit before, during, and after teaching, as well as desirable personality characteristics and evidence of student achievement. The standards should then be adopted as official policy by the local board of education and applied to all teachers. The advantage of district standards is that teachers can be made aware of the criteria used in evaluation. Acheson and Gall recommend having fifteen to twenty standards at most, with from three to five behavioral indicators for each. Principals can use the standards and indicators, they suggest, to judge a teacher's level of competent performance.

Written job descriptions that are consistent with the standards of competent performance should describe the unique responsibilities of teachers with particular assignments in specialized areas. These job descriptions, Acheson and Gall suggest, can be used in conjunction with the general standards for determining if a teacher has neglected his or her duty.

Performance goals should next be established for teachers that are based on the standards and job descriptions. Teachers should concentrate on overcoming deficiency needs, as identified by evaluations, before attending to personal growth needs. Acheson and Gall clearly consider building on one's strengths as less desirable than eliminating weaknesses or adding new skills. Individualized performance goals allow a teacher to focus energy on improving in several areas of greatest need. The goals should be recognized as important by the supervisor as well, however, and should be stated in behavioral terms with specific criteria for assessment.

Formal evaluations should be based on progress that a teacher makes during the year toward achieving his or her performance goals. Mid-year adjustments are advisable if serious problems develop. Annual evaluations along with clearly stated goals for improvement should be stored in computers, Acheson and Gall recommend, for use in making decisions about professional development or dismissal.

Plans of assistance are advisable for teachers with serious deficiencies, according to Acheson and Gall, because such plans meet the "due process" requirements for dismissal under law. They suggest that a three-member committee be formed comprised of a neutral administrator, an advocate for the teacher, and a specialist in the area of deficiency. This committee is charged with developing and implementing the plan to remediate the deficiency.

A *postevaluation conference* should be held between the evaluator and teacher to discuss the evaluation before a copy is placed in the teacher's personnel file. Acheson and Gall advise that the teacher should be able to write a rebuttal. In most cases the conference can be an opportunity for setting new goals for the next year. This conference may also be used, however, for notifying a teacher of impending dismissal.

Postdismissal activities may include grievances, arbitration, hearings, and legal action. To ensure satisfactory results of such proceedings, Acheson and Gall recommend that supervisors should be careful to:
   a) set a reasonable number of performance goals;
   b) provide clear and specific feedback after observations;
   c) avoid evidencing bias or vindictive behavior; and
   d) provide sufficient time for assistance plans to work.

Summary

Acheson and Gall present a highly rationalized, three-step version of clinical supervision that is comprised of thirty-two discrete, specific behavioral techniques for conferencing and observation. Their stated preference is for supervision that centers on teachers' concerns, that is democratic instead of autocratic, and interactive instead of directive.

The freedom to develop a personal style of teaching, Acheson and Gall propose, is accompanied by a responsibility to analyze and improve one's teaching. They suggest that supervisors can help teachers acquire the skills needed to fulfill that duty. Before beginning the clinical cycle, Acheson and Gall suggest that supervisors should meet with teachers individually to identify concerns the teacher may have and translate those concerns into observable behaviors. Ways of improving instruction are then discussed and the teacher identifies goals for self improvment.

During the planning conference, the first stage of clinical supervision, the teacher and supervisor determine a time for the observation, select an observation strategy, and discuss matters like the content of the lesson and the instructional strategy that will be used. During the observation, the second stage of the clinical cycle, the supervisor collects descriptive data using techniques such as selective verbatim transcripts, notations of student behavior, videotaping, checklists, or timelines. The feedback conference, the third stage of Acheson and Gall's model, involves a collaborative analysis of the data and agreement about what it shows happening in the classroom. The teacher is encouraged to express opinions and feelings about the data, then the teacher and supervisor make inferences and propose possible cause and effect relationships among the behaviors and events observed. Finally, they make decisions about possible changes in instructional strategies, objectives, or improvement goals.

Acheson and Gall recommend that supervisors should avoid giving direct advice to teachers. Instead, supervisors are advised to employ an indirect conferencing style characterized by listening, acknowledging the teacher's feelings, paraphrasing, asking questions, giving praise, and providing verbal support. They do not view counseling or curricular support as part of clinical supervision, and suggest that teachers sometimes use problems outside the classroom as a ploy to evade issues related to their teaching.

While they acknowledge that summative evaluation can interfere with collegiality and trust, Acheson and Gall believe that a practical compromise with clinical supervision is possible if certain procedures are in place. They recommend, first of all, that a committee of teachers, administrators, and others should establish district standards for performance which then become district policy. Written job descriptions specifying responsibilities in specialized areas should also be developed. Acheson and Gall further suggest that performance goals should be established for each teacher based on uniform standards and specific job descriptions.

Formal evaluations can be based, according to Acheson and Gall, on progress that teachers make in attaining their performance goals. Assistance plans are then developed for teachers with major deficiencies, they suggest, and a post evaluation conference is held with all teachers to discuss the evaluation before the results are placed in the teacher's personnel file. Acheson and Gall advise that supervisors should be reasonable, specific, unbiased, and patient at all times in order to avoid legal complications if dismissal proceedings against teachers become necessary.

References

Acheson, K. A. & Gall, M. D. (1980). *Techniques in the clinical supervision of teachers.* White Plains, NY: Longman.

Acheson, K. A. & Gall, M. D. (1987). *Techniques in the clinical supervision of teachers*, 2nd edition. White Plains, NY: Longman.

Acheson, K. A. & Gall, M. D. (1992). *Techniques in the clinical supervision of teachers*, 3rd edition. White Plains, NY: Longman.

Chapter 7

Madeline Hunter's
Decision-Making Model

The Model at Work

Mr. Perry has been in education for twenty-one years. He taught in the second and fourth grades for eleven years before becoming an elementary principal, the position he now holds. Six years ago the school board hired a superintendent who introduced Mr. Perry and everyone else in the district to a highly detailed and organized system of teaching and supervision. Skeptical at first, Mr. Perry soon became a "true believer" in the new methods.

Several staff development days were scheduled for the central office staff and school administrators during the summer after the new superintendent came on board. Mr. Perry expected them to talk about planning, scheduling, and budgeting, as they had always done in the past. He was surprised when they spent the entire time learning about teaching, something he thought he already knew how to do. Mr. Perry felt uncomfortable at first when he was told to plan and teach a lesson to the other administrators, *but everybody did it and he ended up enjoying himself.*

The message presented during the training was that teaching is a predictable "science" and that successful classroom learning depends on fundamental cause-and-effect relationships between teacher behavior and learning outcomes for students. Mr. Perry had always believed that good teaching differed somehow at the elementary, secondary, and college levels. But the trainers told them that "research shows" the same skills to be applicable to all types of learners and situations. The skills centered around decisions teachers make before, during, and after teaching.

Mr. Perry and his fellow administrators were introduced to something the trainers called a "common vocabulary" that included terms like "anticipatory set" and "closure." Although these words sounded strange, the idea of presenting a brief overview of a lesson at the beginning and a summary at the end was very familiar. Other elements of effective lesson design, like teaching to an objective, giving examples, and checking for understanding all seemed very comfortable too. During a break one of the high school principals said that the training reminded her of "ED 101 – Introduction to Teaching." Everyone laughed, because the comment rang true, but the ideas presented at the workshop were packaged and delivered so neatly and tightly that Mr. Perry had difficulty finding fault with them.

Later in the year, teachers were given the same type of training. Mr. Perry and the other principals were enlisted to provide some of the instruction to their own faculties. Most teachers seemed to appreciate the workshops and had little difficulty applying the ideas in their classrooms. Many said that the skills they learned were things they already did, but now they knew what those things were called. Some teachers, however, complained that the model of teaching was too constraining or inappropriate for their content area or students. Mr. Perry patiently explained that research showed the same teaching skills to be applicable in all situations.

What Mr. Perry found he liked best, however, was that the sometimes confusing and always time-consuming task of classroom supervision was greatly simplified. Once everyone understood the elements of an effective lesson, there was no need to meet with teachers in a preobservation conference. He also found that an observation could be completed, as the trainers had predicted, in as little as ten minutes. Mr. Perry became skilled at "script taping," a kind of shorthand that enabled him to make a detailed written record of events he observed in classrooms. When he met with a teacher in a conference afterward, they looked for examples of planning, teaching, and student behavior that they learned research has shown to be effective and talked about possible alternatives. At the end of the year when evaluations of teachers were to be made, Mr. Perry was pleased to find that he already had a complete file on the performance of every teacher in the school.

Introduction

In order to understand the version of clinical supervision that Madeline Hunter advocates, one must first understand her position with respect to teaching. Hunter views effective teaching first as a science and then as an art. Teachers should be expert diagnosticians who base their decisions about instruction upon principles derived from the science of human learning, she proposes, instead of relying upon professional folklore or intuition. Research in the area of human learning can be translated, she states, into cause-effect relationships that teachers should use when working with students. By acquiring the skills needed to systematically apply these relationships in their classrooms, teachers can both accelerate learning and ensure that all students learn.

Effective teaching, Hunter believes, can be both taught and learned. Knowledge and application of identifiable cause-effect relationships between teacher behaviors and learning can increase the probability of a teacher's success. Though learning cannot be guaranteed in every instance, Hunter contends that effective teaching can improve achievement among students regardless of their IQ or socioeconomic origin. Furthermore, she suggests, the same set of professional skills can be applied to learners who differ in age or ethnic background, and can be used to teach any type of subject matter, including how to teach effectively.

The essence of teaching, according to Hunter, is decision-making. More precisely, teaching is the constant stream of decisions made and implemented by teachers before, during, and after their interactions with students. These decisions are important, she observes, because they affect the likelihood of student learning. Teachers who are knowledgeable of research-based cause-effect relationships that affect learning in the classroom can deliberately incorporate these practices into the processes of planning and evaluating, before, during, and after teaching. Supervisors can assist teachers by observing them in action and by documenting the presence or absence of those cause-effect relationships.

Effective teaching, Hunter acknowledges, can become artistry that goes beyond proficiency in the use of specific practices. Although aesthetic qualities can be observed, recorded, and categorized, she believes, they cannot be taught with any degree of predictability. Consequently, we must be content at present to concentrate on improving the science of teaching.

Hunter's Model of Clinical Supervision

Basically, the version of clinical supervision that Hunter recommends is comprised of five phases, summarized as follows:

Phase I: Inservice

Both the teacher and the supervisor first receive extensive inservice training in order to develop a common vocabulary concerning events that occur in classrooms. Live demonstrations or videotapes are presented so that teachers can observe and practice the implementation of cause-effect relationships that, according to Hunter, govern successful teaching-learning interactions. Though a preobservation conference is not a part of Hunter's model of clinical supervision, a *planning* conference is sometimes considered appropriate during which the supervisor helps the teacher prepare for a lesson and assumes some responsibility for its success.

Phase II: Observation and Script Taping

The supervisor or classroom observer records an almost verbatim written transcript of teacher actions and subsequent student actions as they occur in the course of a lesson. A detailed record is made of classroom events through a form of shorthand note taking that Hunter calls "script taping." She recommends ten to fifteen minutes of observation as usually sufficient.

Phase III: Analysis

The supervisor in this phase first reviews the transcript of the lesson, and then identifies and labels salient patterns in the teacher's behavior. Important patterns often include, for example, behaviors that Hunter believes improve the chances of learning, that use time ineffectively, or that may interfere with student learning. Next, the supervisor develops a conference plan aimed at promoting growth for the teacher and the maximum positive transfer of what has been learned by the teacher to classroom practice.

Phase IV: The Conference

The interaction between the supervisor and teacher during the supervision conference, Hunter suggests, should build trust. The supervisor provides as much support, stimulation, information, and guidance as the teacher appears to need. But the conference should be directed toward the goal of establishing a collaborative and professional interaction whereby the teacher and supervisor are able to learn from each other.

Phase V: Follow-up

The clinical cycle is repeated throughout the year, with the supervisor providing additional feedback or guided practice to further encourage the stimulation and acceleration of the teacher's professional growth. Hunter's model culminates with the summative evaluation of the teacher. A more detailed description of each of the five phases of Hunter's model follows:

The Phases in Practice: Phase I: Inservice

One of Hunter's fundamental beliefs is that teachers should be expert diagnosticians. Accurate diagnosis of the appropriate level of content, student learning style, and the educational environment in any situation, she suggests, are prerequisites for effective decision-making in teaching. How a teacher can make such diagnoses and apply them to the classroom constitutes the content of the inservice phase.

Hunter draws a clear distinction between diagnosis and evaluation. Both involve the appraisal of various qualities, behaviors, skills, or elements, and the findings from both processes are used to guide decisions. The specific types of information sought and the ways it is used, however, often differ depending on whether one is evaluating or diagnosing.

Information is used in evaluation, for example, to determine the success or failure of an effort to accomplish something. In contrast, the purpose of diagnosis is to select and use information in ways that suggest prescriptions for improvement. Evaluation has an element of finality to it, diagnosis implies a beginning of growth.

Three Types of Diagnosis

Hunter identifies three types of diagnosis that she claims are useful to teachers for guiding instruction. Each of these – formal, informal, and inferential – are described below.

1) Well-designed tests are the most common example of *formal* diagnosis. Such tests focus on either a process (e.g., speaking) or a product (e.g., a written paragraph) and compare specific behaviors or elements against predetermined criteria. An advantage of formal diagnosis is that it provides clear and concise information, but a drawback is that it consumes valuable time and the results are often not immediately available. Hunter also suggests that formal diagnosis has been unproductively over-emphasized in areas relating to cognitive knowledge and skills, with the result that teachers frequently overlook affective and psychomotor learnings that are equally important to the development of children.

2) *Informal* diagnosis is much more useful to a classroom teacher than formal diagnosis, Hunter observes, because large amounts of data are readily available at the moment they are needed and relate to a broader range of considerations. For instance, the teacher can quickly extract important information about classroom processes by closely observing student behaviors. Or, the teacher may solicit feedback from students by asking them to provide nonverbal signals (e.g., raising hands). Informal diagnosis can focus on either processes or products and can guide decisions such as whether to speed up or slow down the presentation of subject matter.

3) *Inferential* diagnosis is based upon the knowledge and insights that a teacher has acquired over time. Experience with individu-

als and groups similar to those with which a teacher is currently working are useful, for example, in predicting how best to begin a lesson and how much difficulty students will have in mastering its content. The major advantage of making such inferences is that time and energy can be saved. The actual similarity of the present situation to the past as well as the sensitivity and astuteness of the teacher, however, determine the validity of conclusions based on inferential diagnosis.

All three types of diagnosis – formal, informal, and inferential – can be helpful to teachers at different times, depending on the situation at hand. However, Hunter suggests that the over-emphasis on formal evaluative procedures such as testing has resulted in valuable learning time being lost to students, while teachers have become recorders and bookkeepers of scores that are so precise they are comparatively useless in daily practice. Also, paperwork associated with testing can be so overwhelming that teachers have little time and energy left to devote to teaching. Hunter advocates encouraging teachers to acquire and rely on informal and inferential diagnostic procedures more often than they do.

The information a teacher gains from formal, informal, and inferential diagnoses, according to Hunter, should guide professional decisions in three areas: content, learner behaviors and styles, and teaching behaviors. A description of how decisions are made in each of these areas follows.

Diagnosis and the Planning of Content

When planning the content of a lesson Hunter believes that teachers should conduct a systematic task analysis of the goals they intend to pursue. Because learning is incremental, she reasons, teachers should consider what their students already know, what they are ready to learn next, and the level of complexity at which they are capable of understanding the new material. Simpler learnings and skills that comprise complex learnings should also be identified.

The teacher should next consider whether the simpler learnings must be acquired in some fixed logical sequence or if they can be secured by students in any order. In the first instance, the lesson should be structured by the logic of the content, while in the second case, the content can be learned as students develop an interest in the subject, as classroom materials become available, or according to preferences of the teacher. The same types of decisions are necessary whether the content to be taught falls into the cognitive, affective, or psychomotor domains.

Diagnosis and Planning for Learner Characteristics

A second major focus of diagnostic information applies to the learners and what they are expected to accomplish. For example, teachers should be aware of students' learning styles when making decisions in order to accommodate individual differences in their lessons. Among the many factors to be considered, the teacher should be aware of: the ways by which students acquire information and skills; how students demonstrate what they have learned; the nature of the learning; and the effort students must expend. The content to be taught, of course, dictates to some extent the kinds of activities in which students will be involved. Writing skills are best taught, for instance, by practicing writing. However, the characteristics of the individual learner and what he or she is capable of doing should not be overlooked.

Hunter does not advocate the use of formal diagnosis (i.e., testing) to identify students' learning styles, only that the teacher be sensitive to individual differences and be prepared to adjust his or her teaching in order to ensure that students learn. Students should be able to learn in a variety of ways – seeing, hearing, reading, doing – rather than just one. But the teacher should have sufficient flexibility to try an alternative modality as soon as it becomes apparent that something is not working with a particular individual or group. Similarly, students should have a variety of means available for demonstrating to the teacher that they have learned the material. Not everyone performs well on written tests, Hunter notes, so oral reports, graphs, drawings, models, and other alternatives should be acceptable forms of expression when learning is assessed.

Other factors to consider when planning for teaching pertain to the learning environment. The teacher must decide whether to use small group or large group instruction, to excite students or calm them down, to introduce novelty or rely upon predictability in a lesson. Such decisions can only be based on a sensitive understanding of individual students, an awareness of who their friends may be, what their interests are, and events affecting them outside the classroom. The teacher should also consider the amount of effort that will be required from the teacher and the student to achieve a certain learning outcome. The student's intelligence, level of motivation, willingness to persevere, likelihood of being distracted, and previous experience all come into play. Again, judgments are best guided by informal and inferential diagnostic procedures and a willingness by the teacher to change his or her approach when it is obvious that a particular strategy is not proving successful.

Diagnosis and the Planning of Teacher Behaviors

The third area of teacher decision-making has to do with teaching behaviors. Decisions in this area should be made, according to Hunter, only after questions concerning the content to be learned and the behavior of the learner have been answered. What the teacher does or does not do during a lesson may be the major determining factor in a student's learning. It is certainly the single element over which the teacher has most control. Four categories of decisions and actions, according to Hunter, should be considered by the teacher:

a) Which teacher behaviors are most likely to increase students' intention to learn or motivation?

b) Which teacher behaviors will increase the rate, degree, and amount of learning?

c) Which teacher behaviors will enhance retention of learning?

d) Which teacher behaviors will encourage the transfer of learning to different situations that require students to solve problems, make decisions, and be creative?

After dealing with these issues the teacher can better plan a lesson that is exciting and interesting to students, enhancing to their self concepts, and meaningful to their experiences.

Hunter suggests that teaching becomes an artform when teachers consciously and deliberately apply the procedures of diagnosis and decision-making she has outlined, but also draw upon intuition to guide their practice. A swiftly flowing, smooth, and comfortable performance then becomes possible. As with other performing arts, she maintains, practice, observation, and feedback are the keys to improving teaching.

Phase II: Observation and Script Taping

Because Hunter believes that the effectiveness and appropriateness of teaching behaviors can only be determined within the context of a particular lesson, she advocates the use of a data collection procedure during classroom observation that captures the wholeness of the fabric of events that occur in a classroom. Hunter refers to this technique as "script taping," which involves making a detailed written record of what is said and done during an observed class session. An example of a script taped record is presented below:

> Opn p. 43 I'm ask ver hd - use mark to find ans whn fnd sho me w/ sig who has lots of pets Every had mark on rt ans Who can't see Mr. Sleeper (wrong ans) that rt if askd who sees but can't see. Now just rt. (Hunter, 1983)

To the uninitiated reader the above quotation may seem indecipherable, but a considerable amount of information is actually present. The abbreviations are necessary in order to quickly preserve an accurate record of what was said and done during the lesson. A full transcript of the observation segment reads as follows:

> Open your book to page 43. I'm going to ask you some very hard questions. Use your marker to find the answer. When you have found the answer, show me with the signal (thumbs up). Who has lots of pets? Everyone had the marker on the right answer. Who can't see Mr. Sleeper? (A girl gave a wrong answer.) That would be right if I asked who sees Mr. Sleeper, but I asked who can't see Mr. Sleeper? (Same child responds correctly.) Now you're just right! (Hunter, 1983)

The supervisor in this example, has documented some important aspects of the teacher's performance. For instance, Hunter notes, the teacher had students answer questions as a group by pointing with their markers. The teacher was thus able to monitor and correct each student's response. When a correction was necessary the teacher responded in a way that elicited the correct response, but did so in a way that did not make the student feel unsuccessful.

The supervisor might also infer from this record that the teacher's behavior contributed to productive student outcomes. Very specific evidence is preserved, in fact, which indicates that this was the case. In terms of this brief excerpt, Hunter observes, it does not appear that the teacher wasted time, energy, or materials on unproductive activities, nor did the teacher do anything that interfered with student learning.

Specific examples of productive or unproductive behaviors can be quickly gleaned from a script tape by the supervisor. Concrete examples of effective and ineffective behaviors can be highlighted for discussion, according to Hunter, making the conference that follows the observation more meaningful, credible, and helpful to the teacher.

The major drawback of script taping is that a little time is required to learn the technique, but Hunter points out that the advantages of script taping over other data collection strategies are many. For example, although audio and videotaping also provide objective records of events, they require expensive and sometimes cumbersome equipment. Problems of analysis can arise with audio recordings because they are indiscriminate in preserving everything that occurs. Video recordings can be problematic because they focus too narrowly and miss much of what happens in a classroom.

Script taping, in contrast, requires only a pencil and pad of paper. A trained observer can record a detailed and objective account that preserves the complexity of classroom events, Hunter reports, yet allows the identification of specific instances of cause-effect interactions. The supervisor can simultaneously monitor multiple events or individuals and can also rapidly change the focus of attention when necessary.

Data generated by script taping is also easily accessible for analysis. Hunter notes that salient events can be quickly located and highlighted for attention during the post observation conference. The data or summary notes and recommendations can be easily and inexpensively stored as documentation of progress over time.

Phase III: Analysis

One of the ways that a supervisor can assist a teacher is by examining, describing, and interpreting the decisions that govern the teacher's classroom practice. The three areas of teacher decision-making discussed earlier – content, learner characteristics and behavior, and teacher behavior – can be used by a supervisor as a template or guide when assessing the quality of a teacher's instruction. Questions such as the following may be asked:

- Is the difficulty and complexity of the content suitable for the students?
- Are student activities appropriate for the content of the lesson?
- Are the activities suited to the learning styles of students?
- Are activities introduced and mastered in a productive sequence?
- Do students have a chance to demonstrate learning in a variety of ways?
- Is the teacher applying principles of learning correctly, making new learning relevant to students' earlier experiences and encouraging its transfer to different situations?
- Does the teacher allow time for students to practice new skills and reinforce new behaviors when they occur?

The Seven Elements of Effective Lesson Design

A second template that can be used for helping teachers improve their effectiveness is what Hunter refers to as "seven elements" of effective lesson design. She cautions that all of these elements are not necessary in every lesson and that the elements should not be used as an observation checklist. Teachers may legitimately decide to exclude one or more of the seven elements in any given lesson, according to Hunter, after taking into account their knowledge of theory and of the current situation. Teachers should, however, thoughtfully consider each of the elements when planning a lesson. Consideration of the elements is very helpful to teachers as a means of determining and understanding how their own behavior may result in students not learning successfully.

Application of the seven elements in planning assumes that the teacher has already considered decisions regarding content and student characteristics, and has identified a specific instructional objective for the lesson. The seven elements of effective lesson design are as follows:

1) *Anticipatory set* is defined by Hunter as any teacher action that focuses student attention and prepares them mentally for the instruction to follow. Set often includes a review of what was learned previously, relating that learning to new material, or relating the new material to students' experiences. Anticipatory set is necessarily brief because it simply sets the stage for the

major portion of the lesson that follows. Set motivates students to participate in learning and gives them an idea of what is to follow. Depending on the responses of students, set can also provide diagnostic data to the teacher concerning how best to proceed.

2) The *objective and purpose* of the lesson are explicitly stated by the teacher to let students know what they will be learning. The teacher also explains why the objective is important or how it will be useful to students immediately or in the future.

3) *Instructional input* is a phrase used by Hunter to describe the introduction of new information pertaining to the knowledge or skill that students are to achieve. In order to successfully accomplish the objective, she notes, the teacher must have identified the prerequisite knowledge, skills, and tasks. This information can be introduced in a variety of ways, such as having students read, view films, listen to a lecture or audiotape, discuss a topic, or draw a picture or diagram.

4) *Modeling* a process or product, according to Hunter, is a means by which the teacher lets students know what they are supposed to do or produce by the end of a lesson. Several examples of stories, poems, solutions, or graphs should be provided in a lesson, she suggests, so that students exercise creativity when completing the objective and do not merely mimic what is demonstrated to them. As students view the process or product, the teacher can verbally describe and label critical elements so that students focus on essentials and are not distracted by irrelevant factors.

5) *Checking for understanding* is important for ensuring that students possess the necessary information and minimum skills, as well as the understanding of exactly what they are supposed to do. Hunter recommends that the teacher check understanding verbally by posing questions to the group, observing student performance, or asking for nonverbal signals (e.g., thumbs up or down) from the students. Checking for understanding should always precede the introduction of new material.

6) *Guided practice* is an opportunity for students to apply their new knowledge or to practice a newly acquired skill under the direct tutelage of the teacher. According to Hunter, careful guidance at the earliest stages of learning increases the probability of subsequent accuracy and success. The teacher can circulate among

students, making certain that they have mastered the content before allowing them to practice independently. Errors in learning are more difficult to eradicate after they have been internalized, Hunter notes, so it is better to catch them early and correct them.

7) *Independent practice* is assigned to students once they can perform a task without making major mistakes or becoming confused. Students are likely to repeat and reinforce errors if unsupervised practice occurs before they are ready, Hunter believes, so teachers should be cautious about introducing independent practice too early.

The Teaching Appraisal for Instructional Improvement Instrument

The *Teaching Appraisal for Instructional Improvement Instrument* (*TA III*) represents a third guide that Hunter suggests supervisors may find useful for describing and interpreting teacher performance during the analysis phase. The TA III was originally developed to document changes in decisions and behaviors made by teachers and the effect of those changes on student academic achievement, self-concept, and problem behavior. Answers to the following five questions are derived from observation data and can serve as a focus for discussion in a conference:

1) *Are the efforts and energies of the teacher and learner directed toward a learning objective?* The classroom behavior of teachers and students should perceivably contribute to the attainment of an objective instead of being random, aimless, or haphazard. This does not mean, Hunter cautions, that teaching should be rigid or unresponsive to changing circumstances. On the contrary, effective teachers are highly adaptable and can adjust appropriately when student behavior or other conditions indicate that a change in activities or even objectives is called for at any point during a lesson. The only real constraint is that the decision that is made should be based upon learning theory and earlier diagnosis.

2) *Has the teacher selected an objective that is at the proper level of difficulty for the students?* In order to select an objective that is appropriate for a particular individual or group of students, the

teacher will have had to apply the procedures discussed earlier: formal, informal, and inferential diagnoses. In other words, the teacher will have drawn upon information from standardized tests, observation of students, and previous experience in planning the lesson.

3) *Does the teacher monitor student learning during a lesson and adjust teacher and student behaviors accordingly?* Information about student achievement is needed most at the very time that a lesson is being taught so that adjustments can be made to ensure that as many students as possible master the material successfully. Valuable information concerning which students do and do not understand the material emerges or can be elicited throughout a lesson. The teacher should continuously check for understanding by means such as: observing covert indications that individuals and groups of students are progressing, sampling individuals within a classroom group, asking for choral responses to questions, or soliciting overt nonverbal signals from students (e.g., holding up colored strips of paper) to indicate that they understand. The resulting information can be used for guiding decisions about whether to slow down a lesson, speed up, repeat, try another approach, or provide remediation.

4) *Does the teacher use the principles of learning properly?* Here, as in assisting the teacher with planning, the supervisor is expected to observe, describe, and interpret the decisions made by the teacher relating to content, learner characteristics and behaviors, and teacher behaviors. Questions are again asked pertaining to:
   - suitability, complexity, and organization of content; appropriateness of activities for communicating content and achieving the learning objective;
   - appropriateness of activities for the learning styles of the students;
   - effective use of positive reinforcement and extinction of negative student behaviors;
   - use of motivational strategies;
   - provision of meaning and relevance to students to improve retention;
   - allowing adequate time for guided practice; and
   - promoting transfer of what is learned to other situations.

5) *How can the supervisor contribute to further professional growth of the teacher?* Hunter advises that the script tapes recorded during a lesson are the best indicator for a supervisor to use when deciding how best to proceed in working with a teacher. Careful observation and analysis of the data can tell the supervisor what the teacher is already doing well, which areas need improving, and what the teacher can or should learn next. The approach used by a supervisor during the post observation conference depends upon the answers to these questions.

Phase IV: The Conference

Hunter observes that conferences between supervisors and teachers are frequently sterile and unproductive. At best, they are not as effective as they might be. According to Hunter, the reason for this state of affairs is that professional knowledge and a common vocabulary have been unavailable to educators, so supervisors have had to rely extensively on their own intuition which is a poor guide for professional practice. Hunter proposes four broad generalizations about the purposes and outcomes of conferences:

Assumption # 1 - Supervisory conferences can contribute to teacher growth, but they are also useful for purposes of evaluation. She suggests using the term *instructional conferences* when referring to conferences that are diagnostic and prescriptive, and aimed at improving instruction. The term *evaluative conference* should be reserved for the summative assessment of a teacher after a series of instructional conferences. Both the teacher's current level of performance and potential for further growth should be considered in such an assessment.

Assumption # 2 - Every supervisory conference should have a primary purpose and most of the time spent during the conference should be directed toward accomplishing a primary objective. Two or more objectives may be pursued, but each should complement the other. It is inconsistent, Hunter observes, to try to bolster a teacher's self-confidence at the same time that the supervisor discloses a major teaching deficit.

Assumption # 3 - The principles of learning that were introduced earlier apply to teachers as well. Unless the principles are applied and modelled correctly by the supervisor, she suggests, the probability of teacher growth will be substantially reduced.

Assumption # 4 - The best way of improving teaching behavior is to analyze it. The application of this assumption requires that the supervisor observe a lesson and carefully record what transpired. The simplest analysis requires the identification and categorization of teacher behaviors that promoted learning, wasted time and energy to no useful purpose, or unintentionally interfered with learning. Interpretations of data should be based on educational research findings and learning theory. By focusing on behaviors during a conference in this way, according to Hunter, the strengths and deficits apparent in a teacher's performance can be highlighted for discussion and improvement, thus replacing unproductive complimentary platitudes and cliches.

Six Conference Types

After a supervisor has analyzed the data collected during a classroom observation a decision should be made as to the primary purpose of the conference. Hunter suggests six different objectives for six types of supervisory conferences (see *Figure 7.1*). The first five conference types concentrate on providing the teacher with formative feedback for improving instruction. The sixth conference type is evaluative in nature and is a summation of the year's diagnostic, prescriptive, and collaborative activities. The six conference types are as follows:

"Type A" Instructional Conference.
The purpose of a "Type A" supervisory conference is to identify and label for the teacher those instructional behaviors that were observed to be effective, and to explain within a framework of research evidence *why* those behaviors are assumed to be productive. The immediate objective is for the teacher to be able to identify by the end of the conference the teaching decisions and behaviors that contributed to student learning during the lesson, and to state the reasons for their effectiveness.

The supervisor proceeds in this instance by calling attention to student behaviors that appeared to be productive and by suggesting that certain decisions and behaviors of the teacher probably evoked those responses. The supervisor then introduces labels to describe those cause-effect relationships and a research-based rationale for their success. The teacher grows professionally from learning which behaviors

Conference Type	When Appropriate	Supervisor's Behavior	Teacher's Behaviors	Desired Outcomes
A	For the first conference or when the teacher is fearful or defensive, to bring effective behaviors to a conscious level.	The supervisor identifies, names, and tells why the iistructional behaviors of the teacher are productive, so that the behaviors can be intentionally repeated in the future.	At the end of the conference, the teacher identifies and explains why particular teaching decisions and behaviors advance student learning.	To generate a positive conference atmosphere and bring effective teaching to consciousness so it can be used later when appropriate.
B	When the generation of a variety of teaching behaviors and reactions is desired.	The supervisor asks the teacher to identify alternatives to the behaviors that were observed and suggests additional ones.	The teacher thinks of various alternative behaviors that fit his or her particular style to be used in similar but slightly different teaching situations.	To broaden the teacher's habitual repertoire to include new behaviors and greater flexibility.
C	To aid a teacher in finding methods, changing unsatisfactory parts of a lesson.	The supervisor stimulates teachers to identify inadequate parts of a teaching event and cooperates in suggesting possible solutions.	The teacher identifies possible solutions for improving unsatisfactory parts of the lesson.	To reduce or eliminate unsatisfactory outcomes in the future.
D	To inform the teacher of an unfavorable teaching performance and to suggest alternative behaviors that might prove more successful.	The supervisor identifies and labels ineffective parts of the teaching episode and offers effective alternative approaches.	The teacher chooses effective teaching strategies to use in place of observed ineffective strategies.	To identify cause effect relationships that lead to problems and to generate alternative teacher behaviors that are more productive.
E_x	To stimulate the continuing professional development of excellent teachers.	The supervisor encourages the teacher to develop professionally beyond his/her own plans.	The teacher and/or supervisor suggest steps to be taken in professional development.	To simulate outstanding teachers to face new challenges and opportunities.
E	At the end of a series of instructional conferences.	The supervisor provides information and conclusions about the teacher's current level of performancc based on diagnostic, prescriptive, and collaborative work done throughout the year.	The teacher listens to the information and conclusions, and should accept them as fair and just.	To assign the teacher into some category reflecting the teacher's current level of performance as assessed over the entire school year.

Figure 7.1
USING HUNTER'S CONFERENCE TYPES

are effective and why. Terms for talking about effective teaching are also introduced which are useful in later discussions.

A "Type A" conference is especially recommended when working with teachers who are apprehensive or overly defensive. Because the message of the conference is entirely positive, the teacher is likely to deliberately use the effective behaviors in future lessons and also approach subsequent conferences more comfortably and more confidently.

"Type B" Instructional Conference.

In the case of a "Type B" instructional conference, the purpose is to encourage a diversity of teaching behaviors beyond those that the teacher already regularly uses. Again the focus is on productive behaviors and decisions, but the interaction is more collaborative. The supervisor and teacher together generate alternative behaviors to those used in the lesson that could be equally effective under different circumstances. Hypothetical situations may be introduced and discussed.

Experienced teachers often come to rely heavily on comfortable behavioral patterns and classroom routines. Over a period of time, such routines limit flexibility and hinder professional growth. A "Type B" conference is designed to introduce new behavioral options for the teacher to consider. The supervisor still maintains responsibility for the success of the conference and should be ready to suggest a variety of possible alternatives while encouraging the teacher to do so as well. Solutions are not imposed upon the teacher. Instead, alternatives are developed which teachers may test against their personal styles, and incorporate into their repertoires if they choose.

"Type C" Instructional Conference.

A "Type C" instructional conference attempts to encourage the teacher to identify events in a lesson which were not satisfactory and to develop with the supervisor strategies to reduce or eliminate unsatisfactory outcomes in the future. The specific objective is for the teacher to identify possible solutions for improving unsatisfactory elements of the observed lesson and subsequent lessons.

The supervisor again retains the obligation to contribute to the conference by proposing solutions. However, the teacher is allowed to take the initiative by being the first to suggest alternatives. This type of conference provides an opportunity for the teacher to critically analyze his or her own teaching, which is a powerful technique for inducing professional growth. Through introspection by the teacher, problems are identified, possible causes analyzed, and alternative solutions suggested.

"Type D" Instructional Conference.
With a "Type D" instructional conference the supervisor introduces less effective aspects of a lesson that may not be evident to the teacher. The identification and labeling of ineffective behaviors by the supervisor is followed by the recommendation of alternatives that might work more successfully. The primary objective is for the teacher to select from among the alternatives suggested to replace behaviors that were perceived by the supervisor as being ineffective.

Although the focus of a "Type D" conference is on unproductive behaviors, the experience itself need not be negative. As an objective observer the supervisor will have unique insight into a lesson that can be helpful to the teacher. By emphasizing the interpretation of information and analysis of problem situations, the supervisor can ensure that the conference is minimally threatening.

The supervisor should remember that a "Type D" conference is not intended to impose particular solutions on the teacher. Alternatives are suggested which the teacher can choose to incorporate into his repertoire and personal style. The emphasis is on analyzing the process of teaching and applying the principles of learning, which bridges the gap between practice and theory. A "Type D" conference is recommended, however, if "Types A," "B," and "C" have resulted in little or no improvement in performance. In such an instance, the message that the teacher's performance is not satisfactory must be communicated. The presentation of data in this way and the actions of the supervisor are, in Hunter's opinion, legally defensible.

"Type EX" Instructional Conference.
The major purpose of a "Type EX" conference is to encourage the continued professional growth of excellent teachers. The main objective in this case is to have the teacher select and plan the next steps in his own professional development. Excellent teachers are often simply left alone by supervisors, Hunter notes, which is actually a form of neglect. With a "Type EX" conference outstanding teachers are stimulated to face new challenges and possibilities. The interaction is collaborative, with the supervisor acting much like a coach. The best ideas and planning skills of both the teacher and supervisor are synthesized and may even lead to some cooperative professional venture.

"Type E" Evaluative Conferences.
Evaluative, or "Type E" conferences, represent a summation and culmination of events and outcomes from earlier instructional conferences. The teacher should not be surprised by the content of a "Type E" conference because the evidence supporting the information and conclusions presented have already been discussed extensively during earlier formative interactions. Because it is built upon diagnostic, prescriptive, and collaborative work throughout the year, a final evaluative conference should be perceived by the teacher as being fair and just.

Supervisors may mix objectives from the first five conference types because they are mutually compatible. The evaluation conference, however, is distinct and separate from the others. In summative conferences the teacher is assigned by the supervisor into some category reflecting the teacher's current level of performance as assessed over the entire school year.

All six types of conferences require that the supervisor be competent in analyzing teaching and suggesting solutions to instructional difficulties. Interpersonal communication skills are also needed, as well as the ability to model the cause-effect teaching behaviors that result in productive learning outcomes for both students and teachers.

Phase V: Follow-up

Hunter distinguishes between the processes of supervision and evaluation, but believes that both can contribute to the improvement of teaching and can be effectively performed by the same individual if they are done sequentially. Supervision is considered a formative process by Hunter, involving diagnosis and prescription by someone who plays the part of "coach" to help remediate or improve teacher performance. Both supervision and evaluation require skills in the areas of classroom observation, script taping, analyzing effective and less effective teaching behaviors, and conferencing. Evaluation, as noted earlier, is considered a summative activity which sums up an extended period of supervision and results in the classification of a teacher into some category ranging from "inadequate" to "outstanding."

The relationship between supervision and evaluation, Hunter contends, closely parallels the relationship between teaching and grading. Thus, the threat of evaluation can be used, she suggests, to stimulate reluctant teachers to improve their performance, just as it is used by teachers for motivating reluctant students in their classes. Evaluation in both instances, however, should occur only after the evaluator has spent time and effort in a sincere attempt to help improve the performance of the person being evaluated.

Supervision is viewed by Hunter as more difficult and more complex than evaluation. She suggests that supervision differs from evaluation in the following ways:

1) Supervisors have to diagnose strengths or deficiencies in a lesson and prescribe specific knowledge and skills that a teacher should acquire in order to improve.
2) A supervisor must monitor the teacher's acquisition of knowledge and skills, and adjust the process accordingly.
3) Supervision requires the supervisor to assume a certain degree of responsibility for the teacher's professional development.

Evaluation, in contrast, only requires assigning a teacher to a category indicating success or failure based on previously accumulated evidence.

Hunter is convinced that teachers cannot conceal deficiencies from well-trained observers. Having supervisors available who do not evaluate, therefore, serves no useful purpose except possibly to augment the ongoing efforts of the principal. But because summative evaluation relies heavily on earlier formative supervision, the principal must remain the central figure in both processes.

As a general rule, Hunter is opposed to assigning the tasks of supervision and evaluation to separate roles. When two or more administrators are available, she favors their sharing responsibility for both processes. Principals should schedule several hours each week exclusively for supervision. By employing what she terms "walk through" supervision, principals can observe as many as six teachers in thirty minutes. Rarely, Hunter believes, should an observation last longer than ten or twenty minutes.

When engaging in summative evaluation, specific performance criteria may vary for beginning and experienced teachers. Professional growth should be the ultimate measure, however, not "adequacy" in meeting some standard. Such growth can be assessed by considering the new knowledge and skills a teacher is currently learning, the eagerness with which they seek constructive assistance, how much effort they put forth in trying to improve, and how much progress they have made over the year. Only someone who has supervised teachers formatively for an extended period of time, according to Hunter, is capable of making such judgments.

In summary, decisions in teaching should be made on the basis of a teacher's knowledge of human learning generally; information that is known or inferred about a student or group of students; information that is available about environmental constraints and requirements of the particular situation; and consideration of future possibilities.

Why No Preobservation Conference?

A noticeable feature of Hunter's version of clinical supervision is the omission of the preconference from the clinical cycle. Hunter maintains that the preconference is a vestige of earlier times when teaching and supervision were poorly understood, ambiguous activities that were mainly guided by intuition. Teachers, she argues, had no way of knowing exactly what was being observed, how interpretations and judgments were made, or what to expect as an outcome of supervision.

Hunter suggests that if teachers and supervisors have a clear understanding of the principles of learning and the elements of effective teaching practice that she has identified, the preobservation conference can and should be eliminated. She believes that information concerning research-based cause-effect relationships between teacher behaviors and student achievement can be better communicated to groups of teachers through inservice sessions. A preobservation conference only biases the teacher and supervisor toward a lesson beforehand, she contends, thus interfering with an objective assessment of reality. In defense of this controversial position, Hunter offers five arguments.

1) Supervisors ought to make teachers aware at the beginning of the academic year that the purpose of classroom observation is to promote instructional success for teachers and students. This can be accomplished, as already mentioned, through inservice meetings where participants discuss elements of effective teaching, view and analyze films depicting classroom events, and learn about relevant research findings.

2) Feelings of trust and support between a teacher and supervisor depend more on what occurs during the post observation

conference than what happens beforehand. Supervisors should display empathy and understanding for teachers and the complex work they do in classrooms. Supervisors should initially seek to understand each teacher's rationale for using particular strategies instead of acting on the basis of untested assumptions. In order to promote continued professional growth in teachers, Hunter further suggests, supervisors ought to concentrate on identifying and reinforcing productive teaching practices rather than trying to impose a particular style on all teachers. Trust and support will result, Hunter asserts, only if the supervisor adheres to these recommendations and can demonstrate in the post observation conference that observation and feedback are effective ways of facilitating excellent teaching.

3) Hunter believes that teaching behavior can only be understood within a larger context that includes other behaviors that precede and follow it. Isolating a particular technique in advance from everything else that occurs in a classroom for focused attention during an observation will result in an artificial performance by the teacher. The technique will inevitably be overused, sometimes inappropriately. The notion that the use of any single technique is good or bad under all conditions is false. According to Hunter, the appropriateness of a teaching behavior is dependent on the circumstances. Absolutes in teaching simply do not exist.

4) The preobservation conference, Hunter claims, is likely to bias the teacher and supervisor with respect to the lesson. For one thing, she suggests, the teacher may feel compelled to continue with an agreed upon plan for a lesson even though it becomes obvious from student behavior that the plan is not working as intended. Also, if the supervisor knows in advance what to expect in a lesson, his later perception of what really happens may be faulty. That is, the supervisor may both perceive and interpret events selectively in accordance with his preconceptions about what the teacher is trying to achieve instead of what the teacher actually does achieve.

5) Finally, Hunter argues that the time required for the preobservation conference is poorly spent. More productive outcomes can be achieved if teachers and supervisors engage instead in observation and feedback sessions.

In some instances, however, Hunter believes that a *planning conference* before an observation is very beneficial. During a planning conference the teacher and supervisor collaborate in developing a lesson that the teacher subsequently teaches, but responsibility for learning outcomes is shared. Such collaborative planning sessions can be stimulating and growth inducing for both teachers and supervisors.

Summary

The essence of teaching, according to Madeline Hunter, is decision making. Principles of effective teaching that are derived from the scientific study of human learning, she believes, can be used to guide teachers' behavior so that more students learn and all students learn faster. Teaching can become an artform when teachers consciously and deliberately combine specific procedures of diagnosis and decision making with intuition to guide their practice. Furthermore, she asserts, these principles of teaching can be both taught and learned.

Hunter combines a five phase clinical sequence with elements of teaching that she considers most important. The first phase of her supervision model, involves inservice training which introduces teachers to three types of diagnoses: formal, informal, and inferential. Teachers are instructed to apply diagnostic information when making decisions concerning content, learner behavior and styles, and teaching behaviors. This inservice training replaces the preobservation conference in this version of clinical supervision.

The second phase of Hunter's model is the observation. Script taping is the recommended method of data collection, a shorthand verbatim account of what is said and done in a lesson. The third phase involves analysis of the data. Hunter offers three templates that may be used to assess a lesson's effectiveness. These include: a) the appropriateness of decisions concerning content, student characteristics and behavior, and teacher behavior; b) the application of seven elements of effective lesson design; and c) a series of questions that comprise what is called the Teaching Appraisal for Instructional Improvement Instrument (TA III).

Six distinct types of conferences are presented as alternatives for planning the fourth phase of Hunter's clinical supervision model. Each is intended to achieve different objectives that are considered appropriate for teachers of varying ability. The fifth phase of this model is called follow-up and involves a summative evaluation of a teacher's professional growth. Hunter distinguishes between supervision and evaluation, but believes that teachers cannot conceal deficiencies from a well trained observer and that the same person who supervises teachers should also evaluate them.

References

Brandt, R. (1985). On teaching and supervising: A conversation with Madeline Hunter. *Educational Leadership, 42*, (5), 61-66.

Hunter, M. & Russell, D. (1977). How can I plan more effective lessons? *Instructor, 87*, (2), 74-75, 88.

Hunter, M. (1979). Diagnostic teaching. *The Elementary School Journal, 80*, (1), 41-46.

Hunter, M. (1979). Teaching is decision making. *Educational Leadership, 37* (1), 62-67.

Hunter, M. (1980). Six types of supervisory conferences. *Educational Leadership, 37* (5), 408-412.

Hunter, M. (1983). Script taping: An essential supervisory tool. *Educational Leadership, 41* (3), 43.

Hunter, M. (1985). What's wrong with Madeline Hunter? *Educational Leadership, 42*, (5), 57-60.

Hunter, M. (1986). Let's eliminate the preobservation conference. *Educational Leadership, 43*, (6), 69-70.

Hunter, M. (1986). The Hunter model of clinical supervision. *A practical guide for instructional supervision: A tool for administrators and supervisors*. Curriculum and Instruction Leaders Committee, Association of California School Administrators.

Hunter, M. (1984). Knowing, teaching, and supervising. In, Philip L. Hosford (ed.), *Using what we know about teaching*, Alexandria, VA: Association for Supervision and Curriculum Development.

Hunter, M. (1988). Effecting a reconciliation between supervision and evaluation – A reply to Popham. *Journal of Personnel Evaluation in Education, 1*, 275-79.

Chapter 8

Joyce and Showers' Coaching Model

The Model at Work

Mrs. Whitman felt just a little nervous with her colleague Joe Cabral sitting in the back of her classroom, even though he smiled and gave her a friendly wink of encouragement. She and Joe have both taught science at Wilson High School for almost four years. As they got involved with peer coaching this last year, however, they have become closer and learned more about each other than teachers in the same department usually do.

Staff development was different this year from the very start. It was ongoing, for one thing, with the same consultants working with the faculty again and again. In earlier years, inservice sessions were typically one-shot, half-day affairs featuring presenters who suggested some interesting new ideas about teaching, and then left. Mrs. Whitman always intended to try out the techniques recommended in these workshops, especially since the presenters almost always said how easy the new methods were to use, but she found that she rarely did so.

The consultants who began working with the faculty last summer, however, began talking about how difficult it is to change the way we do things, especially those things that are habitual. They offered golf and bowling as examples, and said that changing one's grip or stance at first feels awkward and unnatural, and throws off one's entire game. Think about, they suggested, how difficult it must be to change an infinitely more complex set of behaviors like teaching. These consultants had some innovative ideas to offer that they called "models of teaching." They demonstrated several, but warned that the strategies were not as easy to master as they appeared. The consultants also left the teachers with a strange promise: "We'll make you worse before you get better."

The faculty divided itself into "study groups" with two or three teachers in each. The six teachers in the science department, including Mrs. Whitman and Joe Cabral, formed two study groups and together comprised a "coaching team." Some coaching teams, however, were interdisciplinary. In total, there were eight such teams at Wilson High School. One member represented each team on a school council that made decisions about school-wide instructional and curricular improvement.

Mrs. Whitman's study group selected the "inquiry method" of teaching as its focus because it fit what they wanted to do in science. They spent hours reading about inquiry and discussing its fine points after school. They also viewed videotapes of other teachers using the inquiry method and examined instructional materials that could be used in an inquiry lesson.

After about a month, the consultants returned and helped the teachers at Wilson High School prepare lessons that they would teach to their coaching teams. The consultants distributed rating scales on which the team members noted the extent that various behaviors associated with the model of teaching being attempted were enacted. Each teacher received feedback as their coaching teams analyzed their lesson in terms of what went well and what went poorly. Mrs. Whitman began to really appreciate the members of her department as caring and creative professionals who could offer both collegial support and insight into her teaching.

The consultants cautioned the teachers at that point, however, not to begin using the models in their classrooms until they had practiced them several more times with their coaching teams. They explained that the classroom is a much more challenging environment than a workshop setting, and the consultants wanted to be *sure that the teachers experienced success by acquiring what they called "executive control" of their new teaching skills. This had seemed unnecessary to Mrs. Whitman at the time. But as she cleared her throat to begin the lesson and glanced again at Joe Cabral sitting there smiling at her, she felt a sudden surge of confidence about the lesson that she realized she would not have had a few weeks ago.*

Introduction

The Joyce and Showers "coaching" model involves four elements that are based upon research in the area of staff development. The thoroughness of their documentation lends credence to their claim that educational research can help educators better organize curriculum and instruction to improve and accelerate student learning. They suggest that educators need extensive staff development to stay informed about recent research and its implications for classroom practice, in order to make better decisions about instruction. The elements of the coaching model follow one another more or less sequentially, though not always, and may be summarized as follows:

Element 1: *Study*. Teachers begin by reading about a particular instructional method or model of teaching to become familiar with its theoretical basis and rationale. Teachers also discuss what they have read in groups of six. These groups may represent grade levels, departments, teams, or other units.

Element 2: *Demonstration*. Teachers next observe a demonstration of the new teaching strategy by someone who is expert in its use. They may also view videotapes or visit and observe teachers in other schools who are already applying the technique.

Element 3: *Practice and Feedback*. At this point each teacher plans a minilesson and tries out the new method with other teachers who play the role of students. After several trial runs, each teacher plans a real lesson and applies the new teaching strategy in the classroom. Initial success should be encouraged, Joyce and Showers suggest, by selecting students who are capable and fairly easy to teach. Each teacher is paired with a colleague who observes the lesson and offers constructive criticism along with suggestions for improvement. The partners then switch roles and repeat the process. Several such cycles of practice and feedback are recommended to ensure mastery of the strategy before moving on to the coaching stage.

Element 4: *Coaching*. Teachers attempt to use the new teaching method in their regular classes when appropriate and to incorporate the new strategy into their teaching repertoires. To help ensure continued success, partners and coaching teams provide each teacher with companionship, assistance, ideas, and ongoing feedback.

Assumptions and Purposes

Joyce and Showers believe that professional development for teachers should be an integral and ongoing part of daily life in schools. In the past, they observe, inservice sessions have been either inspirational or one-shot helpful-hint affairs which had little impact on practice and little connection to other events in teachers' personal and professional lives. According to Joyce and Showers, research on teaching, teacher behaviors, instructional programs, and curricular designs have recently accumulated to the point where staff development can be more systematically planned and organized.

A comprehensive staff development plan, Joyce and Showers believe, ought to provide time for teachers and administrators to study, prepare for teaching, and cooperatively strive for school improvement. Such a program of continuing inservice education would certainly benefit educators, but students and society would ultimately benefit most from this investment in human resources. According to Joyce and Showers, teaching strategies now exist that can help students learn more now and continue to learn throughout their lives. It follows that getting this information to teachers so that they can apply it in their classrooms is the most important step to be taken if schools are to improve. But staff development must be conducted in a manner that encourages teachers to both learn and use new ideas and approaches successfully, something that has not always happened in the past.

The Content of Training

According to Joyce and Showers, professional growth for teachers is not only a worthy end in itself, it is also an excellent way of improving outcomes for students. A vast number of studies have been conducted in recent years that have direct bearing on student achievement. Unfortunately, the findings of these studies have not been readily available to teachers. Joyce and Showers recommend that staff development should concentrate on research that has emerged in four areas: (1) models of teaching; (2) curriculum and curriculum implementation; (3) school effectiveness; and (4) teacher effectiveness. Each of these areas is described briefly in the pages that follow.

Models of Teaching

One area of training that Joyce and Showers recommend as a focus for staff development is alternative models of teaching. Bruce Joyce and Marsha Weil (1986) have classified numerous models of teaching into four broad families or categories of teaching strategies: a) information-processing, b) personal, c) social, and d) behavioral. While not entirely mutually exclusive, each of the families tends to focus on a particular area of growth needed by students.

Joyce and Weil (1986) recommend that teachers develop a repertoire of teaching strategies and use a variety of approaches in their classrooms to adequately meet student needs. The families of teaching models are summarized below:

Four Families of Teaching Models

Information Processing Family
  Concept Attainment
  Inductive Thinking
  Inquiry Training
  Advance Organizers
  Memorization
  Developing Intellect
  Scientific Inquiry

Personal Family
  Nondirective Teaching
  Synectics
  Awareness Training
  Classroom Meeting

Behavioral Systems Family
  Mastery Learning
  Learning Self-Control
  Training for Skill and
    Concept Development
  Assertive Training

The Social Family
  Group Investigation
  Role Playing
  Jurisprudential
  Inquiry
  Laboratory Training
  Social Science Inquiry

The models of teaching described by Joyce and Weil (1986) vary in terms of their relative instructional and nurturant outcomes. That is to say, some are more efficient for conveying information or changing behavior, while others heighten awareness of feelings or improve interpersonal skills. For the most part, instructional outcomes tend to result from purposefully leading a student in certain directions, while nurturant outcomes result more from the student's interaction with the learning climate that is established by the model. A brief description of the four families of teaching models follows.

The *information processing* family is comprised of models intended to enhance students' abilities to process information. Some models in this category, like "advance organizers" or "memorization," are designed to improve retention of information. Other models in this same family, such as "concept attainment" and "inquiry training," teach students higher level thinking skills.

The *personal* family of models of teaching includes strategies that tend to be student-centered. One example of a personal model is "synectics," which aims to enhance creativity and divergent thinking of students as they develop alternative perspectives of concepts and original solutions to problems. Another example is the "nondirective teaching" model which seeks to develop students' self-concepts and improve intergroup attitudes and interactions.

The *behavioral systems* family of models originates and is based on principles derived from classical and operant conditioning which rely on the stimulus-response-reinforcement sequence for acquiring and extinguishing patterns of behavior. "Mastery learning," for example, is a model that is highly teacher-directed. Students pursue objectives that have been predetermined by the teacher in generally lock-step activities. In contrast, the "assertive training" model is less structured. Students help one another substitute new behaviors for habitual responses through goal setting, role playing, feedback, and encouragement.

The *social* family of models includes teaching strategies that emphasize cooperative learning and lead students in analyzing their own values as well as public policies. Social skills and interpersonal understanding are prominent outcomes. The most complex of the social models is "group investigation" which seeks to apply scientific inquiry and the democratic process to the improvement of society. "Laboratory training" is the least structured model in the social family. Here, a permissive, supportive, and accepting climate emerges through group interaction. Self-expression, tolerance, personal insight, creativity, and openness to change are intended outcomes.

A teacher can acquire the flexibility needed to address a wide range of instructional situations and goals, Joyce and Showers suggest, by mastering a repertoire from the models of teaching described by Joyce and Weil (1986). Because the models of teaching are research-based with proven effectiveness, Joyce and Showers claim, intended instructional effects can and should be anticipated.

Curriculum Studies

The study of innovative curriculum programs represents a second possible focus for staff development recommended by Joyce and Showers. The twenty year period from the mid-1950s to the mid-1970s witnessed the development of innovative curriculum programs in diverse subject areas for various grade levels. Joyce and Showers report that many of these programs were shown to produce measurable effects on student learning. They offer a number of examples of innovative curricula in various subject areas, such as: "Man, A Course of Study" in social studies, "BSCS Biology" in science, "School Mathematics Study Group" in mathematics, and "Headstart" and "Follow Through" in early childhood education.

Implementing these curricular programs to the point where they actually make a difference in terms of learning materials, teaching processes, and content at the classroom level, however, proves very difficult. Curriculum implementation is much more likely to succeed, Joyce and Showers note, when it is accompanied by a well-planned program of staff development that includes coaching.

Effective School Studies

A third area that educators may consider as a topic for staff development is the effective schools research. Recent reports suggest that a number of important factors distinguish effective schools from others that are less successful at improving student achievement. These factors include:
- a clear sense of mission;
- high standards and expectations of success;

- close monitoring of student progress;
- involvement of parents;
- a safe and orderly environment;
- collaborative decision-making; and
- strong instructional leadership.

Joyce and Showers suggest that the implementation of effective models of teaching may provide a framework for faculty to use in determining a sense of mission, establishing an orderly environment, and other characteristics of effective schooling.

Teacher Effectiveness

A fourth possible focus for staff development, according to Joyce and Showers, is the results of teacher effectiveness studies. Although the generalizability of much of this research is limited, according to Joyce and Showers, several studies suggest that more successful teachers tend to:
- emphasize clear goals;
- use whole class instruction;
- display enthusiasm when teaching;
- conduct class in an efficient manner;
- focus on the task of instruction;
- closely monitor student performance;
- provide frequent feedback to students;
- allow sufficient "wait time" for students to respond to teacher questions;
- hold high expectations for students; and
- be relaxed and nonevaluative toward students.

The Coaching Analogy

As in athletics, Joyce and Showers argue, the application of a new skill by a teacher is likely to temporarily upset the delicate balance of complex factors that contribute to a smooth performance. Because a new behavior feels uncomfortable the first few times it is tried, people have a tendency to revert to their original way of doing things even though the old ways may be less effective.

Unlike professional athletes, many educators wrongly assume that a skill can be acquired easily and mastered quickly. In truth, Joyce and

Showers observe, small increments of improvement in teaching or any complex activity usually require enormous effort. Attending one-day workshops, viewing a videotape, or hearing a speaker cannot be expected to make any lasting difference in a teacher's performance, although inservice has traditionally been based on that assumption.

Skills should be learned gradually and practiced extensively by teachers, Joyce and Showers recommend, before they are even attempted in the classroom. Such "overlearning" is needed to incorporate a new skill into the teacher's repertoire as fully as possible.

Once a skill is transferred to the classroom context, ongoing observation, feedback, and reinforcement from colleagues is essential. Joyce and Showers believe that at least one hour per teacher each week is needed to sustain an effective coaching program. They suggest allowing teachers to organize into groups in order to train and support each other during the difficult period of transfer as the best and most efficient way of promoting change in schools.

Ultimately, Joyce and Showers believe that a school should strive toward a "coaching environment" in which all teachers view themselves as each other's coaches. To accomplish this end "coaching teams" comprised of pairs of teachers are formed during training. These teachers serve one another as peer supervisors. The coaching teams provide five major functions as their members observe and conference with one another:

1. *Providing Human Companionship During the Process of Acquiring a New Skill.* Coaching provides teachers with the opportunity to interact with another human being as they embark on the difficult and risky process of learning something new. A coach or companion is someone with whom a teacher can reflect on an idea, check perceptions, share successes and frustrations, and solve problems informally. Companionship is especially important immediately after training, while the teacher is still feeling awkward about attempting a newly acquired skill. Peer coaching lets teachers know that their feelings and failures are not unique, that their colleagues are experiencing similar difficulties.

2. *Providing Technical Feedback on Performance.* Teachers learn to provide technical feedback to each other during training and continue to do so during the coaching phase. Feedback is very important when a skill is tried in the classroom for the first time because other dimensions of the classroom environment re-

quire the teacher's attention, possibly shifting the focus away from the teaching method. An observer can check for omissions and oversights during the lesson, the arrangement of materials, or whether all the elements of the strategy have been orchestrated properly. The observer thus keeps the teacher's mind on the application of the skill and increases the chance that the skill will be improved and perfected. The observer benefits as well from the opportunity to watch a colleague in action. New ideas and valuable insights into one's own performance are obtained from observing another teacher's successes and shortcomings. Joyce and Showers suggest that this benefit can be extended by expanding the number of teachers on a coaching team to four or six, a practice which also provides each teacher with multiple sources of feedback.

3. *Analyzing Application to Enhance Executive Control.* Coaching contributes to the attainment of what Joyce and Showers term "executive control" over a skill. By this they mean that the teacher should be able to apply the skill confidently and effectively when it is appropriate. Executive control can be achieved as teachers mutually analyze the factors that determine when a skill is appropriately applied and what the consequences are likely to be. Close attention should also be given to the curriculum and materials available as a lesson is planned to ensure that the new teaching method will be properly executed and that the outcomes are satisfactory.

4. *Adapting the Skill to Students in Real Classrooms.* An especially difficult task which coaching can facilitate is that of adapting a new teaching skill to the living, breathing students whom teachers face in their classrooms. Students have to both understand and be able to perform the responses that are required from them in order for a teaching strategy to work successfully. The coach can help the teacher to interpret student responses and adapt the model to their level of readiness.

5. *Facilitating Practice for Success.* Finally, coaching provides mutual reinforcement for continuous practice of a new skill. Joyce and Showers believe that the failure of innovative strategies to become incorporated into classroom practice is due in part to the isolation and lack of support that teachers experience. Coaching can foster personal facilitation among teachers to overcome these barriers.

The Problem of Transfer

Joyce and Showers developed the four elements of their coaching model (i.e., study, demonstration, practice and feedback, and coaching) after extensive review of research on the staff development of teachers. They report that most teachers are capable of applying a new teaching approach reasonably well if they are provided with opportunities for studying the theory behind the strategy, for observing demonstrations of the strategy in action, and for practicing the strategy while receiving feedback on their success. Acquiring a new skill, however, is only the first step. Even highly motivated teachers are not necessarily able to immediately transfer a new skill into their regular teaching repertoires. This point of transfer between learning a new skill and applying it is where the element of coaching assumes greatest significance.

Coaching is absolutely essential, according to Joyce and Showers, for ensuring transfer following the acquisition of a new skill. One reason teachers may have difficulty immediately applying a new approach is that the classroom context is entirely different from the experience of the training session. For example, a workshop setting typically lacks the distracting conditions that prevail in most classrooms. A new teaching strategy has to be adapted to fit less than ideal conditions.

A second reason that transfer may be difficult for teachers is that existing behavior patterns may inhibit the ability to master new teaching strategies. The new teaching approach may feel awkward at first and frustratingly slow, Joyce and Showers note, because the teacher has not mastered its subtleties nor grown accustomed to its pace. Only time and practice will make the new strategy feel natural to the teacher.

Facilitating Transfer

Three techniques are suggested, in addition to coaching, for overcoming the problem of transfer. The first technique is to forecast throughout the training process that transfer will be difficult. Rather than telling teachers how "simple and easy" a teaching strategy is to use, Joyce and Showers recommend that teachers be truthfully told from the very beginning that extensive practice is required before a new skill can be fully mastered. Even experienced and competent teachers should recognize that they will not leave the training session fully equipped to immediately implement the new strategy in their classrooms. They should understand that coaching is a necessary part of improvement.

A second technique for encouraging successful transfer is to try to achieve the maximum possible level of skill attainment during the training, before coaching begins. Intensive study of theory requires at least twenty to thirty hours, according to Joyce and Showers. Also, teachers should observe at least fifteen to twenty demonstrations of a new teaching method with various types of students and different content areas before they attempt it. At least ten to fifteen practice sessions are recommended to attain a sufficiently high level of competence in a skill before teachers try to use it in their regular classrooms. Such intensive training is necessary, Joyce and Showers believe, in order to overcome the momentum of current classroom routines.

The third technique for improving the probability that new skills will transfer is to ensure that the preliminary study and training phases are carefully attended to. Teachers should clearly understand the new teaching method, how and why it works, when it is appropriately used, and how it can be adapted to various grades and subject areas. A comprehensive grasp of all the facets of a new approach is needed, according to Joyce and Showers, to attain what they call "meta-understanding" which they consider essential for the achievement of "executive control." Meta-understanding is the capacity to think about and shape the new strategy while actually using it. This capability of modifying any teaching strategy at the very moment it is applied is considered necessary for success.

In summary, the chances that successful transfer will occur are improved substantially if the transfer process is forecast throughout training, a high level of skill attainment is reached, and executive control is established. However, these techniques merely pave the way for the most potent contributor to successful transfer, the process of coaching.

The Purposes of Coaching

Joyce and Showers propose that numerous purposes are served by coaching in schools, such as the following:

a) One intended outcome of coaching is the establishment of a community of teachers within the school who engage in an

ongoing study of their craft.
b) Coaching is also said to promote the development of common understandings and a shared language which permit discussion and acquisition of new knowledge and skills.
c) A professional culture may be established that encourages and reinforces hard work, striving for constant improvement, expansion of teaching repertoires, and collegiality.
d) Finally, coaching provides a supportive structure following training that ensures the transfer of new skills and knowledge into the classroom.

Coaching is especially important, according to Joyce and Showers, when the mastery of teaching strategies and configurations of teaching patterns require teachers to think in new ways about learning objectives and classroom processes. Coaching is less important for fine-tuning existing skills, something which is considered easily achieved by teachers independently.

The Process of Coaching

As noted earlier, the process of coaching follows a period of extensive training that involves studying the theory and rationale behind an innovation in instruction or curriculum, observing demonstrations by experts, practicing in a workshop setting, and getting feedback from colleagues.

If teachers are to function effectively as peer coaches, Joyce and Showers note, they must also become familiar with techniques of observation and feedback. Training in observation and feedback can be provided at the same time that new teaching strategies are introduced. Working first in pairs with a single coaching partner and later in coaching teams of up to six teachers, the new skills of teaching and coaching are acquired simultaneously as each teacher practices the skills required by both roles.

During this training period teachers are introduced to what Showers (1984; 1985) calls "Clinical Assessment Forms." These forms are used to assess whether specific behaviors are present or absent in a lesson as well as the relative degree of completeness with which they are performed. Each teacher uses the clinical assessment forms to check and provide feedback on his own and others' teaching.

For example, when providing feedback on a colleague's attempt to use a particular model of teaching, the peer coach would observe and record whether or not the teacher and students exhibited specific behaviors associated with the model. For the concept attainment model appropriate teacher behaviors include, among others, asking questions that focus students' thinking on the essential attributes of the concept under consideration, asking students to justify their answers, and asking the students to describe their thinking processes.

For the synectics model, the peer coach would use the clinical assessment form to determine whether or not the teacher and students displayed behaviors such as defining a direct analogy, eliciting multiple analogies, selecting one analogy with which to work, and applying personal analogies. The peer coach records on a four-point scale whether each behavior was "thoroughly" or "partially" enacted, "missing," or "not needed."

Three to six weeks after a new teaching strategy is introduced into classrooms, the teachers in a school reassemble as a large group to talk about problems and progress they have made in implementing the strategy. At this point the trainers model a process of collegial dialogue as instructional objectives, lesson plans, materials, and texts are examined in light of the rationale and purposes underlying the model. The intention behind this phase of the training is to focus coaching on questions relating to the appropriate application of the new teaching strategies instead of the execution of interactive classroom skills.

Once the mechanics of a new strategy are established, coaching moves to the more complex task of determining when a new teaching strategy is appropriately used. Teachers must go beyond simply being able to perform a skill. They should develop an understanding of the intricacies of a skill on a cognitive level. Being able to think about a strategy objectively is essential to its successful application in the classroom.

When learning the models of teaching, for example, teachers often find it fairly easy to enact the patterns of various models and to use the materials provided for them. However, creating and planning original lessons, developing new materials, and getting students to respond in nonhabitual ways are usually much more difficult. Coaching necessarily becomes more of a collaborative problem-solving venture as teachers draw on each others' creativity and cooperatively plan lessons.

Successful coaching, according to Joyce and Showers, requires a minimum of three to four months of activity. Even better is a continuation of coaching as an ongoing institutionalized process of mutual assistance and school improvement. Having teachers serve as peer coaches best facilitates this ethos within the organizational context, though principals and instructional supervisors can also participate in coaching.

Coaching and Evaluation

According to Joyce and Showers, the processes of coaching and summative evaluation are entirely opposed to one another and are separate categories of both thought and practice. Coaching emphasizes collegial assistance and requires an environment where new skills can be safely practiced for the improvement of instruction. Joyce and Showers emphasize that coaching is not and should never be confused or used concurrently with summative judgments about a teacher's adequacy. Risk of failure always accompanies an attempt at something new. If teachers are to take such risks, they cannot feel that temporary failure will be used against them.

Coaching differs from supervision as it is practiced in most schools in that coaching is something that teachers do with each other rather than to each other. Hierarchy promotes dependency, Joyce and Showers argue, as does any form of supervision that does not encourage educators to work together as colleagues without the fear of evaluation. Teachers will not experiment, take risks, or practice strategies that still feel awkward if evaluation is the end product. Coaching necessitates a safe environment where new teaching behaviors can be learned, practiced, discussed, and perfected between and among equals.

Principals and central office staff can best contribute to the success of a coaching program by setting it as a priority for the school, allocating resources to it, and planning and supporting its implementation. Coaching, Joyce and Showers claim, requires well-focused, long-term commitments to improvement. Hit-or-miss one-shot inservice sessions should therefore be avoided. Principals must convince teachers that professional growth through observation, feedback, and experimentation is an expectation for everyone. Schedules and incentives should be reorganized to permit and reinforce this effort. The principal is a key factor.

Coaching requires changes as well in the social structure of the workplace, Joyce and Showers maintain, so that the school can become a learning laboratory. Feedback and judgments about processes have to replace evaluative pronouncements about teaching and teachers. A community of professionals who mutually inquire and provide each other with assistance replaces the traditional emphasis on monitoring and inspection by administrators.

Central office staff, principals, and teachers have to cooperate extensively in organizing and implementing the training and coaching components. The technical and social changes required by coaching mean that it cannot be simply added onto the usual way of doing things. It means that fundamental changes have to be made in the way that teachers relate to each other and to administrators.

Overcoming Obstacles to Peer Coaching

A source of difficulty in implementing the coaching model is that schools are usually organized and scheduled in ways that leave little if any time for planning lessons, participating in staff development sessions, observing other teachers, or conferencing. Joyce and Showers recommend seven specific changes that can be made at fairly low cost which allow teachers more time to support one another in their efforts to improve:

1. School principals can teach at least one class period every day. Assuming a ratio of one administrator to twenty teachers, fully 25 percent of the faculty in a school can gain an hour for coaching each week in this way.

2. Have community volunteers or aides cover classes. Hired substitutes, Joyce and Showers believe, should be reserved for releasing teachers for training.

3. Schedule some larger sections of classes for certain subjects. While one teacher instructs a large group, one or more other teachers can be freed to engage in professional development activities. Such an arrangement requires trust that released time will be productively spent.

4. Store materials and information needed for planning in the school library. Teachers can then study and practice instruction in a sequestered area while their students conduct library research or engage in independent study.

5. Use student teachers to free teachers' time. Joyce and Showers advise that student teachers be assigned in teams of two so that they can also benefit from coaching each other.
6. Organize teaching teams for instruction. By combining classes teachers can free each other to conduct observations and have discussions.
7. Audio and videotape classes to reduce the time needed for observations. A coaching partner or group can later analyze the lesson at any convenient time. The principal can offer to take responsibility for taping, and taped lessons may even be viewed and discussed at faculty meetings.

Joyce and Showers do not recommend that all these possibilities be used at once. Using only several should provide sufficient time for coaching.

Transforming the Organization

The isolation and independence that teachers and administrators have traditionally experienced, Joyce and Showers contend, has hindered the emergence of a sense of community among teachers and prevented the development of a professional ethos of common beliefs. Collective efforts at improvement and opportunities for sharing expertise among educators are virtually impossible unless this situation is dramatically changed.

A common understanding of the objectives, rationale, and processes of change is required by educators at all levels for improvements to occur. Joyce and Showers recommend a structure that links small communities of teachers and administrators within and among schools throughout a district. The fundamental unit of the structure is a coaching team comprised of two or three teachers or administrators. Each team is linked to one or two other teams which together form a study group of no more than six individuals.

The principal and representatives from the various study groups comprise a Staff Development/School Improvement Council for each school building. One representative from every school council serves on a District Cluster Network Committee which works with the central office in coordinating staff development efforts across the district. In larger districts, each high school and its feeder schools has its own District Cluster Network Committee (see *Figure 8.1*).

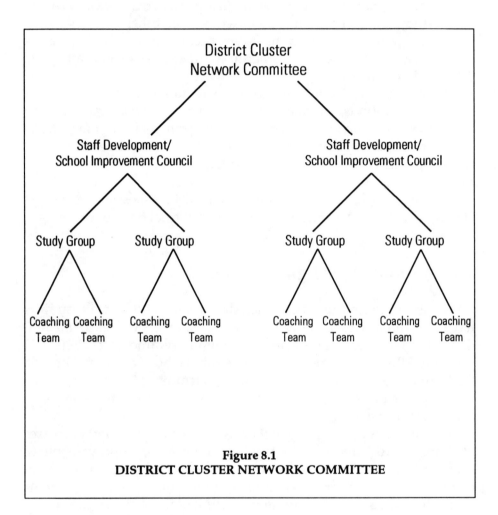

Figure 8.1
DISTRICT CLUSTER NETWORK COMMITTEE

A closely-knit system of the type depicted in *Figure 8.1* is more likely to encourage continued professional development among educators, Joyce and Showers observe, than the haphazard hit-or-miss approach that has characterized inservice in the past. Though requiring more extensive time, effort, and resources, a comprehensive system has the advantage of simultaneously focusing on three strands or dimensions of improvement. First, the academic knowledge and clinical skills of individual teachers and administrators are enhanced through continuous study of teaching and learning. Second, the effectiveness of the faculty as a group is enhanced through the study of school improvement and the planning of collective action. Third, the success of district-level initiatives involving new curricula and instructional technologies are improved by facilitating adjustments at the level where change is implemented, namely, classrooms and schools.

At the individual or clinical level, for example, courses and workshops can be offered that focus on academic content, models and strategies of teaching, characteristics of students, or instructional technology. Similar sessions may be planned by school-level councils for entire faculties, but school effectiveness and the process of school improvement may also be appropriate foci for collective study and action. At the district level, they note, external consultants are often needed to assist in planning and coordinating the implementation of complex district-wide initiatives.

Joyce and Showers recommend that instructional teams comprised of qualified and interested district personnel should be used to provide training and consultation to their colleagues whenever possible. Besides being more credible and accessible, internal experts reinforce the ethos of sharing professional responsibility for educational processes and outcomes.

A comprehensive system of staff development, Joyce and Showers point out, both requires and contributes to a transformation of the social organization of the school. Learning, collaborative activity, and mutual support can flourish only in an environment that is conducive to change, experimentation, and growth. Time and opportunities for study, discussion, and sharing ideas must obviously be provided to overcome the prevailing norms of isolation and complacency in schools. But if collective energy and cohesiveness are to be unleashed, other social processes must also be harnessed to the effort.

The formal leaders of the organization, first of all, must actively support and facilitate the formation of study groups, coaching teams, school councils, and district networks. They should also participate in the training and initiatives emanating from the improvement effort, keeping themselves knowledgeable about issues being addressed and sensitive to changes in the educational climate. Essentially, administrators must become fully committed to the role of instructional and curricular leader.

A spirit of cohesiveness must pervade the organization as well, accompanied by a clear understanding that collaborative action implies shared responsibility. Therefore, Joyce and Showers recommend that decisions made by councils or network committees should be binding on everyone. Furthermore, the district office and local schools must work cooperatively to ensure that change initiatives are focused and not diffused.

On the one hand, coordination is needed so that principals and teachers are not overwhelmed by programs that people in the central office think are important. On the other hand, coordination ensures that those programs that are initiated are implemented with more than superficial compliance. The key to responsible cohesiveness is involvement by teachers at all levels of governance and a willingness on their part to put aside individual interests for the common good of their colleagues and students.

Summary

Joyce and Showers recommend that professional development for teachers should be an integral and ongoing part of daily life in schools. Their model involves four elements that are based on research in the area of staff development: study, demonstration, practice and feedback, and coaching. These elements typically, though not always, follow one another sequentially. Classroom observation and feedback, which comprise the coaching phase, are used primarily for reinforcing a broader program of staff development.

According to Joyce and Showers, professional growth is more likely to occur if teachers begin by reading about and discussing a particular method or model of teaching with a small group of colleagues. Next, teachers should observe several demonstrations of the new strategy by someone who is expert in its use. Teachers then are prepared to try out the new strategy by planning and teaching a minilesson to their colleagues. Teachers should attempt to use the new teaching method in their regular classes only after such extensive preparation. Coaching takes place toward the end of this sequence as two or three teachers observe and provide feedback and encouragement to one another.

Coaching is essential for incorporating a new skill into one's repertoire as a teacher, according to Joyce and Showers, because trying out a new approach invariably upsets the delicate balance of factors that contribute to a smooth performance. Repeated practice with feedback is needed to ensure that the new skill is overlearned and can be enacted easily and naturally when appropriate. Assessment forms are recommended to record data that indicate the extent to which teachers' enactment of a particular strategy conforms to the model they are trying to emulate. Coaching and summative evaluation, Joyce and Showers believe, are entirely opposed to one another and are distinctly separate categories of both thought and practice.

Ultimately, Joyce and Showers advocate the establishment of a coaching environment. A coaching environment requires changes in the normative structure of the workplace so that the school can become a learning laboratory. They recommend that coaching teams of two or three teachers be linked to larger study groups, to school-based staff development councils, and to district-wide cluster network committees. Possible topics of study, discussion, and action for these larger groups include new curricula and its implementation, research on effective teacher behaviors, and research on characteristics of effective schools.

References

Brandt, R. S. (1987). On teachers coaching teachers: A conversation with Bruce Joyce. *Educational Leadership, 44,* (5), 12-17.

Joyce, B. (1985). Models for teaching thinking. *Educational Leadership, 42* (8), 4-7.

Joyce, B. & McKibbin, M. (1982). Teacher growth states and school environments. *Educational Leadership, 40,* (2), 36-41.

Joyce, B. & Showers, B. (1980). Improving inservice training: The messages of research. *Educational Leadership, 37,* (5), 379-385.

Joyce, B. & Showers, B. (1982). The coaching of teaching. *Educational Leadership, 40,* (1), 4-10.

Joyce, B. & Showers, B. (1987). Low-cost arrangements for peer-coaching. *Journal of Staff Development, 8,* (1), 22-24.

Joyce, B. & Showers, B. (1988). *Student achievement through staff development.* New York: Longman.

Joyce, B. & Weil, M. (1986). *Models of teaching* (Third Edition). Englewood Cliffs, NJ: Prentice-Hall.

Showers, B. (1984). *Peer coaching: A strategy for facilitating transfer of training.* Eugene, OR: University of Oregon Center for Educational Policy and Management.

Showers, B. (1985). Teachers coaching teachers. *Educational Leadership, 42,* (7), 43-48.

Showers, B., Joyce, B. & Bennett, B. (1987). Synthesis of research on staff development: A framework for future study and a state-of-the-art analysis. *Educational Leadership, 45,* (3), 77-87.

Showers, B., Joyce, B. & Rolheiser-Bennett, C. (1987). Staff development and student learning: A synthesis of research on models of teaching. *Educational Leadership, 45* (2), 11-23.

Section Four

The Developmental/Reflective Models

The developmental and reflective approaches to supervision described in Section Four represent a recent movement away from the technical/didactic perspectives of teaching and supervision. They express a view that teaching and learning are influenced by the personal, social, organizational, historical, political, and cultural contexts in which they occur. The aim of these newer approaches is to directly influence the thinking of teachers to help them consider, circumvent, resist, or transform those contexts.

Glickman's developmental approach to supervision is based on the idea that certain characteristics of the teaching profession and the work environment of schools (e.g., unrelieved routine, isolation, powerlessness) have traditionally inhibited the cognitive development of teachers. Supervisors should challenge the ineffectiveness that is continuously reinforced in schools, he suggests, by facilitating the development of teachers' decision-making capabilities and capacities for abstract thinking.

Glickman urges supervisors to informally diagnose the levels of cognitive development, commitment to organizational goals, and experience displayed by the teachers with whom they work. He suggests that supervisors should select a directive, collaborative, or nondirective strategy for pre- and post observation conferences that matches each teacher's particular developmental level. The supervisor then gradually uses less control and increases opportunities for choice by the teacher as the teacher gains experience and expertise. Essentially the same procedure is recommended when the supervisor works with groups of teachers in staff development, curriculum development, and action research.

Costa and Garmston also advocate an approach to classroom supervision that is focused on facilitating the cognitive growth and decision making ability of teachers. The basis of their position is that teaching is an incredibly complex activity requiring a high degree of intellectual capability and that the enhancement of teachers' thinking will result in improved student learning. Costa and Garmston's approach, which they call "cognitive coaching," assumes that even inexperienced teachers can be challenged to think at higher levels. The supervisory strategy they recommend is uniformly nondirective.

Cognitive coaching involves a sequence of three interrelated goals: (1) establishment of trust between the teacher and the supervisor, (2) facilitation by the supervisor of the teacher's learning, and (3) nurturance by the supervisor of the teacher's autonomy. Matters relating to observation and data collection are de-emphasized in cognitive coaching, with most attention given to the supervisory conference. Supervisors try to stimulate teacher thinking during conferences by asking questions that are intended to increase introspection, precision, and specificity of thought, while also enhancing conscious reasoning and enlarging the scope of teachers' awareness of alternative classroom techniques and outcomes. As such, the thrust of cognitive coaching is intended to enhance reflective teaching.

The reflective practice models of Schon, Zeichner and Liston, Garman, Smyth, Retallick, and Bowers and Flinders represent emerging perspectives on supervisory practice in education. Schon's version of reflective practice bears a strong resemblance to John Dewey's method of reflective problem solving (1933). However, Schon more heavily emphasizes the cognitive processes and actions of individuals over collective deliberation and action. Zeichner and Liston acknowledge Dewey's work as a basis for their own, and give greater attention than Schon to the social context of teaching and learning, the social construction of meaning, and the social responsibility of educators. Like the originators of clinical supervision, Zeichner and Liston's thinking is informed by their experience with the preparation of beginning teachers. They encourage supervisors to help new teachers examine taken-for-granted values, assumptions, and beliefs. Garman writes in the tradition of Goldhammer and Cogan and corroborates the historical link between clinical supervision and reflective practice. She highlights the importance of understanding personal history to the generation of professional knowledge and the regeneration of oneself as a professional.

Smyth and Retallick write from a position that openly challenges the legitimacy of existing social, economic, and political realities. Drawing on the "critical practice" perspective associated with neo-Marxist philosophy, both call on teachers and supervisors to question and transform classrooms and schools in ways that serve the ends of equality and social justice. Finally, Bowers and Flinders' view of teaching and supervision is the most novel of the emerging approaches. They propose that classroom events and outcomes are less the result of consciously motivated actions of teachers and students than they are manifestations of the cultural ecology of each classroom. According to Bowers and Flinders, reflective problem solving does not go far enough. They call on supervisors to be advocates of cultural, racial, and gender sensitivity in schools.

Supporters of reflective practice thus call on teachers and supervisors to consider the personal, social, organizational, historical, political, and cultural contexts that impinge on learning in classrooms and schools. One aim that the reflective approaches share is for teachers and supervisors to question their taken-for-granted beliefs, assumptions, and theories about teaching and learning. Another aim is for teachers to develop greater empathy for students and sensitivity to the diversity among them. A third common purpose is for teachers and supervisors to willingly act upon principles of justice and equity as guides to their practice.

Advocates of reflective practice urge supervisors and teachers to question the hierarchical nature of interpersonal relationships in schools, to raise issues of gender, race, and culture to conscious levels, and to challenge the knowledge embodied in the books, curriculum, lessons, and examinations that are part of schooling. Teachers and supervisors are encouraged to consider those aspects of classrooms and schools (including their own professional identities) that disempower educators and debilitate students. This potential transformation of schooling is fueled by collaborative inquiry and is guided by moral principles of justice and equity.

Glickman's developmental model marks a transition between the heyday of the technical/didactic approaches and the emergence of reflective practice in the supervision literature. Because it functions as an intellectual bridge, developmental supervision contains elements of both perspectives. For example, it embraces the mastery of techniques developed outside the classroom context and the cognitive development of teachers simultaneously. Also, while the goal of developmental supervision is to expand the scope of teachers' influence, the supervisor is clearly in control of the process at all times. Although Glickman's model acknowledges the existence of organizational constraints to teaching, it does not directly address issues arising from the social, cultural, or political contexts that can impede learning.

Costa and Garmston deliberately distinguish cognitive coaching from the technical/didactic orientation. Their approach to supervision is grounded in counseling and seeks teacher autonomy as its ultimate goal. Cognitive coaching is similar to Goldhammer's model in this respect and in its primary emphasis on nondirective collaboration between supervisors and teachers as a starting point. Like the advocates of reflective practice, Costa and Garmston recommend rational inquiry as the foundation for improving learning in classrooms and schools. They refrain from adopting an ideological position, however, and concentrate almost entirely on the practical matter of how supervisors can guide teachers toward conscious understanding and control of their actions in the classroom to attain desirable learning outcomes for students.

Proponents of reflective practice seek to reclaim the potential of clinical supervision, anticipated by Goldhammer, to liberate students, teachers, and supervisors from the insensitivity, meaninglessness, irrelevancy, and dependency that are often encountered and subtly encouraged in schools. Like Blumberg and Eisner, they criticize technical and bureaucratic approaches to teaching and supervision which they consider narrow, constraining, and oppressive. The willingness of these authors to challenge the assumptions, opinions, and conclusions of other scholars may be a sign of new vitality in the field of clinical supervision.

Chapter 9

Carl Glickman's Developmental Supervision

The Model at Work

During his first year as principal of East High School, Mr. Nelms is making a point of visiting teachers' classrooms regularly and frequently. His predecessor, Mr. Sledge, had retired after serving as principal for eight years. Mr. Sledge had a reputation for "doing things by the book." He followed district policy to the letter and referred teachers who had questions to the Faculty Handbook for answers. His favorite saying was, "If it ain't broke, don't fix it." Teacher creativity, involvement, and assertiveness languished during Mr. Sledge's years as principal, and eventually were replaced with quiet conformity, isolation, and routine behavior in classrooms.

Mr. Nelms believes that supervision can reshape the work environment and promote norms of creativity, collegiality, and collective action. He is especially determined to break up the routine and isolation he sees in classrooms. Recently, Mr. Nelms visited the classroom of Mrs. Silas, an experienced mathematics teacher who often complains that the school used to run more smoothly. He noticed that Mrs. Silas' teaching seemed to center almost entirely around worksheets, which she spent many hours preparing, copying, and grading. Students picked up worksheets on their way into her classroom, and for the most part completed them quietly at their desks. Mrs. Silas rarely interacted with students and there was little interaction among the students themselves. Those who completed their work either stared out the window or began their homework. Mrs. Silas, meanwhile, kept very busy grading papers that had been turned in the day before.

After giving the situation some thought, Mr. Nelms decided that a "directive informational" approach would work best during the follow-up conference. Mrs. Silas, after all, had taught mathematics for over twelve years and the amount of time she invested in her worksheets demonstrated considerable commitment. Mr. Nelms thought that her mechanical approach to teaching was probably due to the debilitating effects of being left alone for so long.

Mr. Nelms began the conference by telling Mrs. Silas what he had observed. He stated that he believed her teaching could be improved if she interacted with students more directly and introduced some variety in their activities. He then asked her what she thought. Mrs. Silas responded that it was important in her opinion for students to learn to work independently and be responsible for their own learning. Rather than pursue an argument, Mr. Nelms simply told Mrs. Silas that other strategies could be used to achieve those ends and that he considered an over-reliance on any single method to be unacceptable. He then suggested several alternatives for her to pursue, ranging from more lecturing to cooperative learning, and asked Mrs. Silas to choose one to work on.

The suggestion she liked best was to allow students to grade one another's papers while she explained the solutions to the problems on the board. Although this was a humble beginning, Mr. Nelms decided to accept her plan and said that he would be observing her again in one week to see how things were going. He had confidence that Mrs. Silas was capable of much more than she was demonstrating and was prepared to gradually build her skills throughout the year. As she begins to choose new actions, Mr. Nelms intends to use a more collaborative approach and ask her for her own ideas.

Eventually, Mr. Nelms plans to get teachers involved in peer *supervision and in making decisions about instruction and curriculum. In fact, he has already taken steps to do so. On the next planning day, a time when teachers are used to working alone in their rooms to catch up on paperwork, Mr. Nelms intends to hold a meeting in the media center to discuss the problem of teacher isolation.*

Because a number of teachers have responded favorably to his thinking about this issue in informal conversations, Mr. Nelms has decided to risk a "collaborative" approach. He will begin the meeting by presenting the problem as he sees it. Then he will listen, encourage, clarify, and reflect the faculty members' perceptions. Next, he intends to ask the teachers to suggest possible solutions which he will list and they can prioritize together. He plans to make his own preference known, but will go along with what the teachers decide. By gradually allowing teachers more opportunity and freedom to participate in decisions, both individually and collectively, Mr. Nelms believes he can improve East High School for both teachers and students.

Introduction

In Carl Glickman's developmental model (Glickman, 1985; 1990), clinical supervision is regarded as a component of "direct assistance" to teachers. Direct assistance, in turn, is viewed as one dimension of general supervision that also includes inservice training and staff development, curriculum development, group development, and action research. Supervisors ought to be knowledgable, Glickman suggests, in a number of areas that are central to his notion of "developmental supervision." These include a knowledge of: effective school characteristics, adult and teacher development, interpersonal skills, and technical skills. Direct assistance, and particularly clinical supervision, require flexibility on the part of the supervisor, ongoing personal contact with individual teachers, and competence in the technical skills of observing, planning, conferencing, and assessing.

Drawing upon the effective and successful schools literature, Glickman suggests several propositions as appropriate tasks for supervision:

Proposition #1: Supervision should encourage teachers to invest in "a cause beyond themselves." Teachers should devote greater time and energy to school-wide instructional concerns beyond their own classrooms.

Proposition # 2: An important task of supervision is to enhance teachers' feelings of efficacy in influencing student outcomes by exercising greater control over classroom management and instruction.

Proposition # 3: Supervision ought to encourage teachers to share materials, ideas, and generally support one another's efforts in striving toward common instructional goals.

Proposition # 4: Supervision should stimulate teacher involvement in planning inservice, curriculum, and action research projects in order to strengthen collective action.

Proposition # 5: Supervision should challenge teachers to think more abstractly about their teaching. This last task is especially relevant to clinical supervision, according to Glickman, because it is accomplished by giving teachers feedback on their performance, and by questioning and confronting teachers to appraise, reflect upon, and adapt their current teaching practices.

Problems with the Status Quo

Traditionally, Glickman asserts, characteristics of the teaching profession, the work environment of schools, the people who have sought careers in teaching, and prevailing views of supervision have shaped the norms of schools in ways that make them less successful than they might be. Specifically, he notes, these factors contribute to pervasively low levels of thinking and commitment among teachers with respect to instructional improvement.

Glickman views many of the difficulties facing education today as arising from what he calls the "legacy of the one-room school house." During the settlement of the frontier, teachers were frequently isolated geographically from colleagues. By necessity, they operated independently and taught in privacy. Furthermore, as early as colonial times, the public accorded teachers and teaching a paradoxical status. Although teaching was considered an honorable calling on the one hand, teachers typically received low pay and were required to perform menial duties.

Vestiges of these traditions, Glickman suggests, continue to haunt contemporary schools and the teaching profession. Particularly troublesome are the following characteristics of the teaching occupation:

- inversed beginner responsibilities;
- an unstaged career;

- a highly routinized and unrelieved work schedule;
- psychological overload;
- isolation of teachers from other adults;
- lack of dialogue about instruction; and
- an absence of participation in school-wide curriculum and instructional decisions.

Glickman points out that the preservice preparation of teachers is generally regarded as inferior to other professions and that traditionally lax entry requirements have allowed teachers to move easily into and out of teaching positions. Teaching careers are also "unstaged" in the sense that responsibilities assumed in the early years of one's career differ little from those of veteran teachers. In fact, novice teachers often receive the less desirable assignments that experienced teachers manage to avoid and are expected to "sink or swim" with little or no help from senior colleagues.

Unlike the medical and legal professions, pay in teaching is tied to number of years of experience instead of on-the-job effectiveness. Also, teachers can leave and return to their jobs without substantially affecting their status, responsibilities, or rewards. Veteran teachers, Glickman suggests, often feel locked into dead-end careers with little chance of promotion or escape. Together, he believes, these factors have contributed to teachers as a group displaying less investment in their careers, their profession, and their jobs than members of other professions.

The typical work environment of teaching is compared by Glickman to that of the factory. He describes schools as being typically characterized by unrelieved routine and repetition. Teachers have little control, he notes, over time, space, and choice of assignments. The intensity and variety of psychological encounters with students that teachers face in a single day are described as overwhelming. As a consequence, teachers routinize classroom events in an attempt to preserve their own sanity. The isolation of teachers from other adults limits opportunities for supervision, for receiving feedback, and for engaging in collaborative activities with colleagues.

Most talented new teachers rather quickly view their work as unexciting, Glickman suggests, and lacking in challenge, variety, and opportunities for advancement. Especially around the third year of experience teachers begin to feel bored and unchallenged by the classroom. The repetition and sameness of teaching leads to unbearable monotony.

In summary, Glickman emphasizes that the absence of a career structure with staged responsibility and rewards fails to provide teachers with an extrinsic motivation for ongoing improvement. The routine, isolation, and psychological demands of the work environment debilitate teachers even further. Therefore, these characteristics of the teaching occupation and the work environment that stifle creative thinking and commitment must be forcefully altered if schools and teachers are to improve.

Encouraging Teacher Thinking

Glickman suggests that most teachers are unlikely to initiate and pursue change independently, because the unchallenging and controlling work environment of schools constantly reinforces conformity and unimaginative thinking. Supervisors, therefore, have the obligation to challenge the ineffectiveness that is continuously reinforced in schools by replacing the view of supervision as controlling the work of teachers with a professional view of supervision as facilitating the decision-making capabilities of teachers. Although supervisors may initially work with teachers in a directive and controlling manner, their goal is to gradually reduce the need among teachers for such structure according to the experience and expertise of the teacher.

Essentially, Glickman believes that direct, one-to-one work with teachers around the issues of teaching, learning goals, and planning for improvement, will help create an environment of thoughtfulness for teachers and their students. Supervisors should provide teachers with time and structures that permit them to think about and plan instructional changes. Beyond time, teachers should be given greater responsibility and choice for making their own decisions about classroom improvements. The impact of the one-room school house tradition – overwhelming beginner responsibilities, an unstaged career, psychological overload, routine, and isolation – can thereby be reduced. Furthermore, new norms that encourage adult dialogue and collective action for the benefit of students can be introduced.

Teacher Development

At the heart of the developmental model of clinical supervision, according to Glickman, are several principles of human development:

1) humans are capable of passing through common stages of development;

2) the stages are ordered in a given sequence of progression from one to another;

3) individuals vary in the rate at which they pass from one stage to the next; and

4) stages of development vary within the same adult depending on the topic or domain under consideration.

Numerous studies suggest that continued cognitive, moral, conceptual, and personality development is possible during the adult years. Generally, human development follows a path from simple and concrete thinking to complex and abstract mental processes, from concerns that are egotistical to concerns that are altruistic. Knowledge of developmental theory and research can be useful to instructional supervisors, Glickman proposes, in selecting appropriate strategies when working with teachers of varying levels of development. After identifying the current level of mental functioning, he suggests, a supervisor can gradually introduce new information that teachers can act upon as individuals or as members of groups when they attempt to improve instruction.

The act of teaching, Glickman notes, is very complex. The number and diversity of students encountered, and the variety of responses required from teachers necessitate complex and abstract thinking in order to be done well. Without appropriate support, teachers who cannot cope with the complexity of teaching develop routines that simplify the richness of classroom reality for students and treat students as if they were all the same. In order to improve, teachers have to generate new behavioral responses in the classroom. But first, they must learn to think at a higher conceptual level.

Because teachers vary greatly in their personal backgrounds and experiences, the ways they view and relate to themselves and others, and their ability to analyze situations and solve instructional problems, Glickman reasons, they need to be supervised in different ways. Generally, teachers who function at lower levels of development need more structure and direction, while those at higher levels need less structure and more active involvement in decisions. The long-range goal of supervision should be to enhance the professional growth of teachers by guiding them, individually and in groups, toward a capacity for reflective self-direction. Only teachers who are able to think for themselves can teach students to think for themselves.

In his recent writing, Glickman has moved away from a lock-step stage progression of teacher development and toward a more comprehensive conceptualization that includes the influence of context and multiple domains of intellect. For example, highly successful teachers may regress to a concrete and imitative operational level when faced with having to teach a new subject area of which they have little knowledge or a grade level with which they have no experience. Teachers' levels of commitment may vary as well depending on the subject area or grade level they are responsible for teaching.

Essentially, this means that teacher development should be considered in a more relative sense. A change in assignment, expectations, or clientele can result in a formerly successful teacher floundering for a time at an early survival stage. Instead of viewing teacher development as a linear and irreversible succession of plateaus, Glickman suggests that supervisors use developmental stages as "lenses" so that they may better view, understand, and assist teachers as individuals.

On the basis of this reasoning, Glickman concludes that supervisors should promote teacher thinking as a way of achieving school effectiveness. Teachers need an environment that simultaneously stimulates and supports their mental and psychological functioning. This can be accomplished most directly by introducing opportunities for teachers to receive feedback, and to observe and interact with each other regularly.

Levels of Abstraction

Glickman defines abstract thinking as a capacity for comparing and contrasting information and experience to generate multiple choices when making a decision. The rationale behind developmental supervision is that by introducing teachers to novel or unfamiliar information and experiences, supervisors can help teachers to think at more abstract levels. He proposes three levels of abstract thought: low, moderate, and high.

Teachers who exhibit lower levels of abstract thinking, according to Glickman, usually have difficulty making rational decisions. Complex situations confuse them and they prefer to be shown how to do things. They fail to see relationships between their own behavior and that of students, and they respond to problems with habitual patterns or impulsive actions. They also tend to blame others for problems. When confronted with instructional difficulties such teachers lack ideas about what can be done and depend on authorities or experts for advice.

Teachers who display a moderate level of abstract thinking recognize that a change in their own behavior is necessary for improvement to occur, but find it difficult to generate alternatives, decide what specific actions are appropriate, and predict the possible consequences of those actions. Because they define the problem poorly to begin with, their actions often are not successful. When faced with a problem these teachers tend to focus on a single dimension at a time. They need assistance from those in authority to plan implementation strategies and weigh the consequences of alternative actions.

Teachers who are capable of higher levels of abstract thought approach and solve problems rationally. They consider information from multiple sources and rely on their own knowledge and experience to accomplish change in their classrooms. These teachers think through a problem by considering its various facets, they identify numerous possible solutions, and anticipate the likely consequences of these responses before they take any action. Highly abstract teachers visualize and verbalize the consequences of their actions easily and are capable of accomplishing change successfully without assistance from a supervisor.

Glickman cites a number of studies which indicate that teachers who function at higher levels of cognitive development are more adaptive, flexible, and tolerant in their teaching styles. Teachers who exhibit higher stages of conceptual and ego development also tend to be less nurturant, more cooperative, and more involved with their work. Further, they address students' needs when planning and evaluating instruction, use a broader range of teaching techniques, ask more precise questions, encourage group involvement, stimulate more positive student attitudes and achievement, and are less susceptible to stress. Finally, teachers at higher levels of conceptual development are also more reflective and self-analytical, hold more complex educational philosophies, relate to students by taking the child's perspective, generate and use a variety of data when making decisions about teaching, and understand rules and authority in more complex ways.

Teacher Concerns

A second major dimension of teacher development is that of teacher concerns, which is related in part to experience. Inexperienced teachers, several studies suggest, are primarily concerned with their own survival on the job. They are very sensitive to how principals, supervisors, and other teachers judge their performance, and they are uncertain about their personal adequacy. In contrast, superior experienced teachers are primarily concerned with student progress and measure their own success against personal standards.

Three levels of concern or motivation are suggested that also follow a developmental sequence. Early in a teacher's career, Glickman observes, egocentric concerns predominate. Novices are insecure, fearful, and preoccupied with proving their adequacy to others. They eagerly seek and cling to whatever seems to work. As teachers achieve some success and become more secure, they focus less on their own needs and begin to adapt their methods and materials in order to improve their instructional technique. They tend, however, to be conventional and conform to group norms and expectations. Their concern for students is limited to the learning needs of the class as a group. Finally, those superior teachers at the highest level of development are motivated by an altruistic interest in individual students. Their actions are autonomous and based on clear personal principles, yet they are eager to help other teachers in the interest of the school and the profession as a whole.

Ideally, teachers are (a) highly committed to students' needs and (b) possess the cognitive capacity to address those needs effectively through their instruction. Because the majority of teachers have not achieved this ideal, Glickman suggests that diagnosing a teacher's level of motivation and cognitive ability is an important first step in the supervisory process. This is best accomplished by listening to teachers' verbal responses and observing their behavior over time. The specific strategy a supervisor employs will then differ depending on the developmental characteristics of the teacher.

By combining the three levels of abstract thinking with the three levels of motivation, Glickman originally suggested that nine developmental teacher types are possible. More recently, however, he has cautioned supervisors against categorizing teachers according to a single stage of development. Rather, supervisors should be cognizant of how the same teacher might be highly abstract in some areas of teaching and low in others. Similarly, a teacher might be highly committed to improve certain aspects of teaching and not stongly committed to others.

In summary, Glickman proposes that individual teachers have unique developmental needs and therefore should not be treated as if they are all the same. Supervisors ought to respond to teachers differently depending on each teacher's motivational level, cognitive abilities, and experience. Responsibilities of novices should be increased gradually to maintain initial enthusiasm. Late in teachers' careers, responsibilities should be reduced to enable them to fulfill broader professional goals.

Supervisory Approaches

Glickman identifies three behavioral approaches that are available to supervisors when working with teachers: directive, collaborative, and nondirective. These three approaches form a continuum ranging from greater teacher control to greater supervisor control. Glickman recommends that supervisors use a supervisory approach that best suits each teacher's particular level of development. A simplified version of the relationship he proposes between teachers' stages of development and various supervisory responses is presented in *Figure 9.1* below.

Each of the supervisory approaches recommended by Glickman is comprised of a different mix of behaviors. A nondirective supervisory approach involves, for example, listening, clarifying, encouraging, and reflecting teachers' thoughts and perceptions. It is intended to help and encourage teachers to make decisions on their own. A collaborative supervisory approach may include nondirective behaviors, but also involves presenting information, problem-solving, and negotiating a resolution. The directive control approach is characterized by giving directions, establishing standards, and reinforcing consequences.

Recently, Glickman (1990) has proposed a fourth approach which he terms "directive informational." With this approach the supervisor represents the primary source of information but asks for and considers teacher feedback while allowing the teacher to choose from a range of alternative actions. More specific information about each of these approaches and how they are used is presented a little later in this chapter.

Stages of Teacher Development	Low	Moderate	High
Teacher's Concerns at Each Stage	Self Adequacy	One's own classroom	Students and other teachers
Recommended Supervisory Approaches for Each Stage	Directive	Collaborative	Nondirective
Examples of Supervisor Behaviors for Each Stage	Modeling, directing, and measuring.	Presenting, interacting, and contracting.	Listening, clarifying, and encouraging.
Direction of Development			⟶

Figure 9.1
GLICKMAN'S STAGES OF TEACHER DEVELOPMENT
AND RECOMMENDED SUPERVISOR RESPONSES

The Developmental/Clinical Model

Direct assistance to teachers is defined by Glickman as an attempt to provide formative feedback to teachers for the purpose of helping them improve their instruction. He suggests that the stages of clinical supervision are an especially useful vehicle for doing so when combined with his developmental approach. Five steps are described by Glickman as follows:

Step 1: Preconference

During the preconference the teacher and supervisor meet to determine the reason and purpose for conducting an observation, decide upon a focus for the observation, agree upon the type of data to be collected, and schedule the observation and postconference.

Step 2: Observation

The supervisor visits the classroom of the teacher during a lesson and describes what is seen and heard in the classroom using an observation technique or instrument appropriate to the purpose determined in the previous step. Narratives, frequency counts, interaction analyses, and checklists are examples. Such techniques and instruments help the supervisor eliminate confusion by clarifying what is actually happening in a classroom.

A description of events that occur in a classroom offers an opportunity for discussion and improvement, Glickman notes, while an interpretation often results in resistance from the teacher. Agreement on the events that occurred during a lesson is important, therefore, because it increases the chances that the teacher will agree to changes that are needed.

Step 3: Analysis, Interpretation, and Strategy

During this step, which includes three distinct components, the supervisor begins analyzing the data by counting frequencies of behavior, identifying recurrent patterns, or determining the presence or absence of certain behaviors in the classroom. After making some sense of the descriptive data the supervisor next makes interpretations and decides what is desirable and undesirable about what was seen and heard in the classroom. Judgments are made at this point concerning the effectiveness of the teacher's behaviors in influencing students. The third component of this step involves the supervisor deciding whether to use a directive, collaborative, or nondirective approach in the postconference. This process, which will be explained in detail later, is absolutely central to the developmental model.

Step 4: Postconference

In this step, the supervisor's analysis of the observation data is shared with the teacher and a plan to improve instruction is developed. Responsibility for the plan can rest with the supervisor, the teacher, or both, depending on the interpersonal approach selected and used by the supervisor. The plan should include at a minimum, an objective for the next observation, activities to be practiced by the teacher in order to accomplish the objectives, human and material resources needed, and a date and time for the next preconference.

Step 5: Critique

Either at the end of the postconference or in a separate conference, the supervisor and teacher discuss what was most valuable and least valuable about the clinical cycle and what revisions are necessary before it is repeated.

The nondirective, collaborative, directive informational, and directive control approaches to supervision that were introduced earlier lie along a continuum ranging from greater teacher control to greater supervisor control. To combine them effectively with the version of clinical supervison described above requires a more detailed understanding of each. A summary follows of the four approaches and how they are applied.

The Nondirective Approach

According to Glickman, a nondirective supervisory approach is considered appropriate given certain conditions: when teachers possess more knowledge and expertise about an issue than the supervisor, when teachers are primarily responsible for carrying out the decision that will be made, or when the supervisor is not particularly concerned about the problem at hand.

Nondirective supervisory conferences vary in terms of the specific sequence of behaviors they exhibit, but an autonomous decision by the teacher should always be the outcome. A pattern typical of a nondirective conference is as follows:

- Listen attentively to the teacher's description of the problem.
- Verbally reflect your initial understanding of the teacher's perspective.
- Clarify understanding by probing for additional information
- Without being judgmental, verbally encourage the teacher to continue.
- Continue reflecting through repeated paraphrasing of the teacher's message.
- Ask the teacher to identify possible actions that might solve the problem.
- Ask the teacher to predict the consequences of the various actions that have been suggested.
- Present an opportunity for the teacher to make a commitment to a particular decision.
- Standardize by asking the teacher to select criteria and establish a timeframe for evaluating success.
- Reflect by restating the teacher's action plan.

The Collaborative Approach

A collaborative supervisory approach is most likely to be successful when used with experienced teachers who function at higher levels of development. It is especially appropriate, Glickman believes, in the following situations: when the supervisor and teacher have similar levels of expertise or when it is necessary to pool information about an issue, when both the teacher and supervisor will be involved in enacting a decision or held accountable for its results, and, when both the teacher and supervisor care deeply about a problem, or if leaving the teacher out of the decision would lead to distrust or lower morale.

Collaborative supervisory conferences also vary in the particular pattern of behaviors they evidence, depending on the specific situation and teacher. Although a frank and open exchange of ideas may lead to conflict between the teacher and supervisor, the intended outcome of a collaborative conference is final agreement through negotiation. A common sequence is as follows:

- Clarify the nature of the problem by asking the teacher to state his or her perception of the situation.

- Listen attentively to the teacher's understanding of the problem.
- Reflect the teacher's perception by verbally summarizing what has been said and then checking for accuracy.
- Present your point of view about the area of difficulty and share any additional information that may not be available to the teacher.
- Clarify by asking the teacher to paraphrase your perspective accurately.
- Exchange ideas concerning possible actions or solutions.
- Encourage the acceptance of disagreement as essential to successful problem-solving.
- Identify a possible solution to the problem by considering where agreements and disagreements lie and being willing to compromise.
- Agree on details of a plan that establishes standards concerning who will be responsible for enacting a solution, exactly what will be done, when, and where.
- Negotiate a final plan of action by checking for agreement on details.

The Directive Informational Approach

The directive informational approach is recommended by Glickman for situations when teachers are inexperienced, confused, lack knowledge, or are simply at a loss for ideas concerning viable goals and strategies. It may also be used when time is short, constraints are clear, and specific actions are needed quickly. Two important assumptions underly this approach: First, the supervisor's knowledge and experience are superior to that of the teacher; and, second, the teacher believes that the supervisor does in fact possess wisdom that he himself lacks. While the teacher exercises a degree of control with this approach, the supervisor is ultimately responsible for the success or failure of the strategies he recommends.

In applying the directive informational approach, the supervisor determines through observation a preferred classroom goal for the teacher to pursue. After seeking and considering the teacher's perceptions the supervisor suggests a range of activities that he believes have a high probability of success. The teacher then chooses the alternatives he prefers and with the supervisor's involvement specifically describes when and how changes will be implemented, along with some criteria for determining success. Finally, the supervisor reinforces the teacher's understanding by repeating what has been agreed upon. An illustrative application of the directive informational approach is as follows:

- Present a summary and interpretation of the data gathered during the observation along with a goal for the teacher to pursue.
- Clarify by asking for the teacher's perceptions of the interpretations and goal.
- Listen carefully to understand the teacher's perspective and to determine whether the teacher accepts the goal, or if further explanation is needed.
- Solve the problem yourself by mentally considering alternatives the teacher might try based on your own experience and knowledge.
- Direct the teacher's actions by presenting alternatives for the teacher to consider.
- Listen for ideas and reactions from the teacher so that alternatives can be revised, modified, or eliminated.
- Direct the teacher's actions by defining the alternatives that remain.
- Clarify by asking the teacher to decide which activities he or she will apply.
- Standardize by guiding the teacher to develop more specifically the actions to be taken and the criteria for measuring success.
- Reinforce the teacher's decision by restating the goal, the actions the teacher will take, the criteria for success, and agreeing on a time for the next observation or conference.

The Directive Control Approach

A directive control approach is characterized by frank and precise language on the part of the supervisor. Directive control behaviors are recommended given certain circumstances: when the supervisor has more knowledge concerning an issue or problem than the teacher, when the supervisor will be primarily involved in implementing the decision or is totally accountable for its outcomes, when the supervisor cares a great deal about an issue or decision and the teacher does not, or in emergencies when insufficient time is available to hold a meeting with teachers.

Evidence suggests that directive control behaviors from supervisors are preferred by many inexperienced teachers who seek quick solutions to immediate problems. A directive conference culminates with the supervisor making decisions for the teacher or suggesting a course of action that the teacher should consider. A directive control conference may unfold as follows:

- Identify the problem by listening, observing, and gathering information before confronting the teacher with the situation.
- Clarify the problem by asking the teacher for input.
- Listen attentively in order to understand the teacher's overt and underlying messages.
- Determine the best solution to the problem by mentally considering alternative courses of action and making a selection.
- Tell the teacher directly what your expectations are.
- Clarify by allowing the teacher to have some input into how the expectations will be met.
- Establish standards by detailing and modifying the directive based on the teacher's input.
- Reinforce the teacher's understanding by repeating the entire plan, including times when progress will be reviewed, and then checking the teacher's understanding.

Applying the Four Approaches

According to Glickman, very few teachers display the very highest and lowest levels of reasoning and concerns. Most teachers, he suggests, operate somewhere in the middle ranges. However, abstraction and motivation can vary considerably from one situation to another, Glickman believes, so selecting the correct supervisory approach is no simple matter. Faced with a new school and different students, for example, an experienced and successful teacher may regress to an earlier stage of self-survival. Also, an individual may display higher levels of cognitive and motivational development in one area of responsibility and lower levels in another.

A number of factors enter into selecting the proper supervisory approach to use with a teacher or group of teachers. For one thing, the supervisor should be aware of whether his intention is to share information or control the situation (Pajak & Glickman, 1989). When the supervisor's purpose is to control and limit the teacher's choices, terms such as "must," "will," "should," and "have to" are useful for ensuring clarity. On the other hand, if the supervisor wishes to encourage the teacher to think through a problem and make an informed choice, the supervisor will be more likely to succeed using less harsh language such as "may," "could," "can," and "might." The amount of information shared with the teacher varies, however, depending on the teacher's problem-solving expertise and competence.

Glickman advises that directive control be reserved for working with inexperienced teachers at the survival stage and for emergency situations. Directive information, along with collaborative and nondirective approaches are used otherwise, according to the teacher's expertise and competence. Expertise is the knowledge a teacher acquires through training and experience that is related to improving instruction. Competence refers to the skill with which desired learning outcomes are actually achieved.

Evaluation and Peer Supervision

Direct assistance works best, according to Glickman, if it is unrelated to the summative evaluation of teachers for purposes of contract renewal. He believes it is possible, however, for one person to fill the roles of both helper and evaluator. Supervisors must work especially hard at maintaining trust and credibility in such situations. They must convince the teacher that their primary interest is that of helping to improve instruction, and not whether the teacher measures up to some standard of acceptable performance.

Peer supervision, Glickman points out, has numerous advantages. For one, teachers usually turn more readily to other teachers for advice and assistance. This may be because the threat of summative evaluation does not exist with colleagues. Another advantage of peer supervision is that the time and energy required by direct assistance can be shared within a group. Participation in peer supervision should be voluntary if possible to ensure high commitment. Though it is most expedient to have teachers pair off with someone with whom they want to work, under ideal conditions each teacher is matched with someone of a slightly higher or lower level of development. Teachers who are less highly developed are expected to be challenged and motivated by their association with more highly developed colleagues. The mixed thought processes that result should be a stimulant for both.

Peer supervision changes the nature of the role of supervisor in important ways. The supervisor becomes more involved in providing training for teachers, coordinating schedules of observations and conferences, hiring substitutes, and trouble-shooting minor problems that arise. With peer supervision, the supervisor is nevertheless always available as a resource to teachers – providing material, ideas, and encouragement – and periodically checking on progress.

Other Applications

Direct assistance through clinical supervision is only one way that supervisors can contribute to teacher development. Glickman suggests that the diagnosis of teachers' motivation and capacity for abstract thinking is important as well in the processes of group work in relation to curriculum development, inservice training, and action research.

As with the direct assistance component, a supervisor's responsiblities when working with groups involve several phases. The first phase is *diagnostic* in that the supervisor must initially assess the current level at which a group is functioning with respect to an instructional or curricular concern. The level of cognitive abstraction exhibited by teachers is a central determinant of the diagnosis. Abstraction is a capacity for forming multiple orientations toward one's environment, including interpersonal relationships. Thus, teachers operating at lower levels of abstraction are less able than teachers who think more abstractly to identify instructional and curricular difficulties and generate alternative solutions.

Supervisors are expected to diagnose levels of abstraction by talking with teachers, observing them in action, and asking them questions about the instructional problems they perceive and ideas for possible solutions. The degree of flexibility and adaptability displayed by a teacher in the classroom, Glickman advises, is another good indicator of level of abstraction. Teachers who rely on habitual routines or random and erratic behaviors when faced with difficulties are probably functioning at lower levels. Teachers at higher levels can change course in midstream when a problem arises, and abandon behaviors that are unsuccessful in favor of others that work. They are also able to justify the new behaviors with a sound rationale.

The second phase is *tactical*. In order to help meet a need or solve a problem, the supervisor matches the appropriate supervisory approach with the teachers' level of abstraction. Groups of teachers at lower levels of abstraction need more information, advice, structure, and alternatives presented to them by the supervisor. Groups at higher levels are merely encouraged to identify problems, generate ideas for addressing those problems, creating action plans, and following through on decisions made.

The third phase of the developmental model as applied to groups is *strategic* in that this is where the developmental goal of increasing teacher abstraction, problem-solving ability, and self-direction becomes operative. The supervisor enacts this phase by gradually introducing new ideas and information to teachers about students, instructional methods, and techniques for solving problems. Over a period of time the supervisor also diminishes the degree of direction and structure he provides while increasing the teachers' responsibility for making decisions. Finally, teachers who function at higher levels of development can influence their lower level colleagues simply by working with them on instructional improvement efforts.

Curriculum Development

When working with teachers in the area of curriculum development, Glickman recommends that supervisors assess the faculty's current knowledge and skills by reviewing such things as their academic preparation, curriculum training, and previous experience on curriculum committees, along with current use of curriculum guides and level of motivation and abstraction as revealed in discussions about curriculum. On the basis of such data, supervisors diagnose the current level of development of the teachers and respond accordingly. Three curriculum development approaches (Tanner and Tanner, 1980) are proposed.

If the majority of the teachers is judged to be functioning at lower levels of commitment and abstraction, Glickman recommends the adoption of an *imitative* curriculum. This curriculum is externally developed and prescribes for teachers what they will teach, when, and how, as well as standards of performance. The curriculum, for these teachers, is to be implemented and not thought about.

When the majority of teachers is determined to be operating at a moderate level of development, a *mediative* curriculum model is recommended. Teachers who function at a moderate level of commitment and abstraction need an established structure to guide their efforts, but are capable of making improvements on a finished product. A mediative curriculum is one that is externally developed, but adapted and modified by the teachers to suit local conditions. Topics, activities, and sequences are changed by the teachers to match the needs of their students.

A *generative* curriculum is suggested by Glickman for teachers who operate at higher levels of abstract thinking and commitment. Beginning with writing objectives for students, teachers develop their own curriculum, search out appropriate texts and resources, and create their own activities and materials according to this last model.

Teacher thought is promoted in curriculum development in two ways. First, teachers acquire knowledge and skills during the process of developing a curriculum related to content, scope, sequence, goals, objectives, resources, evaluation techniques, and curriculum formats. Second, teachers at lower levels of development are expected to learn and grow from their interaction with more highly developed colleagues. Greater opportunities for curriculum generation can be provided as the faculty group grows in experience and insight.

Inservice Training

Supervisors may also extend teachers' thinking, Glickman suggests, when training teachers in groups. In this case, the supervisor is careful to assess teachers' levels of concern (Hall & Loucks, 1978) with respect to the innovation being introduced. Teachers at the lowest level have what are termed *orientation* concerns. These teachers want basic information about the innovation and convincing reasons for adopting it. More time is spent during the inservice session, therefore, on lecturing, explaining how other teachers have found the innovation useful, and demonstrating how the new skills are used.

Teachers at a moderate level possess what are called *integration* concerns. These teachers already know something about the new ideas and are interested in learning more, especially about how to go about introducing them in their classrooms. Training for these teachers should include demonstration of how skills are used along with role playing and feedback within a workshop setting, and classroom application with feedback from the trainer.

The highest level of teacher concern is called *refinement* and characterizes teachers who are already using an innovation, but want to know how to become better at applying it. Since these teachers are already familiar with the skills and activities involved, inservice concentrates on classroom observation and feedback from the trainer followed by peer discussion, observation, and feedback. The emphasis here is on encouraging teachers to help improve, strengthen, and reinforce one another's efforts.

Glickman recommends that in most districts inservice should include a general orientation session for all teachers in a district that provides an overview of the innovation to be implemented. A range of inservice activities can then be provided from which individuals or groups can choose. These activities might include additional lectures and explanation, films and readings, practice and feedback in workshops, watching teachers who are already using the new technique, practice and feedback in the classroom, and peer observations and discussion groups. A range of activities allows teachers to proceed at their own pace. Teachers who are already at the refinement level of concern can be drawn upon as resources for training their less experienced colleagues.

Action Research and Group Development

Teacher development may be facilitated by helping teachers solve instructional problems rationally. A supervisor can guide individuals and groups to identify instructional problems, to gather information relevant to these problems, to propose changes that might solve the problems, to implement these changes, and to judge the success of their efforts. Glickman recommends that teachers be encouraged to take responsibility for finding solutions to real problems that exist in their classrooms, departments, grade levels, or schools.

The supervisor's task in action research is to provide teachers with information concerning both problem-solving and group process skills. More structure is provided by the supervisor as decisions are made and plans formulated early in a group's existence. As teachers acquire skill and experience in solving problems rationally and working in groups, they assume more responsibility for their own progress. By gradually increasing the choices available to individuals and groups, supervisors can develop teachers' thought, autonomy, and capacity for collective action.

When working with inexperienced groups whose members function at lower levels of abstraction, Glickman suggests that the supervisor initially control group process and limit the range of decisions the group can make. The supervisor identifies the problem for the group, and then presents alternative solutions along with the advantages and drawbacks of each alternative. The group decides only which alternative to use.

Teachers operating at moderate or mixed levels of experience and abstraction are allowed to make decisions with the supervisor acting as a facilitator of group process. A data *discussion approach* is applied with the supervisor collecting data from the group, organizing the information in a meaningful way, and presenting the organized findings to the group. The group then discusses the supervisor's analysis, decides if change is necessary or desirable, and chooses an appropriate course of action.

Finally, a *group problem-solving approach* is recommended when a group of teachers is experienced and exhibits a high level of abstract reasoning ability. The supervisor functions as a member of the group and allows the group to develop its own leadership structure. The group members have primary responsibility for identifying problems, generating and analyzing data, and deciding on needed changes.

Some studies of teacher effectiveness suggest that knowledge is best applied to classroom problems through a process of rational decision-making. On the basis of this evidence Glickman proposes a conventional five-stage sequence for solving problems:

a)   becoming aware of the problem;
b)   identifying possible causes of the problem;
c)   suggesting alternative solutions;
d)   selecting a solution; and
e)   assessing outcomes.

By helping members of less abstract groups gradually assume more responsibility for problem-solving, decision-making, and group process skills, the supervisor can contribute to their development. Teachers can be positively influenced as well by associating with groups and individuals within groups who already operate at higher levels of development. Ultimately, the supervisor's goal is to get all groups to function at the group problem-solving level independently, though the supervisor may occasionally facilitate decision-making with nondirective interpersonal interventions.

Summary

Glickman proposes that supervisors ought to encourage teachers to invest time and energy in school-wide concerns outside their own class-rooms, and challenge teachers to think more abstractly about their teaching. In his view, a number of characteristics of the teaching profession, the work environment of schools, the people who have traditionally sought careers in teaching, and prevailing conceptions of supervision have unfortunately made schools less effective than they might be.

Drawing on research and theory in areas including adult develop-ment, cognitive and moral development, and motivation, Glickman proposes three levels of teacher development – low, moderate, and high. He suggests that supervisors should attempt to match the ap-proach they use with each teacher's particular developmental level. Generally, he recommends a directive supervisory approach with teachers who function at lower levels of cognition and commitment, a collaborative approach with teachers who function at moderate levels, and a nondirective supervisory approach with those teachers who function at relatively high levels of cognition and commitment.

Glickman combines his developmental model with the clinical su-pervision cycle. Following classroom observation, the supervisor makes an informal assessment concerning the teacher's developmental level. He or she then plans a conference that provides an amount of structure and control judged appropriate for the perceived developmental needs of the teacher. Over time, the supervisor uses less controlling ap-proaches, and increases responsibility on the part of the teacher.

Clinical supervision works best, according to Glickman, if it is unrelated to summative evaluation. However, he believes that it is possible for one person to fill the roles of both evaluator and helper. Glickman also suggests that peer supervision can be productive, with the supervisor matching stronger teachers with weaker ones and then providing materials, ideas, and encouragement as they work together.

Other applications of the developmental model include curriculum development, inservice training, and action research. In these cases the supervisor works with groups of teachers and applies a three step method. The first phase involves an assessment by the supervisor of the level at which the group is functioning relative to an instructional or curricular concern. In the second phase the supervisor matches the directness of his or her approach with the perceived developmental level of the group. In the final phase, the supervisor gradually introduces new ideas and information while reducing direction and structure in order to help the group assume more responsibility for making decisions and acting upon them.

References

Glickman, C. D. (1980). The developmental approach to supervision. *Educational Leadership, 38* (2), 178-180.

Glickman, C. D. (1981). *Developmental supervision: Alternative approaches for helping teachers improve instruction.* Alexandria, VA: Association for Supervision and Curriculum Development.

Glickman, C. D. (1985). *Supervision of instruction: A developmental approach.* Boston: Allyn and Bacon.

Glickman, C. D. (1986). Developing teacher thought. *The Journal of Staff Development, 7* (1), 6-21.

Glickman, C. D. & Gordon, S. P. (1987). Clarifying developmental supervision. *Educational Leadership, 44* (8), 64-68.

Greiner, L. E. (1967). Patterns of organizational change. *Harvard Business Review, 45,* 119-130.

Hall, G. E. & Loucks, S. (1978). Teacher concerns as a basis for facilitating and personalizing staff development. *Teachers College Record, 80,* (September), 36-53.

Harvey, O. J., Hunt, D. E., & Schroder, H. M. (1961). *Conceptual systems and personality organization.* New York: Wiley.

Hunt, D. E. (1970). A conceptual level matching model for coordinating learner characteristics with educational approaches. *Interchange: A Journal of Educational Studies, 1* (2) 4.

Pajak, E. & Glickman, C. (1989). Informational and controlling language in simulated supervisory conferences. *American Educational Research Journal, 26* (1), 93-106.

Schroder, H. M., Driver, M. J., & Streufert, S. (1967). *Human information processing.* New York: Holt, Rinehart & Winston.

Tanner, D. & Tanner, L. N. (1980). *Curriculum development: Theory into practice.* (2nd edition). New York: MacMillan.

Chapter 10

Costa and Garmston's Cognitive Coaching Model

The Model at Work

Mrs. Rogers was pleased to congratulate Mr. Brown on his being awarded tenure, though she never doubted that he would make it. In fact, Mrs. Rogers rarely worried about the capabilities of beginning teachers. The colleges and universities were doing a better job than ever, she thought, at preparing graduates for the realities of classrooms and schools.

Fifteen years ago, or even farther back when she began teaching, Mrs. Rogers remembered that novice teachers were often naive about real life outside of schools. Although they had a missionary-like zeal, many had lacked the instructional skills and knowledge of subject matter to put their values into practice successfully. Beginning teachers today were more experienced, had a broader view of society, and approached their work in a more rational way.

Mrs. Rogers was convinced that many supervisors made a serious mistake of underestimating the intelligence and capability of teachers. She viewed teaching and learning as intellectual work and strongly objected to the exclusive focus on student and teacher behaviors that had become popular in recent years. Mrs. Rogers preferred to concentrate on cultivating teachers' inner thought processes to help them make better decisions in their classrooms. She understood that good teaching was complex. Instead of installing and reinforcing new behaviors, Mrs. Rogers aimed to expand the understanding and autonomy of every teacher with whom she worked.

Mr. Brown was obviously very anxious the first time they met shortly after he was hired three years ago. His posture and gestures were stiff, his breathing irregular, and the pitch of his voice was a little higher than usual. Mrs. Rogers spent most of that initial meeting trying to gain his trust and reduce the threat of supervision by listening carefully, paraphrasing his ideas, and reflecting feelings he expressed. She paid close attention to the metaphors he used and the concerns he expressed. She tried to communicate to him in ways that made sense to his way of viewing and thinking about teaching. Her aim at that point was to build his personal confidence and sense of self-esteem. Building his knowledge of teaching and capacity for greater empathy with students, however, would soon follow.

Once trust was established between them, Mrs. Rogers began to help Mr. Brown with the planning of instruction and teaching toward a goal. She told him to describe in specific detail the outcomes he wanted to achieve. "What is it, exactly, that you'll be doing?," she asked, and "What, specifically, will students be doing?" Next, they carefully considered the characteristics of the students in his class. Finally, they developed a plan together by which Mr. Brown could achieve the outcomes he wanted, and included alternatives if the lesson had to be redirected in progress. Although his ideas differed somewhat from her way of thinking, Mrs. Rogers recognized that Mr. Brown had to feel that the plan was his if it was going to work at all.

During the next two years Mrs. Rogers helped Mr. Brown explore and define his personal beliefs about teaching. They also worked on developing skills and teaching strategies with an emphasis on problem solving and decision making. Mrs. Rogers used a variety of data gathering techniques to record events in the classes she observed. Because she made a concerted effort to understand Mr. Brown's intentions and perspective, she was able to draw his *attention to discrepancies between what he wanted to happen and what actually did occur in the classroom. Together, they hypothesized relationships, generated more data, and drew conclusions about how he could improve still further.*

Eventually, Mr. Brown became very skilled at monitoring the sequence of events that unfolded in his classroom. He attended closely to behavioral cues that indicated student readiness and motivation, he asked students questions to get more information, he restrained his own impulsive reactions to student behavior, and he consciously selected appropriate responses from a growing repertoire of strategies. During conferences, Mr. Brown exhibited greater confidence and assumed more responsibility for student learning outcomes. He was willing and able to think about his teaching, to criticize it, and develop ways to improve it on his own. Most recently, he began teaching his students to consciously monitor their own thinking to help improve their study skills.

Introduction

A greater proportion of teachers in the United States today, Arthur Costa and Robert Garmston assert, are better educated, have advanced academic degrees, and have more extensive classroom experience than ever before in history. Most teachers are, in other words, mature, rational, and dedicated professionals. Supervision in schools, it follows, should be made suitable for this capable and intelligent clientele. Costa and Garmston view the act of teaching as the result of a constant stream of consciously and unconsciously made decisions, and they believe that supervisors ought to focus primarily on the task of helping teachers make better decisions about instruction.

Costa and Garmston advocate a model of supervision called "cognitive coaching" that they contend can make schools more growth inducing and intellectually stimulating for teachers, supervisors, administrators, and students. Cognitive coaching is based on four assumptions:

1. that all behavior is determined and influenced by our perceptions;
2. teaching *is* decision making: before, during and after instruction;
3. to change behavior requires an alteration or transformation of the mind, and;
4. human beings can continue to grow in their intellectual abilities throughout their lifetimes.

Cognitive coaching, therefore, is a process of mediating, nurturing, and enhancing the intellectual functions, perceptions, and decision making processes of teaching. With cognitive coaching, the supervisor applies a set of strategies that are intended to enhance the perceptions, decisions, and intellectual functions of teachers. Improving these inner thought processes of teachers, Costa and Garmston believe, is prerequisite to the improvement of overt behaviors in the classroom that result in increased student learning. This chain of events may be depicted as follows:

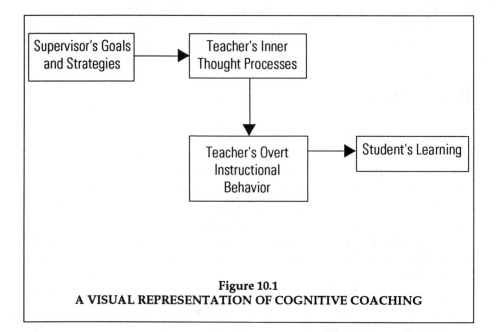

Figure 10.1
A VISUAL REPRESENTATION OF COGNITIVE COACHING

Costa and Garmston question the value of educational research that is focused on the identification of discrete effective teaching behaviors that supposedly correlate with student achievement. They take issue as well with supervisory practices that emphasize the observation, recording, and reinforcement of those behaviors to the exclusion of the cognitive processes that are the basis of good teaching. The important decisions that a teacher makes concerning when to ask questions and which questions to ask, Costa and Garmston emphasize, may be overlooked entirely when a supervisor simply counts the number of higher-level questions that are observed. Issues such as whether the questions were appropriate at that time for that particular group of students may be more crucial than simply the number that was asked.

Costa and Garmston base their thinking on a growing body of research that conceptualizes teaching as an intellectual, decision making process. They agree fundamentally with Shavelson's (1973) hypothesis:

> Any teaching act is the result of a decision, whether conscious
> or unconscious, that the teacher makes after the complex
> cognitive processing of available information. This reasoning
> leads to the hypothesis that the basic teaching skill is decision
> making. (1973, p. 18)

Their view is consistent as well with Joyce and Showers' (1988) more recent observation that the overt, visible skills of teaching are driven by mental activities that comprise "invisible" skills of teaching.

Cognitive coaching is different from models of supervision that attempt to install or extinguish certain teaching behaviors. Supervisors following these other models, Costa and Garmston suggest, focus on instructional behaviors that are associated with student achievement in basic skills and are likely to use conferencing techniques to redirect teachers toward using these specified behaviors.

Cognitive coaching, in contrast, attempts to expand the understanding and autonomy of teachers by appealing to their intelligence and rationality. Costa and Garmston believe that the ultimate purpose of supervision is to modify teachers' capacities to modify themselves. Superior teachers, the authors believe, consciously select certain teaching behaviors from a range of approaches at their disposal. Such teachers decide which behaviors to use on the basis of information about their pupils, an analysis of the teaching task, and an assessment of the instructional situation. Superior teachers also understand how a particular approach fits within a broader strategy and are able to predict the effect behaviors will have on the learning performance of their students. All of these, Costa and Garmston note, are processes of the intellect.

Supervisory Goals and Strategies

The process of cognitive coaching, as described by Costa and Garmston, is directed toward the accomplishment of three interrelated supervisory goals: (1) the creation and management of *trust*, (2) the facilitation of teacher *learning*, and (3) the development of teacher *autonomy*. The strategies and skills used by supervisors in attaining these goals are as follows:

Goal # 1: Trust

According to Costa and Garmston, a trusting relationship is fundamental to the success of supervision and is essential to the attainment of teacher learning and teacher autonomy. Because of its importance, trust should be nurtured and maintained by the supervisor during each interaction with the teacher. An effective supervisory relationship must be long-term (two or more years), Costa and Garmston believe, because the pace of lasting professional growth is necessarily gradual and incremental.

Effective supervisors, according to this model, steadily focus on the end goals of trust, learning, and teacher autonomy. They use each supervisory interaction with a teacher to work toward these goals. In order to maintain rapport, supervisors should be skilled at reading nonverbal cues from the teacher such as posture, breathing, gestures, and tone of voice, and adjust their own behavior appropriately to match these signals. Supervisors should also try to remove as much threat as possible for the teacher by holding conferences in neutral locations, avoiding value judgments, and discussing concerns the teacher may have about evaluation.

Costa and Garmston believe that trust is built over time in a relationship, and that supervisors help to build trust most directly through demonstrations of their own competence, consistency, personal availability, and confidentiality. Supervisors also develop trust through precise, nonjudgmental, and empathic active listening. Important related skills include paraphrasing, clarifying, offering objective and nonjudgmental feedback, and using silence. They also believe that supervisors should be aware of and sensitive to a teacher's preferred style of learning, modality, belief system, and level of concern. The careful guidance of cognitive coaching is intended to help teachers further develop their personal confidence, knowledge, capacity for empathy, and sense of self-esteem.

Goal # 2: Learning

Learning is defined by Costa and Garmston as a rearrangement and restructuring of mental processes. They note that every supervisory conference is an opportunity for both supervisors and teachers to learn more about themselves, each other, the students, and the content of the lesson. Supervisors and teachers can also gain insight into their personal belief systems and understanding of the process of supervision during conferences.

The assumption that teaching essentially involves a series of decisions made before, during, and after instruction, leads Costa and Garmston to conclude that supervision should focus on helping teachers learn how to make better decisions. They identify a series of supervisory behaviors that facilitate this type of learning.

Step One. The first step for the supervisor is to formulate a clear image of the desired long range outcomes of the supervisory relationship. With cognitive coaching the teacher should ultimately acquire intellectual functions that are basic to effective instruction such as planning, teaching toward a goal, self-analysis, and learning from experience.

Step Two. The next step involves asking the teacher to describe in specific detail the elements that comprise his or her image of desired classroom outcomes. The supervisor may elicit from the teacher descriptions of desired student behavior or help to develop observable indicators of, for example, "enthusiasm among primary grade children."

Step Three. Finally, the supervisor and teacher develop a map or plan for achieving the desired outcomes. Strategies for facilitating movement by the teacher from the existing state to the desired state are designed. Possible barriers and alternative approaches are also identified.

Costa and Garmston believe that the outcomes envisioned by the supervisor cannot diverge greatly from what they term the *positive intentions* of the teacher's present behaviors. They suggest that the supervisor's plans, in other words, must be consistent with the teacher's beliefs and purposes or the teacher will unconsciously subvert the process. A supervisor is more likely to succeed by helping a teacher to consciously understand his or her own beliefs, purposes, and preferences and then devise ways of behaving that are consistent with this image. The supervisor assists the teacher in exploring and selecting new behaviors that are more effective, but which are still consistent with the teacher's fundamental positive intentions.

Supervisors need a wide variety of supervisory strategies and approaches to help teachers improve their thinking. Costa and Garmston suggest that these are best used flexibly yet persistently, as behavioral cues exhibited by the teacher change. Questioning strategies, for example, are fundamental to cognitive coaching. Through questioning, supervisors can help teachers clarify and probe inner meanings and intellectual functions. Skillful questioning is also intended to stimulate thinking and contribute to the development of new understandings.

The range and repertoire of choices and strategies that are available to a teacher can be effectively expanded, according to Costa and Garmston, when supervisors diagnose and use the teacher's preferred learning style, and are aware of the teacher's patterns of decision making and inherent motivation. Supervisors can facilitate learning on the part of teachers by helping them identify limitations, omissions, and illogical assumptions in their thinking. This is accomplished by gently and judiciously challenging vague statements that teachers may make, and asking them to be more specific. Several examples suggested by Costa and Garmston follow:

- If a teacher speaks of students generally the supervisor may ask: "Which students?"
- If a teacher says that he or she wants students to behave, the supervisor could ask: "Behave how, specifically?"
- If a teacher suggests that he or she is incapable of doing something, the supervisor might ask: "What is preventing you?"

Goal # 3: Autonomy

Costa and Garmston view the goals of trust and learning as important in themselves, but also consider them as instrumental for developing teacher autonomy. As a result of supervisory interactions over time, they expect teachers to eventually become self-supervising. That is, teachers should internalize and spontaneously apply the thought processes that have been stimulated and refined by cognitive coaching.

Supervisors can promote teacher autonomy, Costa and Garmston argue, by encouraging teachers to engage in "metacognition" or thinking about their thinking. This can be accomplished by bringing to awareness, through discussion and analysis, such things as the teacher's speech patterns and motor skills, values, beliefs, teaching strategies, and approaches to decision making and problem solving. Awareness can also be heightened by helping teachers compare their values and beliefs with those of other teachers, and with values implicit in a variety of curricula and alternative instructional strategies.

Costa and Garmston believe that cognitive coaching will eventually lead teachers to autonomously apply self-analysis, and voluntarily change their behaviors and strategies to improve their performance in the classroom. They define autonomy in terms of five transitory states of mind:

1. efficacy;
2. flexibility;
3. precision;
4. consciousness; and
5. interdependence.

These five states of mind are considered transitory because they are not "fixed" or "static." Rather, all human beings have the capacity for continued development of these five states. But for some reason or reasons - maturational, environmental, emotional, or physiological – a person may function at a "less than" or a "not yet" autonomous state. Costa and Garmston believe that the skillful coach can cause continued growth and assist teachers in becoming "unstuck" at their present state and grow to higher levels of autonomy.

Influencing Teachers' Thought Processes

The second component of Costa and Garmston's cognitive coaching model (see *Figure 10.1*) is the attempt by the supervisor to influence teachers' thought processes. This element seems to represent the heart of the model with respect to supervisory practice.

All individuals make sense of new information, Costa and Garmston note, by trying to fit it within the context of what they already know. Information that conforms to what a teacher already knows about teaching, for example, is assimilated quite readily. Information that is inconsistent with a teacher's understanding of reality, however, must be accommodated with that current understanding in some way.

Supervisors can help teachers process new information by serving as mediators. Supervisors may ask questions to draw the teacher's attention to discrepancies between the learning outcomes that are intended and those that students actually attain, for example, to stimulate teachers' cognitive skills. Supervisors can then make statements and ask questions that help teachers to generate data, hypothesize relationships, and formulate generalizations.

Costa and Garmston suggest that the decisions and intellectual functions of teaching can be clustered into four distinct phases and that teachers and supervisors should attend closely to a sequence of four stages or categories of decisions that affect the quality of teaching: a) the preactive stage; b) the interactive stage; c) the reflective stage; and d) the projective stage. During each of these stages, teachers and supervisors have specific responsibilities. These stages and the responsibilities of the teacher and the supervisor are depicted in *Figure 10.2*:

Stages of Decisions Affecting Teaching	Teacher's Responsibility	Supervisor's Responsibility
Preactive Stage	Planning	Auditing
Interactive Stage	Teaching	Monitoring
Reflective Stage	Analyzing/Evaluating	Validating
Projective Stage	Applying	Consulting

Figure 10.2

The Preactive Stage

The preactive stage includes those decisions that are made by the teacher while planning a lesson. This is referred to as "mental rehearsal" and consists of those intellectual processes that occur prior to teaching. The decisions that take place during planning shape the decisions that are made during the next three stages, so the preactive stage is especially important.

During planning the teacher has sufficient time to consider a wide array of information sources and alternative courses of action. Planning can be conducted during a formal session devoted exclusively to thinking and writing, or informally while the teacher is engaged in some other activity like mowing the lawn or driving to work. In either case, planning is viewed by Costa and Garmston as involving at least four elements:

1. *The Teacher Describes Learning Outcomes in Terms of Explicit and Observable Student Behaviors that are Predicted to Occur.* Research suggests, Costa and Garmston note, that such specificity may initially be a low priority for some teachers.
2. *The Teacher Identifies the Students' Present Capabilities or Current Knowledge by Drawing upon Previous Experiences, Data from School Records and Test Scores, and Hints Provided by Parents, Other Teachers, or Counselors.* This information is synthesized into hunches about the likelihood of student success as a result of instruction. The ability to view the lesson from the student's perspective is useful here.
3. *The Teacher Conceives of a Sequence or Strategy for Instruction that Offers a Probability that Students will Progress from their Present State of Knowledge toward both Immediate and Longer-range Learning Outcomes.* According to Costa and Garmston, the content of the lesson should be broken down into its essential components (concepts, skills, etc.) and then rearranged in a logical sequence of learning activities that are based on a theory or model of teaching.
4. *The Teacher Anticipates some Method of Gathering Data About and Evaluating Learning Outcomes.* Data resulting from this evaluation will provide a basis for decisions about subsequent cycles of instruction.

Supervisors can use a number of strategies to facilitate the teacher's planning during the preactive stage. Costa and Garmston refer to this supervisory process as "auditing," meaning "to hear." The supervisor can help the teacher clarify the goals and objectives of the lesson, describe the teaching strategies to be used, identify appropriate techniques of evaluation, and clarify the evaluation process. Other ways in which the supervisor can assist with planning include the following:

- Encouraging the teacher to mentally rehearse the planned activities and anticipate possible consequences. This essentially means mentally testing hypotheses before teaching actually occurs.
- Getting the teacher to describe behavioral cues that indicate successful student performance, thus clarifying judgments about acceptable and unacceptable student outcomes.
- Eliciting from the teacher alternative strategies and procedures as possible options if the lesson has to be redirected or changed while it is in progress.

The Interactive Stage

The interactive stage is the act of teaching itself. Costa and Garmston's model calls particular attention to the spontaneous decisions that teachers make during the intense immediacy of classroom interactions. Teachers' decisions concerning student readiness, alternative strategies, and learning outcomes are often guided more by informed intuition than rationality during the act of teaching, they suggest, due to the uncertainties and pressures of classroom reality.

The decisions that teachers make during the preactive stage represent a script or plan of sequentially ordered teacher behaviors that are intended to produce certain student outcomes. According to Costa and Garmston, superior teachers keep these immediate and long-range goals and objectives in mind as a guide to their teaching. However, superior teachers also carefully monitor their own thought processes while engaged in the act of teaching. As noted earlier, Costa and Garmston refer to this conscious awareness of interpretations, judgments, perceptions, decisions, and behaviors as metacognition. This awareness of mental activity allows superior teachers to orchestrate the unpredictable elements in the classroom in a way that facilitates student progress toward the preselected outcomes. Other behavioral characteristics of superior teachers include:

1. *Self-monitoring by Simultaneously Looking Backward and Forward on the Sequence of Events Unfolding in the Classroom.* Successful teachers, Costa and Garmston suggest, are mindful of accomplishments, goals achieved, and errors made along the way. Successful teachers also anticipate the sequence of operations that lies ahead possible errors that may occur, and the utility of feedback. Looking both backward and forward simultaneously, enables teachers to keep their place during teaching, to assess the appropriateness of their present activity, and to quickly detect and recover from errors along the way.

2. *Attending Carefully to Data Concerning Student Readiness and Motivation While Engaged in the Act of Teaching.* Students frequently use overt behavior to communicate, Costa and Garmston note, and superior teachers consciously process this information in order to further learning outcomes. Successful teachers are attuned to student behavior and make interpretations about what students are thinking and feeling. Teachers' interpretations of students' cognitive and affective states serve to guide subsequent behavior. Costa and Garmston believe that teachers should verify the accuracy of these interpretations more often than they do.

3. *Probing and Asking Questions to Assess the Readiness and Motivation of Individual Students and the Class as a Whole.* Superior teachers go beyond simply observing student behavior. Diagnostic information can be obtained by asking a question of a single student, for example, and the teacher may decide to praise, extend, clarify, or extinguish the response for that student. On the other hand, the teacher may use this information along with other behavioral cues and student responses to determine whether to move ahead in the sequence of the lesson or to remain at the present step awhile longer.

4. *Possessing a Repertoire of Strategies and Selecting Those That are Most Appropriate for Achieving the Desired Outcomes.* This requires that teachers know when to use a particular strategy in addition to how it is done. For example, Costa and Garmston suggest that at the beginning of a lesson, a teacher may use

questions to stimulate students' curiosity or diagnose their readiness. Later in the lesson, the teacher may ask recall questions to review material covered in earlier sessions. Still later, the teacher might ask questions to generate new ideas and stimulate higher levels of student thinking.

5. *Restraining Impulsive and Emotional Reactions in the Classroom.* The number and intensity of classroom stimuli to which a teacher is exposed can be overwhelming. Costa and Garmston note that these stimuli may be absorbed unconsciously by the teacher and can accumulate to the point where they impede conscious information processing. An appropriate teaching strategy, they suggest, keeps the lesson focused and purposeful by helping the teacher select and reinforce cues from student behavior that are relevant to the intended learning outcomes.

6. *Using Classroom Routines and Management Systems for Reducing the Number of Cues that a Teacher Must Attend to during a Lesson.* The spontaneity and unpredictability of classroom events can be brought to a manageable level when procedures are established for frequently repeated activities such as taking attendance, distributing paper and books, or forming groups. Lesson designs that employ routines, such as math or spelling drills, can help students grow accustomed to expectations. Routines also permit teachers to concentrate on and correct student behaviors that signal discrepancies and irregularities, instead of having to respond to all student behavior at the same time.

During the interactive stage of the cognitive coaching model, the supervisor "monitors" the performance of the teacher and students during the lesson. The supervisor observes the teaching as it occurs and gathers data relevant to the teacher in two areas of performance:

- Student performance of objectives;
- Teacher performance of strategies.

Beyond these two general areas, Costa and Garmston do not recommend any particular approach or guidelines for data collection. Their approach to gathering data is eclectic, with the supervisor drawing upon a range of observation techniques – selective verbatim, verbal flow, at-task, classroom movement, and others – depending on the observation focus decided upon during the preconference.

The Reflective Stage

The reflective stage of the cognitive coaching model is centered around analysis and evaluation. These mental processes involve reflection upon, analysis, and judgment concerning teaching acts performed during the interactive stage. The basis for analysis is the development of understandings derived from comparing the intended outcomes of teaching with those outcomes actually attained. If a discrepancy is found between the student behaviors predicted and those observed, an attempt is made to resolve or explain this result. Costa and Garmston use the term "accommodation" to describe the process of accounting for the discrepancy by hypothesizing cause and effect relationships between the instructional conditions and the behavioral outcomes.

Evaluation involves making a judgment about the value of decisions made during the preactive and interactive stages. The quality of the teacher's thinking both before and after teaching is assessed during evaluation. Although Costa and Garmston prefer for teachers to contemplate and evaluate their own thinking independently, they suggest that not all teachers are capable of doing so in a sufficiently objective manner.

Teachers who feel secure and possess high self-esteem are more likely to accept responsibility for the outcomes of their teaching (i.e, internal locus of control), Costa and Garmston believe, while teachers who exhibit insecurity and low self-esteem have more difficulty interpreting data critically. The latter group may dismiss, distort, or try to explain away any information that threatens their self-image (i.e., external locus of control). In working with such teachers, the supervisor may have to help them confront the reality that the lesson did not produce the outcomes for students that had been intended.

The ultimate goal of cognitive coaching, however, is to increase teacher autonomy. Supervisors strive to encourage teachers to develop three mental capacities for criticizing their own work. These are:
- auto-criticism - the ability to engage in self-evaluation;
- introspection - the ability to be aware of one's thinking while making decisions; and
- retrospection - the ability to reflect upon one's thinking after making a decision.

Costa and Garmston imply that the task of the supervisor during the analysis and evaluation stage is primarily to "validate" the teacher's efforts. This is because most teachers, they believe, possess sufficient feelings of security and self-esteem, as well as experience and competence, to engage in honest and open self evaluation. Supervisors can help teachers validate their own performance, according to Costa and Garmston, by inviting the teacher to:

- Share data collected during the observation that relates to student and teacher performance;
- Compare intended outcomes with those actually achieved;
- Make inferences about the students' achievement of objectives;
- Make inferences about the teacher's performance;
- Suggest cause-and-effect relationships between the teacher's decisions and behavior, and the students' achievement.

The Projective Stage

The projective stage of the cognitive coaching model involves the application of what was learned from experience to future actions. Generalizations are abstracted from experiences encountered in the earlier stages (preactive, interactive, and reflective) and are carried forward to future situations. The supervisor assists the teacher in comparing, differentiating, categorizing, and labeling new cognitive and technical skills. The teacher then becomes adept at recognizing and making sense of classroom events, departing from routine behavior, and making the most of novel occurrences. In essence, the teacher becomes better at making decisions and predicting the consequences of various alternative courses of action in the classroom.

The supervisor's task during the projective stage of cognitive coaching is that of "consulting" with respect to both teaching and supervision. Consulting is a process by which the supervisor helps the teacher to:

- Evaluate the appropriateness of desired objectives;
- Prescribe alternative classroom strategies;
- Develop insight into the process of supervision;
- Evaluate the supervisory process.

This final projective stage provides a basis for returning to the preactive stage of planning for instruction. Each cycle of cognitive coaching is intended to make the teacher better able to reflect upon experience in the classroom, to conceptualize and apply understandings to new situations, and to select teaching strategies that are likely to result in the attainment of desired student outcomes. During this stage of application, teachers begin to formulate hypotheses to be tested or make plans to be implemented in subsequent lessons.

Sources of Autonomy

What is the source of autonomy? What conditions need to exist internally, cognitively, emotionally? What perspectives in orientations need to exist for people to behave in autonomous ways? Costa and Garmston propose that the five major states of mind identified below are the wellsprings of autonomous behavior:

Efficacy: People who are efficacious have an internal locus of control. They engage in cause and effect thinking. They pose problems and search for problems to solve. They are optimistic. They are self-actualizing and self-modifying. They are able to operationalize concepts and translate them into deliberate actions.

Flexibility: People who enjoy the state of mind of flexibility are empathic. They are able to see through the perspectives of others. They are open and tolerant of ambiguity. They create and seek novel approaches. They envision a range of alternative consequences. They have the capacity to change their mind as they receive additional data. And they also engage in multiple and simultaneous activities and outcomes.

Precision: People who are autonomous strive for precision. They seek perfection and craftsmanship. They seek refinement and specificity in communications. They generate and hold clear visions and goals. They strive for exactness of critical thought processes.

Consciousness: People who enjoy a state of consciousness monitor their own values, their own thoughts, their own behaviors, and their own goals. They have well defined value systems that they can articulate. They generate, hold, and apply internal criteria for decisions they make. They practice mental rehearsal and the editing of mental pictures in the process of seeking improved strategies.

Interdependence: Autonomous people have a sense of interdependence. They are altruistic. They seek collegiality. They give themselves to group goals and needs. They contribute to a common good. They have a sense of patriotism and volunteerism. They know that all of us are more efficient than any one of us. They value a sense of consensus. They are able to hold their own values and actions in abeyance in order to lend themselves to the achievement of group goals.

Costa and Garmston suggest that supervisors should use a "language of empowerment" to lead teachers toward greater autonomy. The language of empowerment is a set of coaching strategies consisting of linguistic tools which promote greater autonomy among teachers while maintaining trust and enhancing learning. The language of empowerment is used by coaches to mediate teachers' movement along the five major states of mind as illustrated in *Figure 10.3* below:

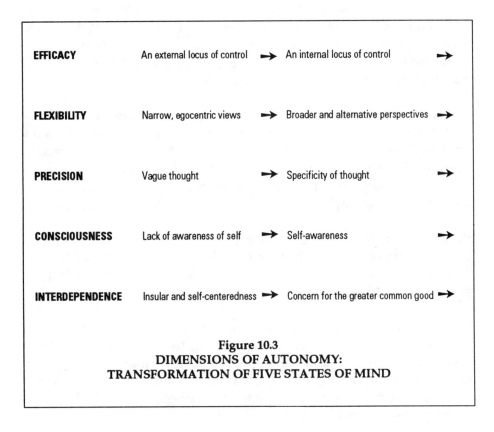

Figure 10.3
DIMENSIONS OF AUTONOMY:
TRANSFORMATION OF FIVE STATES OF MIND

The coach first diagnoses the present state of the teacher's autonomy and envisions a more desirable state of autonomy. The coach then applies linguistic tools to transform the teacher's thinking and intellectual functioning. The examples that follow suggest appropriate responses by supervisors to hypothetical statements made by teachers that indicate low levels of efficacy, flexibility, precision, and consciousness:

Efficacy

Teacher States	Supervisor Responds
"If the parents can't motivate them to learn, how do you expect me to teach them?"	"What might you do within your own classroom to motivate them?"

Flexibility

Teacher States	Supervisor Responds
"I want him out of here! He constantly disrupts the class. He leaves without permission."	"Was there ever a time when you were successful with him?"
"Yes."	"Do you recall what you were doing at the time?"

Precision

Teacher States	Supervisor Responds
"Wow, that was really a great lesson!"	"How, specifically, was it great?"

Consciousness

Teacher States	Supervisor Responds
"In the middle of the lesson I changed my plan."	"What led to your decision to modify your teaching plan?"
"The kids' answers were very creative."	"What went on in your head when the students responded like that?"
(Upon completion of the post conference.)	"When I ask you questions in these conferences, what impact does that have your thinking?"

Modelling

Finally, supervisors should try to bring their beliefs, values, words, actions, and goals into harmony. By modeling the kinds of behaviors they want teachers to attain, they can help students acquire desirable behavior patterns as well.

Costa and Garmston draw a parallel between the acquisition of athletic skills and intellectual skills. While acknowledging that the latter are more elusive and difficult to define, they believe that both athletic and intellectual capacities can be improved through practice, concentration, and coaching. Costa and Garmston advocate the ongoing development of thinking skills for everyone in schools. Teachers should facilitate thinking among students while principals, supervisors, and teachers should facilitate thinking among themselves as well.

Teachers and administrators are encouraged to create conditions in classrooms and schools that contribute to children's thinking. For example, the school environment can be structured to demonstrate that thinking is valued. Time and materials can be provided for enhancing thinking for all staff, students, and parents. Teachers and administrators can model behaviors of thinking and respond to students in ways that build trust and permit risk taking by being positive, experimental, and creative.

Critical thinking, metaphorical thinking, problem solving and other higher level cognitive skills can be taught directly as part of the regular curriculum. Teachers can instruct students in the skills and strategies involved. Teachers can "teach for thinking," for example, by posing problems, asking questions, or presenting paradoxes and dilemmas for students to resolve. Teachers can also help students become aware of their own cognitive processes and the processes employed by others in facing real-life situations and problems. This might include teaching about the human brain, thought processes, memory, emotions, and learning. Students can also be encouraged to consciously monitor their own thinking to improve learning, studying, and reading skills.

Summary

Costa and Garmston advocate a model of supervision that they call "cognitive coaching." They propose that supervision should focus on the inner thinking processes that underlie teaching in addition to overt teacher behaviors. Because research indicates that more complex, higher intellectually functioning teachers produce higher intellectually functioning students, Costa and Garmston suggest that an enhancement of teachers' cognitive abilities will result in improved student learning.

The cognitive coaching model emphasizes three goals: trust, learning, and autonomy. Trust is viewed as fundamental to the success of supervision and essential to the attainment of learning and autonomy. Learning involves a rearranging and restructuring of mental processes that is facilitated by the supervisor during conferences by encouraging the teacher to imagine, describe, and prepare for a lesson in specific detail. Autonomy refers to the teacher's ability to monitor his or her behavior and make consciously deliberate decisions about teaching.

The process of influencing teachers' thinking involves a sequence of four related elements: (a) the pre-active or planning stage, (b) the interactive or teaching phase, (c) the reflective or analytical/evaluative phase, and (d) the projective or applying phase. The pre-active stage includes decisions made by the teacher prior to teaching. The supervisor can facilitate planning by helping the teacher mentally rehearse the lesson, by asking for descriptions of student and teacher behaviors, and by proposing the inclusion of alternative strategies.

The interactive phase is the act of teaching itself, where the teacher enacts the plan of teaching that was prepared while consciously monitoring the lesson's progress, student readiness, motivation, and involvement, and his or her own reactions and responses. Supervisors can help by monitoring the lesson as well through classroom observation, paying especially close attention to the relation between teacher strategies and the achievement of learning objectives.

The reflective stage of cognitive coaching is centered around analysis and judgment of teaching, with a special focus on the discrepancy between the intended outcomes of a lesson and the outcomes actually attained. The supervisor tries to help the teacher engage in self-evaluation, introspection, and retrospection concerning the lesson. Finally, the projective stage involves the application of what was learned to future actions, thus completing the cycle by providing a basis for returning to the preactive stage. Here, teachers formulate hypotheses or make plans to be implemented in subsequent lessons.

By addressing teachers' intellects and emphasizing thinking skills for students, Costa and Garmston believe that schools can become "homes for the mind." Students, teachers, supervisors, and administrators can acquire certain orientations – efficacy, flexibility, precision, consciousness, and interdependence – that contribute to individual autonomy. Through deliberate effort and modelling of higher order thinking by teachers and their coaches, schools can become more growth inducing and mentally stimulating for everyone.

References

Costa, A. L. (1985). "The behaviors of intelligence." In A. L. Costa (Ed.), *Developing minds: A resource book for teaching thinking*, pp. 66-68, Alexandria, VA: Association for Supervision and Curriculum Development.

Costa, A. L. (1985). "Toward a model of human intellectual functioning." In A. L. Costa (Ed.), *Developing minds: A resource book for teaching thinking*, pp. 52-65, Alexandria, VA: Association for Supervision and Curriculum Development.

Costa, A. L. & Garmston, R. (1985). "Supervision for intelligent teaching," *Educational Leadership, 42*, 5: 70-80.

Costa, A. L. (1986). *Supervision for intelligent teaching*. Orangevale, CA: Search Models Unlimited.

Costa, A. L. & Garmston, R. (1986). "Cognitive coaching: supervision for intelligent teaching." *Wingspan, 3* (1): 38-

Garmston, R. (1990). "An interview with Robert Garmston by Dennis Sparks. What is cognitive coaching?" *Journal of Staff Development*, Spring, *11* (2), pg. 12-15.

Garmston, R. (1988). "A call for collegial coaching." *The Developer* (August), pp. 1, 4-6. National Council of Staff Devleopment.

Garmston, R. & Preiskorn, J. (1990). "Leadership for intelligent teaching: Superintendents' responses to cognitive coaching." *Thrust for Educational Leadership*, pp. 36-38. Association of California School Administrators, May/June, 1990.

Joyce, B. & Showers, B. (1988). *Student achievement through staff development*. New York: Longman.

Shavelson, R. (1973). *The basic teaching skill: Decision making*. (R & D Memorandum No. 104). Stanford, CA: Stanford University, School of Education, Center for R & D in Teaching. p. 18.

Chapter 11

Reflective Practice

The Model at Work

Sitting alone in her office, Ms. Peterson thought that in many ways it was much more challenging to coach an already successful teacher than a teacher who is having difficulty. Mr. Meyers, the teacher with whom she just met, taught high school chemistry and physics for eighteen years at Westview High School. Five years ago he received the district's "Teacher of the Year" Award. He said at the time that the "secret to his success," was the personal attention that he gave to each student.

For many years, Westview high school served students who came mainly from middle to upper middle class backgrounds. At one time, ninety percent of the students attended college after graduation. Over the years, a number of Mr. Meyers' students have gone on to major in chemistry or physics in college. Every year, one or two return to thank him for the excellent foundation in science that he provided them.

During the last five years, however, the composition of the student population at Westview has changed. Lower income families have moved into the community as real estate developers built and opened less costly tracts. Apartment houses have also appeared in the neighborhood, attracting single parent and two-income working class families. As a consequence the student body is becoming considerably more diverse – economically, ethnically, and culturally – than it was the year that Mr. Meyers won his teaching award.

Mr. Meyers invited Ms. Peterson into his class because, he said, he hoped she could give him some ideas for working with students. She suggested that she ought to drop by to observe his class to get a sense of what was happening.

Ms. Peterson was fascinated by a lively and informative demonstration and lecture on the expansion and contraction of metals at varying temperatures during the class period she observed. Six students participated in an animated question and answer exchange with Mr. Meyers, which he obviously enjoyed. She noticed, however, that many students in the class did not actively participate and that several were obviously not paying attention at all. One appeared to be sleeping.

When they met in a conference afterward, Ms. Peterson was at first relieved when Mr. Meyers mentioned the lack of participation by some students before she had to point it out. But she was troubled when he kept asking her for specific ideas on how to work with the students who were not participating. A couple of times, when she offered suggestions, he simply nodded silently and wrote them down.

Ms. Peterson suggested suddenly that they begin again. This time she asked Mr. Meyers what he thought was the source of the students' lack of participation and attention. He confided that he was feeling less and less successful recently because he didn't seem able to relate to students in the way he had in the past. He also said that he was thinking about asking for a transfer to another high school in the district, one where he thought he might relate better to the students.

Mr. Meyers was one of the best teachers that Ms. Peterson had ever seen, and she wanted the students at Westview to benefit from his talent. But she also understood that helping him under these circumstances would not be simple and was going to take some time.

Over the next several weeks they discussed how the social, economic, and cultural characteristics of students in Mr. Meyers' chemistry and physics classes had changed during the last five years. Ms. Peterson introduced some statistics that suggested a trend toward greater diversity among students nationally as well. They then shared their beliefs and assumptions about teaching with each other, and discussed where these beliefs and assumptions originated. Mr. Meyers' grandparents were immigrants, he revealed, and he had obtained the view from his parents that education was an avenue toward social mobility and economic security.

At their next meeting Mr. Meyers stated that he was fundamentally committed to the principle that all students would learn. He acknowledged that he would have to make an effort to understand the way that students from nontraditional backgrounds thought about and experienced his classes. As they continued working together, Mr. Meyers began planning lessons that relied more on inquiry into puzzling phenomena and he used examples from students' everyday experiences. He continued with an occasional lecture and demonstration, but he began using discussions and group projects as well. Ms. Peterson was most pleased, however, when he told her that he would not be asking for a transfer to another school afterall.

Introduction

Several emerging models of teaching and supervision are included in this chapter under the rubric "reflective" practice. To some extent, they all echo the sense of outrage expressed in Goldhammer's 1969 edition over the meaninglessness and irrelevance of much of what students experience in school. In the first chapter of his book, Goldhammer severely criticized the hypocrisy and ritualism encountered in classrooms, and the remoteness of curriculum and instruction from the real lives of many students. Schooling often fosters dependency and complacency among children, he argued, and does little to encourage a love of learning. He was especially angered by the insensitive treatment received by children who come from families that are economically impoverished or culturally different.

A central concept in the reflective approaches is the notion of "problematizing" teaching and supervision, in other words, challenging taken-for-granted assumptions, beliefs, theories, and practices. Procedurally, the reflective approaches to supervision closely parallel the first four stages of Goldhammer's clinical cycle. They generally include a preobservation conference, an observation phase, data analysis, and a feedback conference. The post observation analysis is typically omitted as a distinct stage of the process, but the reflective approaches emphasize ongoing introspection by the teacher and supervisor.

The versions of reflective supervision described in this chapter address issues related to the nature of professional knowledge and the social, political, historical, and cultural contexts of teaching and learning. Each of the approaches discussed has a slightly different focus, although each cuts across at least several of these issues to some degree. The authors associated with the various approaches to reflective supervision described here are listed in *Figure 11.1* along with the primary emphasis of their perspectives.

Author	Primary Emphasis
Schon	nature of professional knowledge
Zeichner & Liston	social reconstruction
Garman	historical embeddedness
Smyth & Retallick	political justice
Bowers & Flinders	cultural responsiveness

Figure 11.1
APPROACHES TO REFLECTIVE SUPERVISION

Schon's Reflective Coaching

Donald Schon (1983; 1987) views the problems encountered by teachers and supervisors as untidy, puzzling, uncertain, and complex situations. The intended outcomes of practice and the methods available for attaining those outcomes, he notes, are often unclear and interrelated. The neat theories and technical procedures that teachers and supervisors are typically taught during their professional training, Schon believes, simply do not fit the reality of classrooms and schools.

According to Schon, successful professionals possess repertoires of images and understandings about their work that they acquire through experience. Teachers and supervisors draw on this store of practical knowledge to understand problems they face everyday in their work. In Schon's words, practitioners use past experiences as "lenses" to "frame" new situations that they encounter. The greater the range and variety of lenses available to an individual, the more likely he or she is to be successful in solving professional problems.

Schon's notion of framing a problem involves selecting the goals that will be pursued while consciously ignoring others. The practitioner then performs mental experiments that include formulating and testing alternative hypotheses by imagining how manipulations of contextual factors might influence the situation or resolve the problem at hand.

Schon (1988a) describes "reflective teaching" very specifically as listening carefully and responding appropriately to students in order to help them understand something with which they are having difficulty. Reflective teaching also involves helping students to discover and build on knowledge that they already possess but cannot express, and helping them to integrate their existing knowledge with the knowledge of the school.

Schon describes an example of reflective teaching as including the following phases:
a) allowing oneself to be surprised by an odd or unexpected thing that a student says or does;
b) framing the interpretation of this surprising event as a puzzle, with the teacher's problem being to understand how the student's behavior makes sense to the student;
c) getting more curious and inquiring into the puzzle by inventing experiments to explore it on-the-spot (e.g., by asking questions or presenting new evidence or information for the student to

consider); and

d) as a result of such experiments, helping the student to connect his or her understanding to school knowledge.

This type of teaching, Schon explains, involves "reflection-in-action" or reflecting on a phenomenon and on the ways one spontaneously thinks and acts. Reflection occurs at the same time that one is teaching and serves as a guide to further teaching. Reflection-in-action requires "thinking on your feet," or thinking "about doing something while doing it" (1983, pp. 49,66).

All activities that support, guide, or encourage reflective teaching, Schon suggests, may be considered instructional supervision. Such supervision may be conducted formally by principals or supervisors, he notes, or informally by colleagues, students, and parents (1988a).

Reflective teaching can be facilitated, according to Schon, when one person advises, criticizes, describes, demonstrates, or questions another about his or her practice. A reflective supervisor tries to help, encourage, and provoke the teacher into reflecting on events in the classroom. The teacher's reflection is supported by the supervisor's own reflection-in-action on the process of supervision. The supervisor models reflection, in other words, by verbalizing what he or she sees, how it is interpreted, how it might be tested, and what actions might follow from that interpretation.

In order to help teachers develop the capacity for reflective teaching, Schon (1988a) suggests, a supervisor should assume the stance of a coach. In doing so, the supervisor must pay attention to three levels of interaction:

- **level 1** – the student's interaction with some phenomenon, such as a concept to be learned.
- **level 2** – the teacher's interaction with the student – how the teacher interprets what the student is saying or doing, how the teacher thinks about it, explores it, tests his or her understanding, and draws conclusions about what to say or do next.
- **level 3** – the supervisor's interaction with the teacher – the coach's understanding and response to the teacher's understandings, feelings, and inquiry.

Supervisory tasks and relevant questions appropriate to each of these three levels of interaction are presented in *Figure 11.2*:

Levels of Interaction	Supervisor's Tasks	Relevant Questions
Level 1 Student's interaction with some phenomenon.	**Task 1** Making sense of and responding to the substantive issue of learning and teaching being considered.	What is the nature of the student's spontaneous understanding and know-how? What is the substance of the student's confusion? What difficulties arise in connecting everyday knowledge with the knowledge of the school?
Level 2 Teacher's interaction with the student.	**Task 2** Entering into the teacher's ways of thinking about the issue and tailoring the dialogue to the teacher's understanding.	What structures, strategies, and styles of reflection-in-action does the teacher use? What is the logic of the teacher's on-the-spot experimentation? Are these experiments appropriate for this situation?
Level 3 Supervisor's interaction with the teacher.	**Task 3** Doing task 1 and 2 in a way that minimizes defensiveness on the part of the teacher.	What are sources of defensiveness in the relationship between teacher and supervisor? What responses might be effective in reducing defensiveness?

Figure 11.2
**LEVELS OF INTERACTION, SUPERVISORY TASKS, AND
RELEVANT QUESTIONS IN SCHON'S REFLECTIVE SUPERVISION**

Schon cautions that simply asking teachers about what they do will not suffice, because what they do and what they say often diverge. He proposes that direct, recorded observation is needed for deliberation, that permits a very detailed description of behavior and a reconstruction of (the teacher's) intentions, strategies, and assumptions. Schon notes further that "the confrontation with directly observable data often produces an educational shock, as teachers discover that they act according to theories of action different from the ones they espouse" (Schon, 1988b).

Partly due to this initial shock, teachers may respond defensively to attempts by a supervisor to get them to reflect-in-action, because to do so requires that they accept the uncertainty of practice (Schon (1988a). Being surprised and puzzled by events in the classroom means not being in control of the situation and not having the right answer. This confusion can lead to feelings of vulnerability, which trigger defensive reactions. Schon suggests that supervisors should respond in such cases with sensitive understanding (see *Figure 11.2*).

Reflective teaching and reflective coaching are often uphill struggles, Schon notes, because of the institutional constraints of schools, and the sometimes contrary expectations of administrators, colleagues, and parents about the content that should be taught, when, where, and how. Instead of *reflecting* on their practice, teachers and supervisors often spend time *worrying* about things like "covering material" so that students will "know the answers," because of these expectations that others impose.

Schon believes that although many real obstacles exist, some very powerful constraints are self-imposed. He suggests that practitioners always have available a certain zone of freedom where they can find room to experiment with reflective teaching and reflective supervision if they choose to do so. As they experience success and get accustomed to taking risks, individuals become aware of how their own assumptions and behaviors – their "theory-in-use" – contribute to the reality that they find constraining (Schon, 1988a). Their zone of freedom then naturally expands.

Zeichner and Liston's Reflective Action

Kenneth Zeichner and several associates, most recently Daniel Liston, argue that learning for students and teachers can be improved when teachers make consciously moral decisions about the content and processes of teaching and contribute as partners in shaping schools as learning environments. The means of accomplishing this aim is by encouraging reflective action among teachers, which involves an active, persistent, and careful consideration of the rationale and consequences of beliefs and knowledge as applied to practice.

Zeichner's work relates most directly to the preparation of preservice teachers. He and his colleagues express the hope, however, that more democratic decision-making structures will soon evolve in schools. They also believe that teachers should assume more active roles in reconstructing society to ensure greater social justice. Grant and Zeichner (1984) emphasize that the most compelling reason for encouraging reflective practice is that the wide range of classroom settings and the diversity of students and cultures represented in schools today requires that teachers be highly flexible and sensitive to these differences.

Drawing on Dewey's work (1933), Grant and Zeichner distinguish between "routine action" and "reflective action" to explain what is meant by reflective teaching (1984). Routine action is determined by impulse, habit, tradition, circumstance, or authority and occurs within a definition of the social reality that is taken for granted. Routine action is useful at times, but it can become an obstacle to experimentation and the recognition that alternative realities are possible. *Unreflective teachers* rely on routine action almost exclusively. They accept the "reality" of their classrooms and schools as it is defined by others without question. They may work effectively and efficiently on tasks and problems defined for them, but they tend to neglect their own intentions and purposes.

Reflective action, according to Grant and Zeichner, involves an active, persistent, and careful examination of practices and beliefs, including the grounds on which they are based and the consequences to which they lead. *Reflective teachers* think consciously and carefully about their teaching and about the social and political contexts in which it occurs. Reflective teachers also: (a) understand the kind of teacher they want to be, (b) know what their position is on various issues, and (c) are aware of the kinds of knowledge and skills they need to acquire to put their beliefs into action (Grant & Zeichner, 1984).

The popular technical approach to teaching is viewed as doing little to encourage reflective action. Fundamental perceptions that distinguish the technical view of teaching from reflective practice, are illustrated in *Figure 11.3*, as outlined by Zeichner and Liston (1987):

	Technical View	Reflective View
Knowledge	Certain, fixed, and given	Emergent, negotiated, and centered around inquiry and reflection
Authority Relations	Static and hierarchical	Collaborative and inquiry oriented
Teachers	Efficient technicians	Reflective, moral craftspersons
Supervisors	Technical experts	Self-renewing, reflective, moral craftspersons

Figure 11.3
TECHNICAL VERSUS REFLECTIVE VIEWS OF KNOWLEDGE, AUTHORITY RELATIONS, TEACHERS, AND SUPERVISORS

Grant and Zeichner (1984) discuss three orientations or attitudes identified by Dewey (1933) as *prerequisites* for reflective action: openmindedness, responsibility, and wholeheartedness. These are presented below, along with some implications for teaching:

1) *Openmindedness* is the active desire to consider more than a single side of an issue or perspective, to give full attention to alternative possibilities, and to recognize the potential for error even in our dearest beliefs. It involves examining rationales, seeking conflicting evidence, questioning procedures, and keeping an open mind about traditional subject matter and methods.

2) *Responsibility* requires carefully considering the consequences of an action. Purposes of actions and possible unanticipated outcomes are questioned. Moral implications and the influence of actions on the lives of students are considered from multiple perspectives including gender and culture.

3) *Wholeheartedness* is taking active control of ones' education as a teacher. Openmindedness and responsibility are pursued and integrated into philosophy and behavior. Wholehearted teachers critically analyze their own work and act on a commitment to teach *all* students.

The following are examples of questions offered by Grant and Zeichner (1984) that teachers may consider in attempting to become more reflective:

- What are my current beliefs about teaching and the assumptions underlying those beliefs?
- How do my beliefs compare with those of others?
- What are the origins of my beliefs? How and why were they acquired?
- What are the consequences of holding these beliefs for myself and others?
- How are my beliefs and their consequences linked to the current social, political, and economic order?
- What kinds of knowledge and skills do I need to successfully enact the kind of teaching that is consistent with my educational beliefs?

In order to enact the attitudes of open-mindedness, responsibility, and wholeheartedness, Zeichner and his associates (Grant & Zeichner, 1984; Zeichner & Liston, 1987) see a need for teachers to develop technical skills of inquiry and problem solving, such as keen observation and reasoned analysis. These technical skills are subsumed, however, within the broader context of reflective action. Technical improvement is not an end in itself. Reflective teaching remains the central goal. Inquiry, seminars, journals, and supervisory conferences are suggested as ways of attaining this broader view of teaching. A description of each strategy is summarized below.

Inquiry

Teachers should become skilled in methods of inquiry, such as observation, action research, ethnography, and curriculum analysis (Zeichner & Liston, 1987). Inquiry can facilitate a view of classrooms as social laboratories for study, as opposed to models of practice, where teachers can create as well as consume educational knowledge. Curriculum, teaching, and schooling can be understood in their social and historical contexts, rather than as technical skills.

Action research is a form of inquiry that can be especially aimed at understanding or eliminating social conditions that interfere with student learning. A sequence of steps can be followed – plan, act, observe, and reflect – but not necessarily in a lock-step fashion. Teachers may also employ limited ethnographic studies to better understand varying backgrounds and abilities of students and the effects that teacher actions and curriculum have on students (Liston & Zeichner, 1991).

Seminars

Seminars can be planned cooperatively by a supervisor and groups of teachers. Content may be linked to classroom practice, but Zeichner and Liston (1987) argue that discussion should not be focused directly on classroom experiences nor on the direct application of specific techniques and methods. Seminars should aim to broaden teachers' perspectives on topics such as multicultural curriculum, cooperative learning, grouping, and student assessment. Teachers can consider alternatives for classroom practice and their conceptual underpinnings, discuss dilemmas of practice, critically examine educational research, and assess the development of personal perspectives toward teaching.

Journals

Written accounts of personal development can be kept by teachers and shared regularly. These journals provide a vehicle for communication between the teacher and supervisor and for systematic self-reflection on professional development and actions as a teacher in the classroom, school, and community (Zeichner & Liston, 1987). A variation is for teachers to write autobiographies that examine early experiences as learners and how those experiences influence the kind of teacher they have become (Liston & Zeichner, 1991).

Supervisory Conferences

As is common with other models of supervision, Zeichner and Liston (1987) recommend that supervisory conferences should follow formal observations. Detailed narrative accounts of events in the classroom are recorded. These accounts serve to document critical incidents and patterns of behavior.

Zeichner and Liston suggest that supervisory conferences concentrate on both the teaching activities in the lesson that was observed and the ongoing professional development of the teacher. Consistent with traditional clinical supervision, an emphasis is placed on rational analysis (1987) of classroom behavior. However, supervision that aims to promote reflective teaching is different from traditional clinical supervision in several respects, according to Zeichner and Liston (1987):

  a) attention is given to analysis of teacher intentions, beliefs, and theoretical commitments and their relation to observed behaviors;

  b) the institutional and social contexts of teaching can be considered problematically as acceptable topics for analysis in relation to matters of teaching technique;

  c) justification for the appropriateness of the content taught to particular students is considered, in addition to the analysis of instructional processes;

  d) besides considering whether or not the teacher's objectives were achieved, the supervision conference often considers unanticipated and hidden outcomes of the curriculum, instructional practices, and social relations in the classroom.

In essence, while consistent with clinical supervision, reflective practice conferences are geared more toward "critical inquiry" (Zeichner & Liston, 1987, p. 34), which means that teachers use moral as well as technical criteria when evaluating their classroom practice. Liston and Zeichner (1991) emphasize the importance of encouraging teachers to view events in the classroom as related to broader issues and structures existing in schools and society. They believe that issues of gender, social class, and race associated with everyday teaching activities, should be openly discussed. The intention is to awaken teachers to moral and ethical considerations and to help them establish and maintain relationships with students that exhibit compassion and care.

Zeichner draws on work by Van Manen (1977), who identified three levels of reflectivity. These can be useful for understanding the different emphases that reflection may take when supervisors and teachers work together:

  1. *technical reflection* - The main concern of teachers and supervisors at this level is to efficiently and effectively apply educational knowledge to achieve outcomes that are accepted as

given. Neither the outcomes nor the context of learning are questioned.

2. *practical reflection* - The concern of teachers and supervisors at this level is to explicate and clarify assumptions, beliefs, and predispositions that underlie practical affairs and to assess the educational consequences of their actions. Actions are viewed as linked to values at this level. Competing educational ends are considered and how well students are attaining the intended learning goals.

3. *critical reflection* - Teachers and supervisors consider moral and ethical dimensions of teaching practice at this third level, such as justice, equity, and fulfillment. The means, ends, and contexts of teaching and learning are questioned and considered against alternative possibilities that include the satisfaction of human needs and purposes.

Thus, reflection can be stimulated about teaching and its context at all three levels (Zeichner & Liston, 1987; Liston & Zeichner, 1991). However, more emphasis should be given to educational and moral criteria because of the traditional emphasis on technical mastery and instrumental definitions of success in education. It is important to understand that reflective teaching, according to Zeichner's view, is not intended to result in any particular changes in behavior. Rather, the intention is to make behavior change possible by increasing teachers' awareness of themselves and their work environments.

Supervisors should encourage teachers to actively grapple with the concepts and frameworks that are offered to them, Zeichner and Liston (1987) propose, and to consider broader issues like curriculum, instead of focusing solely on acquiring instructional skills and behaviors. Teachers and supervisors should both continuously reflect upon, re-examine, and renew all aspects of their relationship in terms of knowledge gained from experience and research.

Garman's "Reflective Heart" of Clinical Supervision

Writing in the tradition of Cogan and Goldhammer, Noreen Garman asserts that reflection lies at the heart of clinical supervision. Like Schon and Zeichner, she views educational practice as uncertain and problematic, and favors collegial deliberation as the preferred means of contending with that uncertainty.

The process of reflection can serve as a way of generating knowledge, as a means for attaining personal empowerment, and as a path to developing a mature professional identity (Garman, 1986). Garman sees every professional as having the responsibility to forge a personal rationale of teaching through inquiry and self-understanding. This rationale should make sense in terms of everyday events, she suggests, and also contribute to the teacher's professional community.

Garman elaborates on two aspects of reflective practice that contribute to the uniqueness of her view. First, she expresses greater willingness to admit research and theory into the dialogue between supervisors and teachers as they reflect on data derived from observations of teaching. Second, she describes a procedure for reflecting on significant events that are remote in time and emotionally meaningful as an additional source of data for informing practice (1986).

Accordingly, Garman (1986) describes two types of reflective inquiry. The first, she refers to as *"reflection on action"* which is appropriate for studying immediate events in the present. The second, she calls *"reflection on recollection"* in which memory of incidents from the past are used as data (1986). Both of these are described below.

Reflection on action involves a series of steps that are very consistent with the original clinical supervision frameworks. The supervisor's overall purpose is to encourage the teacher to be the primary generator of knowledge. *Reflection on Action*, according to Garman involves the following:

a. *Involvement* - The teacher and supervisor first agree on the nature of the involvement in the class, including events to focus on, the types of data to be collected, and how the teacher will deal with the data.

b. *Observation* - the supervisor makes as complete a record of classroom events as possible. A verbatim transcript or critical incidents can be written by an observer, or video or audio recordings can be made. Garman considers checklists and rating scales to be "unstable" and inappropriate as a basis for reflection on action.

c. *Analysis/interpretation* - the supervisor assists the teacher in interpreting the data, looking especially for patterns. Experienced supervisors also help teachers learn the skills of inquiry by withholding judgment, suggesting ways of making the data meaningful, and providing a language for teaching. The supervisor also models the process of reflecting on his or her own

practice. Professional educational literature can be drawn upon
at this point to help interpret data.

d.   *Construal* - The supervisor helps the teacher translate the results
of reflection into a useful insight, concept, portrait, or principle.

e.   *Confirmation* - The teacher and supervisor concur on the results
of the process, and seek to widen understanding by consulting
significant writing by scholars and researchers.

Garman's second procedure, *Reflection Through Recollection* (1986),
focuses on the past to help inform the present. It involves the following:

a.   *Recall* - The teacher begins by rummaging around in his or her
memory for pictures or images of past events. Accuracy is less
important as long as significant events and their emotional
attachments are recalled.

b.   *Representation* - The image of the event is captured, usually
through journal writing. Representation through painting or
music are other possibilities.

c.   *Interpretation* - The representation is interpreted in terms of issues
such as the meaning of the past event on the present, new insights
into the event, hidden meanings, revealing words or phrases in the
representation, emotional tone, and subliminal motives.

d.   *Confirmation* - Writings in the field of education are used in an
attempt to determine if one's interpretation makes sense to
others and how it may be useful. The literature can provide both
insight and appropriate language for understanding.

Garman calls for clinical supervision to be more purposefully conscious and less ritualistic in its application. She considers collegiality,
collaboration, skilled service, and ethical conduct to be conceptual
cornerstones of clinical supervision (1982). While her perspective is
grounded more firmly in phenomenology than in social criticism,
Garman's work has influenced more politically conscious advocates of
reflective practice.

Smyth's and Retallick's Critical Consciousness

John Smyth (1984a, 1984b, 1990) and John Retallick (1990), like the
proponents of reflective practice already discussed, argue against the
view that clinical supervision is a technical-rational process. They are
entirely opposed, in fact, to its association with bureaucratic functions
like monitoring and evaluating. Smyth and Retallick both prefer what

they consider to be the original intent of Goldhammer and Cogan – supervision as a collaborative action that can liberate teachers from the assumptions they take for granted about their practice. This outcome can be achieved, they believe, by involving teachers in reflective analysis and theorizing about their own teaching, with an emphasis on its social context and political consequences. Smyth believes, like Garman, that teachers can better understand and challenge their own practices, and eventually transform them by discovering and reconstructing personal histories (1984a).

Smyth (1984a) and Retallick (1990) go farther than other advocates of reflective practice in their belief that instructional supervision has traditionally served the purposes of social control. They link certain applications of clinical supervision to the "scientific management" principles of Frederick Taylor and are therefore suspicious about the use of technical knowledge by "experts" to control the choices and actions of other people. Smyth and Retallick seem to perceive teachers as a persecuted, coerced, dominated, and oppressed class, and view technical applications of supervision as attempts to get teachers to improve while keeping them in their subservient place.

Smyth and Retallick want teachers to reclaim the critical tradition begun by Goldhammer. This would mean a radical re-examination of current beliefs and relationships within schools, and their connection to prevailing larger social structures. They call for enabling teachers to transform schools into critical communities. Ideally, they foresee teachers becoming politically involved and working toward changing the conditions that comprise their own work lives and the lives of students.

Teachers should move outside the limitations of tradition, Smyth and Retallick propose, to examine how teaching and schooling are distorted by the existing social order. Teachers should address their practice morally, ethically, and politically by asking questions that involve equity and justice. They argue that clinical supervision can be more than simply fine-tuning what teachers are already doing. It can also serve to question the social, economic, historical, and cultural circumstances in which teaching and learning are embedded. Although writing separately, both Smyth (1990) and Retallick (1990) propose four procedures that are quite similar for adapting clinical supervision to facilitate this outcome. The headings of the steps described below are those of Smyth (1990):

(a) *Problematizing teaching.* Smyth recommends dialogical relationships wherein observers help teachers recognize the political dimension of their teaching. Teachers are called upon to examine the social and political purposes and ends of teaching that often go unquestioned. In challenging conventional wisdom and established practice, Smyth suggests, they may come to view mandated curricula and prescribed textbooks as debilitating bureaucratic intrusions. Retallick views this first step as an opportunity to problematize supervision as well, by focusing on issues of power and control between the teacher and supervisor.

According to Smyth, the observer can help the teacher become more conscious of subtle questions concerning the lesson. Issues related to the content, its presentation, teaching strategies employed, and desired outcomes may be raised. These questions focus on issues of whose established interests (economic, political, etc.) are served, how those interests can be exposed, and whether the interests of certain groups of students are denied. Smyth admits that some teachers may not be ready to grapple with political issues of this sort, and so specific teaching skills or classroom problems can provide an initial focus.

(b) *Observing and creating text about teaching.* This step requires the observer to create a descriptive or narrative text of classroom events that retain elements of value, cultural significance, and meaning. This is in line with Garman's (1986) view that such textual representation offers the "stable data" needed to understand and uncover implicit agendas in one's teaching. The observer functions as a consultant to the teacher, who helps interpret the teaching episode observed. The observer, according to Smyth, should be prepared to have his or her own professional practice critiqued in turn. Like Retallick, Smyth is concerned that the power to make interpretations be shared as equally as possible between supervisors and teachers.

(c) *Confronting personal biography and professional history.* Smyth concurs with Garman's belief in the utility of unraveling one's personal history to understand why one is the teacher one turned out to be. This aspect of reflection includes examining the origins and outcomes of the values, definitions, practices, and content that come into play when one teaches. It requires confronting oneself, one's ideas about teaching, and one's ideals and practices. Questioning authoritarian assumptions and practices that contribute to dependency and docility among students is viewed by Smyth as especially important.

Smyth (1984b) contends that the basis for change in schools ought to be the interpretations and theories that teachers have about what works in their classrooms. He recommends beginning where teachers currently are in their understanding of themselves and their practice, and then expanding the scope to include their personal histories and school contexts. Like Zeichner, Smyth notes Dewey's (1933) interest in encouraging critical inquiry among educators, which included looking back to past experiences as a guide for future action, open-mindedness, consideration of multiple perspectives, and understanding that even cherished beliefs and practices may be challenged by conscious reflection.

Retallick (1990) is more concerned with analyzing language within the classroom and between teachers and supervisors. Discovering and reflecting upon previously unacknowledged patterns of discourse, he believes, can result in insights into the subtleties of teacher-student and teacher-supervisor relationships. He proposes that these insights can be used to consciously reconstruct and redirect both teacher and supervisor behavior.

(d) *Refocusing and action.* Smyth (1984a) suggests that the following questions pertaining to justice, practicality, and realism should be addressed by teachers and supervisors in order to develop shared frameworks of meaning and to ascertain the efficacy of clinical supervision:

(1) To what extent are the practices of clinical supervision *just* in treating teachers as rational and capable of participating fully in the determination of their own destiny?

(2) To what extent is the process of clinical supervision *practical* in allowing teachers to discover aspects about their own teaching through actions?

(3) To what extent is clinical supervision *realistic* in acknowledging the facts of school and classroom life?

Retallick (1990) urges supervisors to encourage ongoing reflection on the process of supervision throughout the cycle. Such reflection can redirect supervision while it is in process and helps verify agreement on the results. Along with Smyth, Retallick believes that a critical practice of clinical supervision can lead to the emergence of a critical community within schools and across schools that are centered around the values of equality and social justice.

Although he calls for more collaborative inquiry and colleague consultation in schools, Smyth's recent writing (1991) cautions that efforts by administrators to get teachers to collaborate more and participate in decisions may represent a "contrived collegiality." The spirit of interdependence gets lost, he warns, when a narrow definition of appropriate professional behavior is adopted and collectively enforced. An outward appearance of collegiality can mask rigid control and centrally prescribed behavior. Under such circumstances, he fears, collegiality may become a way of controlling teachers indirectly by having them police one another.

Bowers and Flinders' Culturally Responsive Supervision

Although similar in procedure to other models of classroom supervision, Bowers and Flinders (1990, 1991) offer a radically new premise. They argue that it is time for supervision to move away from the view that classroom events are solely the outcomes of rationally motivated actions of individual teachers and students. Instead, they propose an understanding of these events as manifestations of the cultural ecology of the classroom.

This shift to an ecological perspective is needed, according to Bowers and Flinders, because of changes in our understanding of knowledge and how organizations function, as well as the need for greater sensitivity and respect for culture, gender, the environment, and the issue of cultural reproduction in the classroom. They further propose that supervisors should consider new areas of awareness. These include: metaphorical thinking by the teacher, the teacher's role in the primary socialization of students, nonverbal communication, cultural differences among students, and the balance of power and affiliation between teachers and their students.

Bowers and Flinders call their approach "culturally responsive supervision." They want to replace the dominant task-oriented technical approach to supervision with an emphasis on the social and cultural dimensions of classroom life. They believe that teachers and supervisors should become more sensitive and responsive to the fact that the classroom is embedded in a social and cultural context, and they offer specific guides for supervisors to use when considering the many facets of what they call the classroom ecology.

Social issues like drug abuse, poverty, gender and racial discrimination, absence of adult role models, and environmental concerns, Bowers and Flinders maintain, all influence events in the classroom. They point out that culturally determined, taken-for-granted assumptions related to rationality, individuality, and spatial relations also affect perceptions and behavior patterns of students, teachers, and supervisors. Bowers and Flinders argue that supervisors should inform and sensitize teachers to these issues. Recognition of the social and cultural embeddedness of classroom events should guide the teacher's actions, they believe, as well as the supervisor's observation, and the relationship between the supervisor and teacher.

Bowers and Flinders view the classroom as a medium of language and culture. Knowledge and understanding are considered open to negotiation and interpretation by students in terms of past, current, and future relevance and usefulness. They maintain that the supervisor's job should be (a) to bring to consciousness the taken-for-granted patterns of language and behavior that a teacher uses or responds to among students, and (b) to interpret these patterns through the lenses of social issues and cultural differences.

The intention of this emphasis is for teachers to recognize that culturally determined patterns of language and understanding can interfere with communication and impede student learning. Bowers and Flinders (1990) suggest that teachers should be aware of the following sorts of issues:

- Some students from some cultures may not be familiar with linear, topic-centered narratives.
- The meanings of nonverbal behaviors like eye-contact, pauses, and body movements differ from one culture to another.
- Some cultures value cooperation and group relations over competition and individual achievement.
- Metaphors and examples that communicate clearly to students of one gender or culture may have little or no meaning for students of other genders or cultures.
- Some students rely more on subjective impressions and intuition when making decisions and forming judgments instead of relying on objective data and rational thinking.
- Traditions of some students may emphasize oral over written forms of discourse.

Bowers and Flinders state that they are less interested in compiling a complete list of such concerns than they are in having teachers understand the classroom as an ecology of language and culture in order to improve communication and learning. Teachers, like everyone else, take for granted their own culturally determined patterns of belief, communication, and behavior. Unlike most people, however, teachers have the unique responsibility of orchestrating lessons that require a high degree of clarity. The supervisor, Bowers and Flinders suggest, can serve as a third-party consultant to teachers in two respects:

  (1) helping teachers recognize how their taken-for-granted lan-
        guage and cultural patterns influence student learning, and;
  (2) helping teachers clarify their judgments and adapt their prac-
        tices in ways that take student differences into account.

These two functions encompass many of the traditional concerns of supervision related to teacher questioning, wait-time, student engagement in tasks, and introducing and summarizing lessons. Supervisors and teachers should consider these concerns, however, within the context of the multiple meanings possible in a culturally diverse classroom and society. The place to begin, Bowers and Flinders (1991) suggest, is for supervisors to develop sensitivity to their own cultural assumptions, including unquestioned beliefs in objectivity and individual autonomy. Although they assert that the supervisor should avoid partisanship, the culturally responsive supervisor is by no means politically neutral.

Bowers and Flinders provide eleven written guides that are intended to serve as aids for supervisors. Seven are termed "mental" ecology guides because they focus on what students are learning. Four are termed "social" ecology guides because they primarily refer to student-teacher relationships. In part, the guides call attention to traditional issues in classroom observation such as clarity and style of teaching, the introduction and closing of a lesson, providing an overview of key concepts, the use of nonverbal behavior, and encouraging student involvement.

Guide #1, for example, includes a subheading entitled, "A. Introduction of the Lesson: Framing (establishing a common footing of understanding and participation)." The following items are included under this subheading:

  1. Clear opening frame that establishes the purpose or
       context of the lesson.
  2. Acknowledgment of how the main issues of previous
       lessons relate to current lesson.
  3. Overview statements.
  4. Clarification of how students are expected to participate
       in the learning experience....
(Bowers and Flinders, 1991, p. 30)

The guides also include items that focus on nontraditional issues such as: providing for cultural and gender differences among students; avoiding cultural and gender bias in language, humor, and examples; encouraging ecological (environmental) awareness; emphasizing the tentativeness of knowledge; and avoiding references to individualism, self-determination, competition, and ownership as virtues.

Guide # 4, for instance, lists a heading entitled, "Cultural Assumptions, Patterns of Thought, and Values That May Be Either Outmoded for All Students or Problematic in Terms of the Ethnic Composition of the Classroom." The following items then follow:

1. Competition.
2. Individualism.
3. Technology as neutral.
4. Mechanistic view of environment, society, or person.
5. Change as progressive.
6. Thought as data-based or data-driven.
7. Rational process as culture-free.
8. Language as conduit.
9. Success as individual achievement.
10. Work for money.
11. Consumerism indicates success.
12. Modernization viewed as progress.
13. Traditional cultures viewed as backward or unenlightened.
14. Literate people viewed as more socially advanced....
    (Bowers and Flinders, 1991, pp. 36-37)

During the pre-observation phase, Bowers and Flinders (1991) recommend that supervisors can begin to observe and take notes on the teacher's traditions, values, assumptions and cultural presuppositions. These may be inferred, they suggest, from the teacher's use of metaphors, body language, use of space, sense of humor, and voice tone. Supervisors should review the content of the observation guides during the preobservation conference so that teachers understand the kinds of things the supervisor will be looking for.

Bowers and Flinders argue *against* allowing teachers to determine the focus of supervision. They believe that supervisors should define the scope and content of supervision by offering insights into aspects of teaching, students, and the curriculum that the teacher takes for granted. Supervisors thus deliberately set the agenda in the culturally responsive approach. They assist teachers in formulating new problems, rather than solving problems of which teachers are already aware. "Reflection alone," Bowers and Flinders state, "simply does not provide for the types of learning that we hope teachers will model" (1991, p. 25).

During the *observation* phase the supervisor uses the methods of anthropology to gather data on cultural patterns and subtle dimensions of social interactions in the classroom. The observation guides may be used as memory aids if needed or as complements to fieldnotes which record ongoing events in detail.

Bowers and Flinders (1991) refer to the third phase of the clinical cycle as the *review*. During this time the supervisor uses the observation guides to help make sense of the fieldnotes collected during the observation. The guides can serve in this instance, they recommend, as frameworks against which the supervisor can associate isolated events and recognize broader themes.

Providing feedback is the final phase of the culturally responsive approach to supervision. Feedback can be provided in writing or orally. Written reports should provide detailed descriptions of events, through expressive, figurative, and propositional language. Bowers and Flinders suggest that supervisors may want to consider what a handwritten versus a typed report communicates to the teacher, or what the quality of the paper says about their relationship. When making an oral report the supervisor should pay attention to meanings communicated by the tone of the conference and its location, as well as the use of space, turn taking, facial expressions, dress, and other nonverbal cues.

Supervisors should be selective, Bowers and Flinders believe, in providing teachers with feedback. They should attend most closely to issues that they consider most relevant to the broader purposes of education. Supervisors can use the guides to provide focused comments such as the following:

- "Your use of humor does not exclude anyone in the class and thus contributes to feelings of solidarity." (1991, p. 28)
- "Your nonverbal cues, especially how close you stand to the students and your body language, are well coordinated to signal that you're interested in what students have to say." (1991, p.28)

In a sense, the supervisor serves as a connoisseur of culture, rather than a neutral observer, who focuses the teacher's attention on issues of race, gender, culture, and environmental concerns. Bowers and Flinders suggest that objectivity is an illusion and is in fact impossible because we are all shaped by our cultural experiences and contexts. Supervisors and teachers ought to deliberately work toward developing sensitivity toward others, they argue, rather than be swayed unconsciously by the biases, preferences, and predispositions embedded in the perspectives of a dominant culture, race, or gender.

Summary

The perspectives on reflective practice outlined in this chapter are premised on the assumption that successful teaching is much more than simply a matter of mastering a certain body of knowledge and skills. Like Goldhammer's original model, each raises moral, ethical, and political issues in calling for sensitivity to students and the diversity among them. The clinical supervision cycle is directed toward careful self examination on the part of teachers and supervisors, as well as greater empathy for students and a willingness to act upon principles of justice and equity.

Reflective teaching and supervision contrast sharply with the technical/didactic notion that professional practice is a series of dispassionate instrumental decisions built upon externally derived principles of scientific research and theory. Reflective professionals are intensely engaged with their work and in developing expert capabilities by intellectually confronting puzzling situations that they encounter daily.

Although discussion of teaching strategies and instructional materials is not ruled out, the primary emphasis of reflective practice is a critical reassessment of taken-for-granted values, theories, beliefs, and assumptions that underlie and guide both teaching and supervision. Teachers are encouraged, through observation and conferencing, to consider the connections between their beliefs and actions, and the social, historical, political, economic, and cultural contexts of schooling and their students' lives. Reassessment of values, beliefs, theories, and assumptions may require a close examination of one's personal and professional life history. Journals and dialogue with colleagues can be useful for determining how one became the teacher or supervisor one has turned out to be. Action research can be used to understand and even reshape the organizational and social contexts of teaching and learning through the development of critical communities in schools and across schools.

References

Bowers, C.A. & Flinders, D.J. (1990). *Responsive teaching: An ecological approach to classroom patterns of language, culture, and thought.* New York: Teachers College Press.

Bowers, C.A. & Flinders, D.J. (1991). *Culturally responsive teaching and supervision: A handbook for staff development.* New York: Teachers College Press.

Dewey, J. (1933). *How we think: A restatement of the relation of reflective thinking to the educative process.* Boston: D.C. Heath.

Garman, N.B. (1982). The clinical approach to supervision. In T. Sergiovanni (Ed.) *Supervision of teaching* (Alexandria, VA: Association for Supervision and Curriculum Development), 35-52.

Garman, N.B. (1986). Reflection, the heart of clinical supervision: A modern rationale for practice, *Journal of Curriculum and Supervision, 2* (1), 1-24.

Grant, C.A. & Zeichner, K.M. (1984). On becoming a reflective teacher. In Carl A. Grant (Ed.) *Preparing for reflective teaching,* pp. 1-18. Boston: Allyn and Bacon.

Liston, D.P. & Zeichner, K.M. (1991). *Teacher education and the social conditions of schooling.* New York: Routledge.

Retallick, J.A. (1990). *Clinical supervision and the structure of communication.* Paper presented at the Annual Meeting of the American Educational Research Association, Boston, MA, April 1990.

Schon, D.A. (1983). *The reflective practitioner: How professional think in action.* New York: Basic Books.

Schon, D.A. (1987). *Educating the reflective practitioner: Toward a new design for teaching and learning in the professions.* San Francisco: Jossey-Bass.

Schon, D.A. (1988a). Coaching reflective teaching. In Peter P. Grimmett & Gaalen L. Erickson (Eds), *Reflection in teacher education.* New York: Teachers College Press.

Schon, D.A. (March, 1988b). *Teachers as reflective practitioners.* Presentation made at the annual conference of the Association for Supervision and Curriculum Development, Orlando, FL, March 1988. Cited in Schon, D.A. (1989). Quotations, *Journal of Curriculum and Supervision, 5* (1), p. 9.

Smyth, W.J. (1984a). Observation: Toward a 'critical consciousness' in the instructional supervision of experienced teachers. *Curriculum Inquiry, 14* (4), 425-436.

Smyth, W.J. (1984b). Teachers as collaborative learners in clinical supervision: A state-of-the-art review. *Journal of Education for Teaching, 10* (1), 24-36.

Smyth, W.J. (1985). Developing a critical practice of clinical supervision. *Journal of Curriculum Studies, 17* (Jan.-Mar.): 1-15.

Smyth, W.J. (1986, April). *Cinderella syndrome: A philosophical view of supervision as a field of study.* Paper presented at the annual meeting of the American Educational Research Association, San Francisco, April 1986.

Smyth, W.J. (1990, April). *Problematizing teaching through a 'critical' approach to clinical supervision.* Paper presented at the annual meeting of the American

Educational Research Association, Boston, MA, April 1990.

Smyth, W.J. (1991, April). *Instructional supervision and the re-definition of who does it in schools.* Paper presented at the annual meeting of the American Educaitonal Research Association, Chicago, April 1991.

Van Manen, M. (1977). Linking ways of knowing with ways of being practical. *Curriculum Inquiry, 6,* 205-228.

Zeichner K.M. & Liston, D.P. (1987). Teaching student teachers to reflect, *Harvard Educational Review, 57* (1), 23-48.

Chapter 12

Toward a Democratic Learning Community

As stated in the Introduction, this book was intended to clarify what each of the most popular models of clinical supervision has to offer and to help educators make informed choices about the options that are available to them. This final chapter suggests ways of making those choices so that educators can successfully meet the pressing challenges posed by today's changing organizational and social contexts, while preserving and even enhancing the dignity of their profession.

Earlier chapters traced the evolution of supervision in education beginning with the late 19th century. It was noted that John Dewey's combination of democracy and scientific thinking exerted tremendous influence on the literature of educational supervision during the first half of the 20th century. Clinical supervision became popular during the 1960s and refocused Dewey's legacy of democracy, cooperative planning, practical problem solving, and action research on events and processes occurring in the classroom, while de-emphasizing issues of school-wide change and large-scale curriculum implementation. Four "families" or "classifications" of clinical supervision that appeared during the last thirty years were identified. These are briefly summarized in *Figure 12.1*:

Family	Emphasis
Original Clinical Models	The models proposed by Goldhammer, Mosher and Purpel, and Cogan offer an eclectic blending of empirical, phenomenological, behavioral, and developmental perspectives. These models emphasize the importance of collegial relations between supervisors and teachers, cooperative discovery of meaning, and development of individually unique teaching styles.
Humanistic/Artistic Models	The perspectives of Blumberg and Eisner are based on existential and aesthetic principles. These models forsake step-by-step procedures and emphasize open interpersonal relations and personal intuition, artistry, and idiosyncrasy. Supervisors are encouraged to help teachers understand the expressive and artistic richness of teaching.
Technical/Didactic Models	The work of Acheson and Gall, Hunter, and Joyce and Showers draws on process-product and effective teaching research from the 1970s. These models emphasize techniques of observation and feedback that reinforce certain "effective" behaviors or predetermined models of teaching to which teachers attempt to conform.
Developmental/Reflective Models	The models of Glickman, Costa and Garmston, Schon, Zeichner and Liston, Garman, Smyth, Retallick, and Bowers and Flinders are sensitive to individual differences and the organizational, social, political, and cultural contexts of teaching. These models call for supervisors to encourage reflection and introspection among teachers in order to foster professional growth, discover context-specific principles of practice, and promote justice and equity.

Figure 12.1
FAMILIES OF CLINICAL SUPERVISION

Which Model To Use?

The number and variety of existing clinical supervision models, approaches, and strategies can be overwhelming to anyone. By this point the reader may be wondering:

- Which of the clinical supervision models is best?
- Which one should I use?
- Can more than one model be used in the same school?
- Can I "construct" a new model by combining elements from several that already exist?

The answers to these questions depend on one's previous experiences, personal beliefs, and values; the experiences, beliefs, and values of one's professional colleagues; and the context in which one is a teacher or supervisor. In other words, there is no single model of supervision or combination of strategies that is correct for everyone in every situation. The answers to these questions will vary from one teacher or supervisor to another, from one group of teachers to another, and from one school to another. The answers are also likely to change as teachers and supervisors gain experience in classroom observation and conferencing over time.

Selecting a Single Model

The easiest way for you, the reader, to initially select a model of clinical supervision for yourself is to review the introductions and summaries of earlier chapters and recall what you were thinking when you read about each model. It may also be helpful to consider your answers to the following questions which were posed in the Introduction in deciding which model seems to "feel right" for you:

- How might this model of supervision contribute to the learning of students in my classroom or school?
- What does this model of supervision imply about teachers and how they should be treated?
- Do I feel comfortable with this model of supervision as a teacher? Would I want to be supervised in this way? Why or why not?
- Would I feel comfortable using this model of supervision as a mentor or a peer coach? Why or why not?

- Would I feel comfortable using this model of supervision as a supervisor or principal? Why or why not?
- What might I learn about myself as a teacher from this model?
- What might I learn about myself as a supervisor of teachers from this model?
- Would this model of supervision work in my school? Why or why not?

As a general rule, the decision to use one model of clinical supervision over others should be made cooperatively with the teacher or teachers being supervised. Involving teachers in decisions about the purposes and expected outcomes of supervision, how observations and conferences will proceed, and the nature of the relationship between the supervisor and teacher is clearly the most professional thing to do. Involving teachers acknowledges their competence and autonomy as well as their own responsibility for personal growth. Teacher involvement is especially important in mentoring or peer coaching relationships, which are explicitly intended to promote collegiality and open communication.

Choosing a single model that feels right personally may be especially suitable for mentor teachers, peer coaches, and supervisors who have limited experience with classroom observation and conferencing. In such cases, you may want to reread the chapter that describes the model you most prefer and consult the resources listed at the end of that chapter for more information. It may also be helpful to form a study group to discuss and practice the model with your colleagues.

Establishing familiarity and expertise with a single model, however, should be just the beginning. It is a good idea to develop a working knowledge of at least several clinical supervision models. A repertoire of approaches will enable you to adapt flexibly to the preferences of different teachers and the requirements of various classroom situations.

Using an Eclectic Approach

Constructing your own unique approach to clinical supervision by selecting ideas, strategies, and techniques from the range of existing models is another way to proceed. No single model may suit an individual or a situation perfectly, but certain elements from several of the models may seem appealing. You may already be using some of the strategies if you are an experienced supervisor, mentor, or peer coach, and may want to add others to your existing set of skills.

Knowledge of the array of clinical supervision models can provide experienced supervisors with better understanding of the various perspectives that exist concerning teaching and supervision. You can use this knowledge to examine your own beliefs about teaching and supervision, and to assess the approaches that you use most frequently when observing and conferencing with teachers.

The earliest models of clinical supervision described by Cogan, Goldhammer, and Mosher and Purpel were very eclectic, both in their theoretical orientations and in the techniques they advocated. We now recognize, however, that ethical, philosophical, and practical assumptions are important to consider before a particular strategy is employed. A difficulty with drawing indiscriminately from the array of available models is that an erratic, confusing, and inconsistent conglomeration may result. A uniquely tailored eclectic model may indeed be most appropriate for an individual or a particular situation, but it should be carefully thought out, especially with respect to underlying assumptions, intentions, actions, and outcomes.

A Question of Values and Beliefs

The model of supervision that you choose or construct initially depends upon your personal values, assumptions, and beliefs. The statement, "I think that every teacher should develop a unique style of teaching that is right for her," clearly indicates a value position. An individual who holds such a belief might have difficulty with an approach to supervision that monitors teacher conformity with predetermined behaviors. Another individual may believe that, "All successful teachers share a common set of fundamental skills." This person might have difficulty with an approach to supervision that focuses heavily on the social context of instruction and the meaning behind behaviors.

A thorough understanding of your values and assumptions about teaching and supervision is therefore essential as a guide to practice. The families and models of supervision described earlier in this book represent very different philosophical and theoretical views of teaching, learning, supervision, and the nature of professional knowledge. The strategies and techniques included within each family and model are expressions of the specific philosophy or theory in action. You should be sure to consciously select or construct an approach to supervision that is consistent with your own ethical and intellectual assumptions, intentions, and actions.

Treating technical mastery and reflective thinking as polar opposites, however, is inconsistent with the reality of practice. Outstanding teachers readily combine technical expertise with reflective thought, artistic expression, and responsiveness to students (Shulman, 1988). The models of supervision described in this book represent, in a sense, different facets of clinical supervisory practice. All can contribute to improved teaching and professional growth in some respect depending on the outcomes desired by the teacher and supervisor using them.

As discussed in Chapter 11, Zeichner and Liston (1987) suggest that three levels of reflectivity are possible – technical, practical, and critical. Similar frameworks for understanding how supervisors can help teachers reflect on practice at different levels have been identified by others (Garmston, 1987; Grimmett, 1989; Lasley, 1992). A synthesis of these various frameworks and how different levels of reflection – technical, conceptual, and moral/ethical – can be achieved is presented in *Figure 12.2*.

Greater emphasis may need to be given to the two levels of conceptual and moral/ethical reflection to balance the traditional emphasis on technical mastery in education. It is important to note as well that no developmental sequence is necessarily implied by these levels of reflectivity. Beginning teachers as well as veterans can benefit from thoughtful examination of their practice from all three perspectives simultaneously.

You may want to use the levels of reflectivity outlined in *Figure 12.2* to clarify the purposes of a clinical supervision cycle before it begins. Do you and the teacher with whom you are working intend to consider thoughtfully and translate technical knowledge and skills into practice? Or, is your aim to transform practice by increasing awareness of yourselves and the social and political context of your work? You should keep in mind that the consequences of a particular strategy for classroom observation or conferencing that you select may be influenced by the philosophical orientation of the model from which it is drawn. Figure 12.1 may be helpful for examining these assumptions that underlie the various families of models.

Levels of Reflection	Central Issues
Technical Level	Addresses how best to achieve given outcomes within an established context. Involves thoughtful consideration and translation into practice of knowledge and skills acquired through staff development and other experiences.
Conceptual Level	Questions assumptions and beliefs about teaching and learning, as well as their relation to actions and consequences. Involves thinking and deliberating about philosophical and theoretical bases of practice and selecting approaches that are most appropriate for students.
Moral/Ethical Level	Considers issues like justice, equity, and responsibility as well as their relation to the means, ends, and contexts of learning, teaching, and supervision. Involves an attempt to transform practice through deliberation and action centered on persistently encountered problems, the professional self, and institutional, social, and political forces that impinge on teaching.

Figure 12.2
THREE LEVELS OF REFLECTIVE PRACTICE

Emerging Issues in Supervisory Practice

Another factor to consider when choosing or constructing a model of supervision is that new and emerging views of learning, teaching, professional knowledge, and schools as organizations are challenging established practice (Glickman, 1992). These new perspectives suggest that educators should begin thinking and making decisions as members of learning communities. Some of the distinctions between established and emerging supervisory practice are offered in *Figure 12.3*:

	Established Practice	Emerging Practice
View of Learning	Predictable, with standard procedures and outcomes possible.	Complex and differentiated.
View of Teaching	Mastering simple *effective* routine behaviors.	Exercising informed *reflective* judgment.
View of Supervision	Reinforcing specific prescribed teacher behaviors and skills.	Helping teachers discover and construct professional knowledge and skills.
View of Professional Knowledge	General teaching methods exist that are both context- and content-free.	Principles of practice are dependent on context, subject specific, and responsive to individuals.
View of Teachers and Supervisors	Isolated and independent technicians.	Collegial team members, mentors, and peer coaches.
View of Schools	Bureaucratic teaching organizations.	Democratic teaching and learning communities.

Figure 12.3
COMPETING VIEWS OF LEARNING, TEACHING, SUPERVISION, AND PROFESSIONAL KNOWLEDGE

Supervisors across the United States and Canada are becoming less concerned, it seems, with prescribing and reinforcing simple conceptions of teaching and learning. They are focusing instead on whether teachers' decisions are appropriate to student needs, and to the purposes and contexts of instruction. The emerging view suggests that teaching behaviors that might be appropriate under some circumstances (e.g., teaching basic skills in math) might be inappropriate in others (e.g., teaching creative thinking in problem-solving). Teachers as well as supervisors, therefore, should be ready to examine the effectiveness of current practice, explore alternatives with colleagues, and adjust their behaviors according to a variety of instructional situations. Supervision of this sort implies a reliance on groups or teams of teachers who share ideas, plan, evaluate, and learn together (Darling-Hammond and Sclan, 1992).

Learning to teach is beginning to be viewed as a process that should continue throughout one's career. Such lifelong learning contrasts with the more traditional view that a teacher is finished with learning upon graduation from college. Teachers can participate in determining the direction of their professional growth through clinical supervision, coaching, collaboration, reflective practice, and action research (Holland, Clift, Veal, Johnson, and McCarthy, 1992). Supervisors and teachers thus construct and create professional knowledge about teaching and learning through collaborative inquiry (Nolan and Francis, 1992).

Emerging practice in supervision seems to confirm the prediction of many experts that an outgrowth of today's diverse and information-rich society is the rise of "learning organizations" that have the capacity and flexibility to seek out, discover, and invent new knowledge (Dumaine, 1989; Senge, 1990). Such organizations will be able to adapt to change by solving problems creatively. Most work in learning organizations is expected to be completed by semi-autonomous task-focused teams. Leadership is expected to emerge from these short-term, problem-focused teams as needed, instead of emanating solely from a single formal position in the organization (Senge, 1990). Self-disciplined individuals who recognize their responsibility for maintaining relationships and open communication with others are needed to make such an arrangement successful (Drucker, 1989).

Research indicates that successful schools often exhibit the open communication, flexibility, problem solving capability, and team focus attributed to learning organizations. Little (1982), for example, reported that in successful schools teachers value and uphold norms of collegiality and continuous improvement. In successful schools, she suggests, teachers:

- Engaged in frequent, continuous, and increasingly concrete and precise talk about teaching practice.
- Frequently observed each other teaching, and provided useful critiques.
- Planned, designed, researched, prepared, and evaluated instructional materials together.
- Took responsibility for teaching the practice of teaching to one another.

Rosenholtz (1989) similarly discovered that "high consensus" or "learning enriched" schools displayed a marked spirit of continuous improvement in which no teacher ever stopped learning how to teach. Teachers in these schools defined, communicated, and experienced ongoing self-renewal as a fact of professional life. Fullan and Steigelbauer (1991) argue convincingly for the creation of "learning enriched" cultures in schools where academic, social, and personal learning by students and professional learning by adults are taken for granted as natural aspects of the school environment.

A challenge facing leaders in education is how to facilitate the learning process in schools so that new knowledge and creative innovations are continuously generated and internalized (Senge, 1990). Establishing an environment where teachers and supervisors are continuously learning and helping one another to learn may be the primary task of supervision today. Clinical supervision appears to have real potential for generating information and producing professional knowledge through the processes of classroom observation and collegial conversation.

The notion that groups of teachers can work together productively as active members of a community of learners cuts across the various families of clinical supervision models. For example, Mosher and Purpel, Blumberg, Joyce and Showers, Glickman, and Zeichner and Liston, all point out the advantages of cooperative inquiry of this sort. Roles, status, and hierarchy should diminish in importance in learning communities as the power of ideas and persuasion emerge to guide behavior. Supervisory techniques ought to be selected collectively on the basis of the ideas and values they represent, therefore, rather than focused on interpersonal or organizational control. As suggested in the Introduction, the following questions are important to address when a faculty is considering moving toward becoming a learning community:

- Where are we now and where do we want to be in terms of values and assumptions about teaching and supervision in our school or district?
- Where are we now and where do we want to be in terms of how classroom observation and conferencing are practiced in our school or district?
- What forces are likely to help and hinder our progress?
- What series of steps is necessary for us to get to where we want to be?
- Who needs to be involved in these efforts?
- What resources are available?
- How will we know when and how well we have achieved our goal?

Sharing, Introducing, and Inventing Professional Knowledge

Adults who work in schools possess tremendous insights into instruction, curriculum, staff development, the needs of students, and the dynamics of schools as organizations. Unfortunately, as several authors whose work has been discussed in this book have lamented, schools are usually structured in ways that impose isolation and inhibit communication among adults. One issue supervision faces, therefore, involves creating the conditions under which the *existing* rich craft *knowledge* of teaching *can be shared* and made part of an ongoing professional discussion (Barth, 1984).

The original models of clinical supervision seem to be especially well-suited for this purpose. A group-focused approach to supervision, as described by Mosher and Purpel (Chapter 2), can be an economical and nonthreatening way to initially stimulate the sharing of insights among teachers. Teachers report that their professional growth needs are met and feelings of isolation alleviated through discussion of videotaped teaching episodes (Phelps & Wright, 1986; Anastos, 1987). If teachers feel comfortable in visiting each others' classrooms and analyzing and talking openly about teaching, the nonjudgmental approaches to clinical supervision described by Goldhammer (Chapter 1) and Cogan (Chapter 3) can serve to generate valuable objective data about current practice and suggest avenues for growth. Peer supervision or "colleague consultation" of this sort can provide a reciprocal foundation for collaborative assessment, identification of teacher and student patterns, consideration of intended and unanticipated learner outcomes, and enactment of teachers' goals and principles (Little, 1985; Goldsberry, 1986). The observer and the observed can both benefit as equal partners under such an arrangement.

Teachers may further refine and perfect their personal teaching styles by applying the interpersonal and artistic approaches to supervision suggested by Blumberg (Chapter 4) and Eisner (Chapter 5). These perspectives also encourage the expansion of professional dialogue and inquiry beyond the classroom, and into the organizational and curricular contexts that affect learning. Blumberg's and Eisner's approaches can be especially appropriate, therefore, for stimulating discussion that can eventually lead to school-wide improvement efforts. Indeed, interpersonal and organizational issues like time, trust, decisiveness, and mutual confidence may have to be addressed at the school level if collegial clinical supervision is to succeed (McFaul & Cooper, 1983).

A second issue facing supervision with respect to building learning communities involves creating conditions by which *new knowledge about teaching can be introduced* and incorporated into classrooms and schools. Cogan (Chapter 3) was the first to recognize the potential contribution of clinical supervision to the thoughtful, thorough, and systematic implementation of new technologies, curricula, teaching methods, and organizational patterns. The approaches to clinical supervision described by Acheson and Gall (Chapter 6), Hunter (Chapter 7), Joyce and Showers (Chapter 8), and to some extent Glickman (Chapter 9) are highly suited to establishing and maintaining innovative techniques and ideas by reinforcing their use through classroom observation and feedback.

Ideas and insights originating outside a classroom or school can be introduced and discussed within study groups that examine recent research and emerging theory related to teaching and learning (Joyce & Showers, 1982; Glatthorn, 1987). Of course, formal staff development is another valuable source of innovations. Goals can be established and plans developed individually and collectively to guide progress as teachers blend new strategies into their existing repertoires (Roper, Deal, & Dornbush, 1976; DeBevoise, 1982). Considerable evidence suggests that teachers who are coached by peers tend to use innovations more successfully, more frequently, more appropriately, with greater retention, and feel more comfortable using innovations than teachers who are not coached (Baker & Showers, 1984; Showers, 1984; Kurth, 1985; Hosack-Curlin, 1988; Gilman & Miller, 1988).

Mentoring programs that pair a more experienced teacher with a beginning teacher are a popular variation of peer coaching. Goldhammer (Chapter 1), Mosher and Purpel (Chapter 2), and Glickman (Chapter 9) speak directly to the unique needs of new teachers. Although the difference in experience between a veteran and a novice may raise the issue of hierarchy between them, both can gain from pooling their ideas and experiences. The newer teacher can gain from support and assistance provided by the experienced teacher, while the experienced teacher can benefit from being exposed to the idealism and enthusiasm of youth and the latest materials and techniques.

Organizational norms of collegiality, openness to innovation, collaboration, and experimentation (Little, 1982) as well as trust and support (Sparks & Bruder, 1987) must be fostered by the social organization of the school for peer coaching to succeed. The team-oriented approaches advocated by Joyce and Showers (Chapter 8) and Glickman (Chapter 9) can be useful in building the kind of culture that encourages a willingness to try new ideas and commitment to persist with innovations that prove successful.

A third issue facing supervision that is especially relevant in today's diverse and ever-changing world is the need to *invent* and act upon *new knowledge* about teaching and learning. The approaches proposed by Glickman (Chapter 9), Costa and Garmston (Chapter 10), and the various reflective models of clinical supervision (Chapter 11) intend to generate the open-mindedness, critical thinking, creative problem solving, and experimentation that are necessary to help individual teachers better meet the learning needs of students (Goldsberry, 1988). The reflective models, especially, seek to increase teacher empathy for students and sensitivity to differences, and enhance understanding of how teachers may unconsciously contribute to the reproduction of inequities in society. Action research, which the reflective models advocate, may be viewed as an expanded version of supervision in that it represents a form of inquiry conducted by teachers, either individually or collectively, that is aimed at understanding and improving professional practice (McCutcheon & Jung, 1990).

Although similar in some respects to the original models conceived by Goldhammer (Chapter 1) and Cogan (Chapter 3), the contemporary reflective approaches to supervision imply more drastic changes in the conditions that affect teaching and learning. The reflective approaches suggest the possibility of acknowledging and changing the unspoken rules of the game through conscious, thoughtful, deliberate, collective effort. Such change might include reconstituting the relationships among students, teachers, parents, supervisors, and administrators to give them all greater voice and control over what happens in classrooms and schools.

The Need for Democratic Supervision

Preparing students to live in a technologically sophisticated, information-based, global society is itself a challenging task. However, educators must somehow also address the more pressing reality that many families and communities can no longer be depended upon to provide the kind of environment that students need for personal and academic growth (Cunningham, 1990). Opportunities for teachers, administrators, and others to observe one another teach and engage in conversations about common concerns and goals as members of a learning community can be empowering to a degree. But the definition of community and the arena of inquiry must be expanded if the social reality and external environments of schools are to be transformed.

Perhaps it is time for supervision to widen its scope as a field of practice and study to include the conditions that affect the learning of children outside the classroom as well. Opening the curriculum and organizational context of schooling for critical examination and action-focused inquiry is a good place to begin. But poverty, homelessness, child abuse, discrimination, teenage pregnancy, and drug and alcohol abuse are such serious problems that schools cannot be expected to solve them alone. Educators must work with the general public to develop broader participation and wider responsibility for student success (Hodgkinson, 1991; Welker, 1991).

Supervision in education has long drawn on democratic principles for a sense of direction and meaning. In an increasingly unstable and unpredictable world, this professional value is needed more than ever. Democratic leadership declined in popularity after the 1950s, partly because it appeared inefficient. Recent world events have demonstrated, however, that democracy is an extremely efficient form of organization, especially under conditions of change. No viable, credible, or potent conception of supervision may be possible in modern society without democracy as a central tenet. Dewey's cooperative, action-oriented inquiry is the basis of clinical supervision and it also remains a most promising way of generating new knowledge and creative innovations through group consensus rather than majority rule (Torbert, 1990; Schwartz, 1991).

A complicating factor in addressing the challenges facing education today is that students are extraordinarily diverse in their cultures, languages, and past experiences. While cultural assimilation may not be entirely possible or even desirable, *political* assimilation is essential (Giroux, 1991). Democratic values must be shared by members of society while allowing and encouraging diversity of cultures. Educators need to recognize the fact that education is more than a system for transferring knowledge, skills, and even culture from one generation to the next. Education is more fundamentally a system for *inventing* and *reinventing* knowledge, skills, and culture as well. Schools must become models and incubators of democracy.

The current decade requires an image of the teacher as leader, both in the sense that leaders are responsible for teaching those they lead and in the sense of genuine involvement by teams of teachers in learning-focused schools. This image resembles the democratic educative leadership advocated by supervision authors during the 1940s and 1950s in that it unites teachers with administrators, and schools with their communities in cooperative, action-oriented, problem-solving (DSDI, 1943; ASCD, 1946). Our ethical responsibilities as educators must keep pace with our ability to accomplish change in schools. Educational supervision as a specialized area of practice and study must renew its traditional dialogue about social and political responsibilities in a democratic society, and especially the implications of those responsibilities for curriculum and instruction.

Because democracy takes time, energy, effort, and commitment, the process can lose advocates in a society and a profession that prefer quick fixes and ready-made solutions. Teachers and supervisors must recommit themselves to democratic values such as equality, participation, social justice, and personal responsibility as they create action-oriented, learning-focused communities in schools. Democracy can provide the direction, goals, purposes, and standards of conduct that our profession and society desperately need. Clinical supervision can provide the means of translating democratic values into action.

References

Anastos, J. (1987). A teacher-directed peer coaching project. *Educational Leadership, 45,* (3), 40-42.

Association for Supervision and Curriculum Development (1946). *Leadership through supervision,* 1946 Yearbook. Washington, D.C.: Association for Supervision and Curriculum Development of the National Education Association.

Baker, R.G. & Showers, B. (1984, April). *The effects of a coaching strategy on teachers' transfer of training to classroom practice: A six month follow-up.* Paper presented at the Annual Meeting of the American Educational Research Association, New Orleans, LA.

Cunningham, L.L. (1990). Educational leadership and administration: Retrospective and prospective views. In Brad Mitchell and Luvern L. Cunningham (eds.), *Educational leadership and changing contexts of families, communities, and schools,* Eighty-ninth Yearbook of the National Society for the Study of Education. Chicago: University of Chicago Press.

Darling-Hammond, L. & Sclan, E. (1992). Policy and supervision. In Carl D. Glickman (Ed.), *Supervision in transition,* 1992 Yearbook of the Association for Supervision and Curriculum Development. Alexandria, VA: Association for Supervision and Curriculum Development.

DeBevoise, W. (1982). *Collegiality may be the password to effective inservice programs.* Eugene, OR: University of Oregon, Center for Educational Policy and Management. (ERIC Document Reproduction Service No. ED 221 943).

Department of Supervisors and Directors of Instruction (1943). *Leadership at work.* Washington, D.C.: Department of Supervisors and Directors of Instruction of the National Education Association.

Drucker, P.F. (1989). *The new realities.* New York: Perennial Library.

Dumaine, B. (1989). What leaders of tomorrow see. *Fortune, 120* (1), 48-62.

Fullan, M.G. & Steigelbauer, S. (1991). *The new meaning of educational change.* New York: Teachers College Press.

Garman, R.J. (1987). How administrators support peer coaching, *Educational Leadership, 44* (5), 18-26.

Gilman, D. & Miller, M. (1988). *An examination of teachers teaching teachers.* Terre Haute, IN: Indiana State University, Professional School Services. (ERIC Document Reproduction Services No. ED 302 878).

Giroux, H.A. (1991). *Postmodernism, feminism, and cultural politics: Redefining educational boundaries.* Albany: State University of New York Press.

Glatthorn, A.A. (1987). Cooperative professional development: Peer-centered options for teacher growth. *Educational Leadership, 45,* (3), 31-35.

Glickman, C.D. (Ed.). (1992). *Supervision in transition,* 1992 Yearbook of the Association for Supervision and Curriculum Development. Alexandria, VA: Association for Supervision and Curriculum Development.

Goldsberry, L. (1988). Three functional methods of supervision. *Action in Teacher Education, 10,* (1), 1-10.

Grimmett, P.P. (1989). A commentary on Schon's view of reflection, *Journal of Curriculum and Supervision, 5* (1), pp. 19-28.

Hodgkinson, H. (1991). Reform versus reality. *Phi Delta Kappan, 73* (1), 9-16.

Holland, P.E., Clift, R., Veal, M.L., Johnson, M., & McCarthy, J. (1992). Linking preservice and inservice supervision through professional inquiry. In Carl D. Glickman (Ed.), *Supervision in transition,* 1992 Yearbook of the Association for Supervision and Curriculum Development. Alexandria, VA: Association for Supervision and Curriculum Development.

Hosack-Curlin, K. (1988, April). *Measuring the effects of a peer coaching project.* Paper presented at the Annual Meeting of the American Eduational Research Association, New Orleans, LA.

Joyce, B. & Showers, B. (1982). The coaching of teachers. *Educational Leadership, 40,* 4-8, 10.

Kurth, R.J. (1985, April). *Training teachers to improve comprehension instruction.* Paper presented at the Annual Meeting of the American Educational Research Association, Chicago, IL.

Lasley, T.J. (1992). Promoting teacher reflection. *Journal of Staff Development, 13* (1), 24-29.

Little, J.W. (1981, April). *The power of organizational setting.* Paper presented at the Annual Meeting of the American Educational Research Association, Los Angeles, CA.

Little, J.W. (1982). Norms of collegiality and experimentation: Workplace conditions of school success. *American Educational Research Journal, 19* (3), 325-340.

Little, J.W. (1985). Teachers as teacher advisors: The delicacy of collegial leadership. *Educational Leadership, 43,* (3), 34-36.

McFaul, S.A. & Cooper, J.M. (1983). Peer clinical supervision in an urban elementary school. *Journal of Teacher Education, 35,* (5), 34-38.

McCutcheon, G. & Jung, B. (1990). Alternative perspectives on action research. *Theory Into Practice, 29,* (3), 144-151.

Nolan, J. & Francis, P. (1992). Changing perspectives in curriculum and instruction. In Carl D. Glickman (Ed.), *Supervision in transition,* 1992 Yearbook of the Association for Supervision and Curriculum Development. Alexandria, VA: Association for Supervision and Curriculum Development.

Phelps, M.S. & Wright, J.D. (1986). *Peer coaching – A staff development strategy for rural teachers.* Tennessee Technological University. (ERIC Document Reproduction Service No. ED 277 513).

Roper, S., Deal, T., & Dornbush, S. (1976). Collegial evaluation of classroom teaching: Does it work? *Educational Research Quarterly, 1,* 55-65.

Rosenholtz, S. (1989). *Teachers' workplace: The social organization of schools.* New York: Longman.

Senge, P.M. (1990). *The fifth discipline: The art and practice of the learning organization.* New York: Doubleday/Currency.

Showers, B. (1984). *Peer coaching: A strategy for facilitating transfer of training.* Eugene, OR: Center for Educational Policy and Management.

Shulman, L. (1988). The dangers of dichotomous thinking in education. In P. P. Grimmett & G. L. Erikson (Eds), *Reflection in teacher education.* New York: Teachers College Press.

Sparks, G.M. & Bruder, S. (1987). Before and after peer coaching. *Educational Leadership, 45* (3), 54-57.

Torbert, W.R. (1990). Reform from the center. In Brad Mitchell & Luvern L. Cunningham (Eds.), *Educational leadership and changing contexts of families, communities, and schools,* Eighty-ninth Yearbook of the National Society for the Study of Education. Chicago: University of Chicago Press.

Welker, (1991). Expertise and the teacher as expert: Rethinking a questionable metaphor. *American Education Research Journal, 28* (1).

Zeichner, K.M. & Liston, D.P. (1987). Teaching student teachers to reflect. *Harvard Educational Review, 57* (1), 23-48.

INDEX